THE
WEEKEND
GARDENER

THE

WEEKEND GARDENER

A Guide to Low-Maintenance Gardening

VALERIE SWANE

ANGUS
& ROBERTSON

AN ANGUS & ROBERTSON BOOK

First published in Australia in 1990 by
Collins/Angus & Robertson Publishers Australia

Collins/Angus & Robertson Publishers Australia
Unit 4, Eden Park, 31 Waterloo Road, North Ryde
NSW 2113, Australia
William Collins Publishers Ltd
31 View Road, Glenfield, Auckland 10, New Zealand
Angus & Robertson (UK)
16 Golden Square, London W1R 4BN, United Kingdom

Copyright © Valerie Swane 1990

National Library of Australia
Cataloguing-in-Publication data:

Swane, Valerie, 1926–

   The Weekend Gardener; a guide to low-maintenance gardening

   Includes index.
   ISBN 0 207 16457 6
   1. Gardening–Australia. I. Title.

   635. 0994

Designed by Karen Ball

Typeset in Baskerville by Midland Typesetters, Maryborough, Victoria, Australia.
Printed in Singapore
5 4 3 2 1
95 94 93 92 91 90

*To my mother
Gwen Swane,
with many thanks*

Contents

Acknowledgments

Very special thanks are due to Cec Featherstone and Michael Collins, two keen gardeners who shared their gardening knowledge with me; to Melva Manning who put up with papers everywhere while the book was being written; and to Iris Coffey who typed the manuscript. Thanks must also go to Gregory's Publishing Company for permission to reproduce Weed Tables and Climate Map from *Gregory's Australian Gardening Guide* and to Jennie Churchill, who provided photographs.

Grateful acknowledgment is also made of the following references:

Baxter and Tankard, *Growing Fruit in Australia*, Nelson, 1981.

Brooke, J., *The Garden Book*, Doubleday, 1984.

CSIRO Division of Soils in association with Rellim Technical Publications, *When Should I Water?*, reprinted 1979.

Hillier, H.G., *The Hillier Colour Dictionary of Trees and Shrubs*, David and Charles, 1981.

Macoboy, S., *What Flower is That?*, Lansdowne-Rigby, 1986.

McMaugh, J., *What Garden Pest or Disease is That?*, Lansdowne, 1985.

Readers' Digest Illustrated Guide to Gardening, 1979.

Rowell, R.J., *Ornamental Flowering Shrubs in Australia*, Reed, 1980.

Seale, A., *Alan Seale's Garden Doctor*, Doubleday, 1981.

Sunset Magazine editors, *Sunset Western Garden Book*, Lane, 1978.

Stackhouse, S., *Shirley Stackhouse's Gardening Year*, Angus & Robertson, 1980.

Swane, V., *Gregory's Australian Gardening Guide*, Gregory's Publishing Company, a division of Universal Press, 1985.

Swane, V., *The Australian Gardener's Catalogue*, Angus & Robertson, 1989.

Victorian Schools Nursery, *Growing with Horticulture*, Cambridge, 1988.

Wrigley J. and Murray Fagg, *Australian Native Plants*, Collins, 1979.

The illustrations appearing in the book were based on the following references:

Bridgeman, P.H., P.J. Jordan, D. Patch, *Tree Surgery*, David & Charles Inc., 1976.

Brookes, J. *The Small Garden*, Marshall Cavendish Ltd, 1979.

Hadlington, P.W., J.A. Johnston, *Australian Trees—A Guide to Their Care and Cure*, New South Wales University Press Ltd, 1977.

Lesiuk and Pholeros, *Greenhouse—12 Ways to Make the Most of your Garden House*, 1984.

Sunset Magazine editors, *Sunset Western Garden Book*, Lane, 1978.

Swane, V., *Gregory's Australian Gardening Guide*, Gregory's Publishing Company, a division of Universal Press, 1985.

The photographs appearing in "Pests and Diseases" were supplied by the Department of Agriculture, Sydney, New South Wales.

Preface

Do not have a large garden unless you can afford a gardener, or have plenty of leisure time on your hands; it would cause you too much trouble. Make the gardening a pleasant recreation, a labour of love, not a slavery and a worry.

If you have too much land to look after, lay a portion of it down with good kinds of perennial grasses and you produce a beautiful green carpet requiring little labour.

The Happifying Gardening Hobby by E.W. Cole, published in 1918.

This recipe for a happy relationship with your garden still holds true today. The modern low-maintenance gardener may lack the time or inclination to garden, but he or she still wants the pleasure of owning a beautiful garden. You do not need "green fingers" to garden, all you need is common sense and a knowledge of how plants grow and what causes their death. Thereafter logic should control what you do.

In the past, plants have been used in home gardens mainly as ornaments. But gardens can be more than ornamental oases—they can also contribute to the environment. Plants can insulate houses against heat and cold and replace pollution-causing "conveniences" such as air-conditioning and heating. The paling-fence-high shrubs, the imprisoned circles of rock around letter boxes and the rapidly growing shrubs planted to hide the neighbours can be replaced by trees that will air-condition houses, hold the soil in place, preserve the water table and help make people's lives less stressful and

more agreeable. Indeed, research has shown conclusively that gardening is therapeutic.

Gardens will always be superimposed on the landscape, but in the low-maintenance garden the manipulation of plants is minimal. Plants are chosen to be sympathetic to the environment, to suit a particular purpose, site, aspect and climate. Then they are left alone. The traditional gardeners' chores of watering, feeding, pruning, weeding, pest and disease control are kept to a minimum.

The low-maintenance garden is the thinking person's garden. It allows you to enjoy the garden by spending as much or as little time working in it as you are able. Guilt is eliminated because the garden has been planned to be undemanding. The purpose of this book is to act as a reference—to advocate a laissez-faire approach and to show why one such approach may work and what to do if it fails. Heed E.W. Cole and make your garden "a labour of love, not a slavery and a worry".

The concept

Your garden begins in your imagination when you envisage how you would like it to look. It does not matter how much you know about garden-making, whether your picture is original or a version of someone else's garden, or whether it is practical to build. At this stage your vision is the most important thing because it gives direction to your garden.

Inspiration for your vision could come from many sources. It may be a composite picture that is gleaned from seeing or reading about gardens at home or abroad. It may rely on a particular tradition, becoming your notion of an English, Japanese, Mediterranean, Australian, or Italian garden. You may decide to base your garden on a colour, or a particular plant or group of plants, for example, camellias, azaleas, native plants or roses, and make a garden suited to their needs.

Perhaps you will decide to follow "The Room Principle", which divides a garden into "rooms" to serve different purposes such as an entertainment or outdoor living area; a utility space where the clothes line, storage shed and compost heap are kept; a play lawn for the children; a pool and/or spa garden; a glasshouse or hobby section and so on.

You may want to attract birds, bees or butterflies to the garden or cater for your cats, dogs or other animals, caged birds, ducks or fowls. Or perhaps you need a night-time garden because your busy life mostly precludes its enjoyment during the day.

The imaginary garden produces the concept that you or your designer and/or landscaper will follow and alter where necessary. You will soon realise the constraints as you relate your dream garden to the climate and aspect, the amount of maintenance time you can spend on it, and the likes and dislikes of those who will share it. Being prepared to compromise is an essential ingredient in garden-making as factors such as site, climate, plants and family will inevitably change your ideas. Your mind will also change because you are dealing with living plants. These may grow too large, or fail to grow at all through insect or weather damage.

Every change will help you to learn more about plants and their relationship to their environment. Moving a plant for the third time is not a sign of weakness, it is a sign that you are recognising the needs of the plant and/or the plan, which must be balanced if your garden is to be a low-maintenance success. **Plants that are happy with their environment will require less care from you.** This is the foundation of your low-maintenance garden and if you seriously want to reduce work, this becomes your first constraint. Plant selection should be limited to low-maintenance plants—avoiding those that require excessive maintenance.

It is essential to accept this fact otherwise you could end up with plants that look appealing, but are not easy to grow under your conditions. When conditions have to alter to suit the plants, time-consuming maintenance begins and your purpose is defeated.

Be firm with yourself and confine selection to the plants that are known to suit your climate and conditions without much input from you. If you apply this principle to boundary and shade tree plantings until the garden is well established and a protected environment is created, there will then be enough shelter for some of the higher maintenance plants. Trying to grow these without adequate protection, however, will involve too much care and time for low-maintenance gardening.

Lack of time is the main reason for creating a low-maintenance garden, but obviously no matter how carefully you plan your garden, it will demand some time. A few years ago the United States gardening industry estimated that between work and the weekend chores, even a dedicated gardener is lucky to be able to spend five hours a week in the garden. For the less than dedicated or extremely busy, two or three hours a week is more usual.

Calculate the time you will have for the garden and then plan and plant accordingly. There is little point in putting down a lawn that takes three hours a week to mow if you only have two to spend on the whole garden, or putting in shrubs that require daily watering if the weekend is your only gardening time. Setting your heart on a herbaceous border that needs annual replanting, pruning and staking is not practical without ample time. Gardening depends on time!

Young married couples with a new house and a mortgage spend more time at home gardening than they do when their children are older and weekend sport requires parental participation as a spectator or driver. In their middle years, the garden may come second to other interests. Golf, for example, often wins over lawn mowing. Sometimes it works the other way and the low-maintenance gardener becomes dedicated to gardening. In their old age some people sell their homes and move into units because "the garden is too much for them" while others become absorbed in the garden.

Practical and aesthetic constraints will also influence design and style, for example, the physical nature of the site. A steep site will call for a different garden to one on a flat site. A plan for a house on a busy road where car access is difficult would be impractical if it did not allow parking space for visitors as well as a car turn-around.

Australia's climate contributes to making gardens into outdoor rooms. Gardens are a natural extension of the house; they are rooms without walls or roof so closely related to the house that its interior has a bearing on the garden's style, planting and design. When there is contrast between the two, for example, a mock-Tudor house surrounded by a cactus garden, the result is restless. Far from adding value to the house (an important function of gardens), an incongruous garden will downgrade it.

In a new home you will need to imagine how the garden is to be used and plan accordingly. You may decide to live in the house without a garden for a few months to decide from practical experience what is needed in your plan. The form the garden takes is directly related to its various functions and simple things have to be provided for, such as the need to hang out the washing, a place to wash the car and a play area.

A garden leads into and out of the house. It is seen everyday from doorways and windows and inevitably something of the flavour of the house will be found in the garden. It will reflect your taste as clearly as your living room does, though much more publicly. The garden may be designed to alter the light indoors by filtering out the sun, or to take on the role of an effective air-conditioner, keeping the house cool in summer and warm in winter. If it is badly designed it will do the opposite, making indoors

dark and dreary—cold in winter and hot in summer.

Memorable gardens appeal because there is a sense of cohesion between the house and its interior, the garden and the locality, which makes all appear to be part of the area's general landscape. This is especially apparent in heritage houses where time has developed the plants, mellowed the architecture and the landscape and given the owners the opportunity to remove mistakes and perfect even the smallest details.

Style relies on details. A house filled with French gilt furniture needs the box hedges and formal planting of the grander European gardens to complement it. It would be strange to walk from its gilt glory into either a "Japanese" or an "Australian" landscape.

When used out of context some plants can destroy style. Giant-leaved tropical plants like philodendrons and monstera are magnificent in their native climates and in "tropical" style gardens, but they would be out-of-character in a traditional temperate climate garden with lawns, trees and roses.

Rocks, stonework and paving can either contribute to or rob a garden of its style. Rocks are specific to a locality and change colour and texture according to the geology of their area. If you moved the pitted rocks of the Blue Mountains in New South Wales to a flat, naturally rockless garden, they would seem out of context because they had no link with their new locality. It is also essential to keep planting and construction works in scale with the house and garden. An obvious example is the large tree in a small garden—it dwarfs both house and garden.

Country style furnishings in a modern house or a modern version of a traditional Australian house need a sympathetic garden. The clean lines of contemporary houses and their furnishings suit the restrained planning and planting of Japanese influenced gardens. Cottages and chintz belong to the flowery look of cottage gardens. But take care—true cottage gardens have mostly perennials and these require high maintenance in the form of dead heading, pruning and clump division. But do not close your mind to all perennials or you will miss out on colour and interest. Choose those that will give effect without too much work.

These generalisations are a starting point—a way of activating your eye for detail. The beginning of a garden is a time of confusion, excitement and awareness. You begin to think about plants in a way you never have before—seeing each one through your garden! Now you should also relate their scale to your garden, not simply their usefulness or their appearance. It is good to do this because under or oversized plants are the most common way of ruining a garden and decreasing house values.

Be aware that your proposed garden will also be part of a locality. With this awareness your mind is extended beyond your pre-conceived ideas and the well-meant but often wrong theories of friends or relatives. The pleasure you will find in your garden has begun.

Planning an undemanding garden

Regardless of whether you follow the do-it-yourself approach or engage professional help you will need a plan of the house that shows doors and windows. You will also need photographs of the garden and house taken from and towards every fence, and a survey or rough sketch that shows any existing features you intend to retain. Often the survey can be dispensed with and the site plan used instead, but if the site is steep, a survey will be essential to determine changes in levels.

Collect illustrations of gardens and garden details that you would like to copy or use as inspiration, and draw up lists of the features and the plants you would like included in your garden. Expand your thinking to include everything you hope for even if you cannot afford it! Most gardens are built in stages over the years as funds become available. The swimming pool or gazebo that is out of the question now may be a reality in a few years and will be easier to fit in if you have planned for it.

Also decide whether this garden is to be for the long or short term. Are you planning to move in the near future? Will you be adding an extension to the house? Do you want to put in a watering system and/or garden lighting? The answers have a bearing on your plan and will allow you to work out priorities and budget.

PROFESSIONAL HELP

The perfect time to engage a designer or a designer/landscaper is when the plans for your house or extension are being drawn up. When the designer/landscaper and architect and/or the builder work together from the beginning you will save a great deal of money on the garden simply because you are using the same tradesmen on both the house and the garden.

The bricklayer could build garden retaining walls and paths. The builder's excavating contractor could dig out the pool or foundations for pathways and so on. The plumber and the electrician could continue their work according to the designer/landscaper's instructions and move to the garden as soon as their part in the house is finished.

Every time equipment or tradesmen leave a site and have to be brought in again or others engaged, extra cost is involved. When the landscaper, the builder and the pool builder get together in the planning stage they may make this money-saving arrangement. At the very least they will work together and coordinate their activities.

The landscaper will also be able to rescue your soil from both the builder and the pool man, creating a lifetime saving for you. The site works of each of these trades can ruin garden

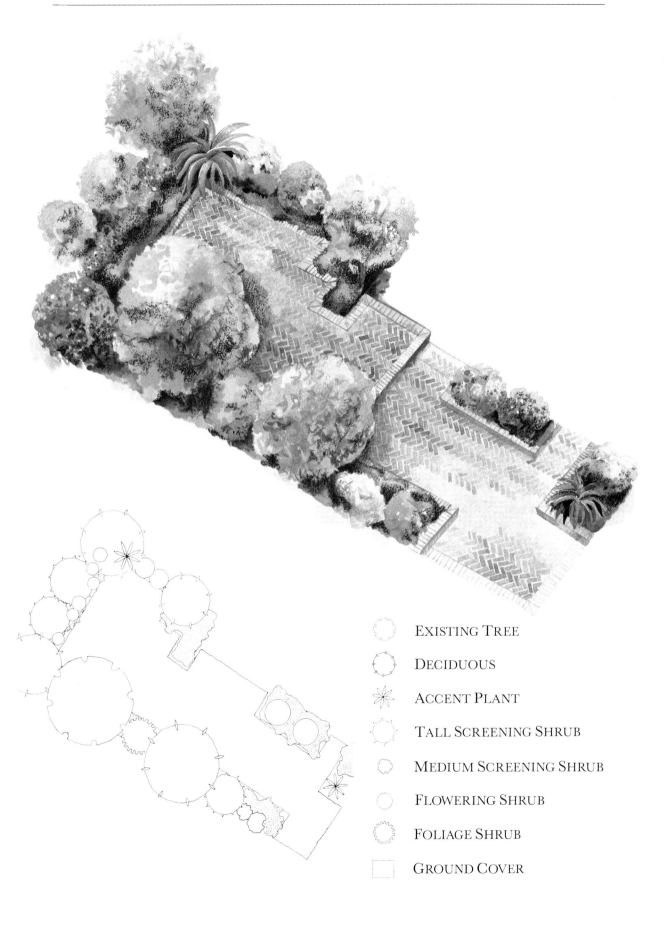

EXISTING TREE

DECIDUOUS

ACCENT PLANT

TALL SCREENING SHRUB

MEDIUM SCREENING SHRUB

FLOWERING SHRUB

FOLIAGE SHRUB

GROUND COVER

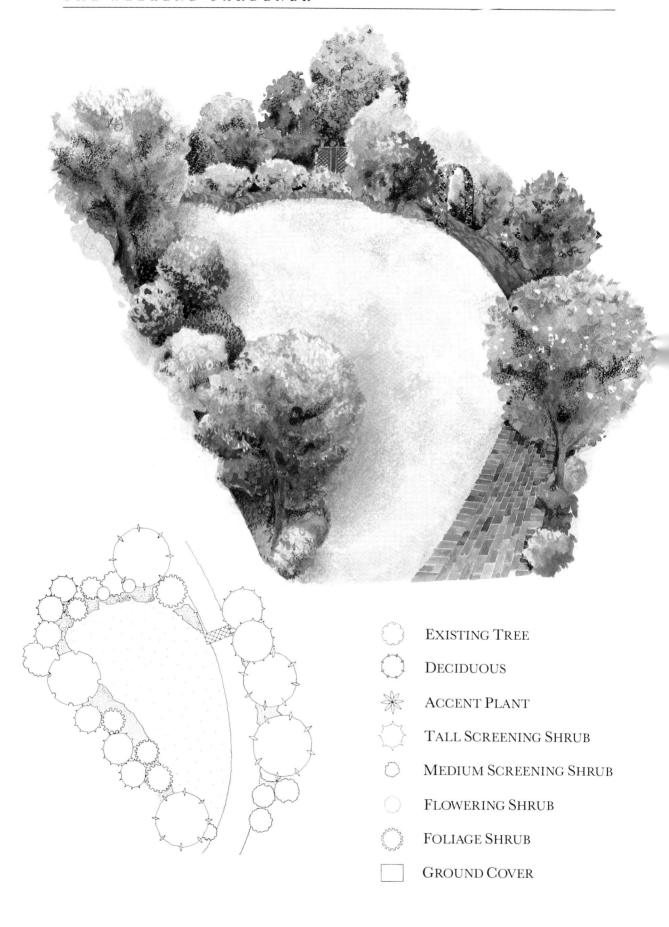

EXISTING TREE

DECIDUOUS

ACCENT PLANT

TALL SCREENING SHRUB

MEDIUM SCREENING SHRUB

FLOWERING SHRUB

FOLIAGE SHRUB

GROUND COVER

soil. If the land is graded or altered in any way to accommodate the house or when it is excavated for the pool, topsoil is usually treated as one with the subsoil.

If topsoil ends up underneath subsoil, you could spend the rest of your gardening life trying to repair it. The designer or landscaper knows this story from experience. They will see that if the topsoil is disturbed it is stockpiled and returned to its rightful place when the building is over. They might also be able to persuade the builder not to leave rubbish all over the site or worse, cover it lightly with soil for you to remove later.

If you drive around new subdivisions you can observe the changes grading has made in an attempt to make the blocks more appealing from a building viewpoint. Take a closer look and you may notice that the large buttress roots of trees are overexposed and the soil is a different colour to that of nearby gardens. This means that the topsoil has been removed and sold, probably to pay for the grading costs. Though this practice is illegal in many areas, only the naive imagine that it does not happen. Buying topsoil to cover the stripped land that now surrounds your house is an expensive and dangerous business. Perennial weeds, such as onion and nut grasses and oxalis, might be introduced with the soil; the soil itself might be poor—either nearly impervious to water, too sandy or too clayey. These faults are all repairable, but at a cost—one your landscaper could help you avoid.

Include the pool builder in your garden and house plans but get the designer or landscaper to site the pool. They will be concerned to place it in the sunniest aspect, whereas the pool company will often put it in the most convenient one from a construction viewpoint. Shade patterns, wind direction and the ultimate size of trees and shrubs near the pool are only a few of the considerations your designer or landscaper will take into account when siting the pool.

Home-owners on a tight budget may be tempted to think that acquiring a few plants

every now and then constitutes the low-maintenance garden. But like the fussiest hobby garden, a low-maintenance garden works well only with informed planning and thorough preparation. It becomes low-maintenance *after* the establishment period, not *during* it!

You will enjoy spending money on your low-maintenance garden because it will soon occur to you that plants *increase* their value by becoming more beautiful with age, unlike other household goods, which deteriorate with time and must be replaced.

Real estate valuers estimate that an attractive garden adds about 20 per cent to the value of the house, but there is no way to measure how much pleasure it brings to the owners' lives. Medical research has proven that gardens and gardening are therapeutic and make us *feel* better. The National Heart Foundation maintains that the exercise of gardening is good for you, especially if you suffer from stress or are in the potential heart attack age bracket.

In the beginning these benefits are often unrecognised. Because of cost, limited time or lack of gardening knowledge, the low-maintenance gardener may see the garden as just one more expense on top of the large investment of the house. They may aim for effect with minimal initial effort and subsequent easy-care maintenance.

At this stage, maintenance and garden-making are often confused and there is an expectation that making the garden will be easy to accomplish. Low-maintenance gardens are a reality but there is no quick or easy way to make a garden! If the benefits of a truly low-maintenance garden are to become part of your life, the same carefully planned and executed groundwork is required as for that of a highly maintained garden.

The professional help you receive may come from a landscape architect, a designer, or a landscape contractor who is also a designer. The landscape architect or designer will draw up plans based on your brief. You then use these to obtain two or more competitive quotes from landscape contractors. The architect or the designer usually concentrates on design and does not participate in garden construction. Many landscape contractors are trained in design and will carry out all the work involved from design to construction and planting.

Before engaging a professional, check their qualifications. Make sure that your architect is a Member of the Australian Institute of Landscape Architects or that your designer is qualified with a certificate or higher qualification from a School of Horticulture of the Department of Technical and Further Education. They may work alone or be attached to a reputable nursery or landscape firm. Ask to see some of their work. Check that your landscape contractor is a Member of the Landscape Contractors' Association, which is a selective body accepting and retaining only those members whose work meets its standards. This is an important point because if things go wrong, you do have some recourse to these organisations.

The finished plan will be based on your brief so if you leave things out when briefing your designer, do not expect to find them in the plan. This is one reason why you should present your designer with lists of features required and plants liked and/or disliked, as well as your collection of inspirational gardens.

The cost of drawing up a plan will vary with the reputation of your architect, designer or landscaper. You could obtain a couple of prices before engaging anyone, but this is not always indicative of value because one plan may be more detailed than another. It is more reliable to decide by reputation and go to someone whose work you have heard about or seen. The designer's good ideas should inspire you for the duration of the garden making.

Once you have the plan, check that it reflects your brief. If it does not, discuss it with the designer and insist on the changes you want, or be convinced that their suggested changes are for the better.

After that do not seek a second opinion! The views of your aunt or your grandmother or the neighbours will only confuse you. Keep in mind that others will see the plan differently and their taste may not coincide with yours. You will waste time arguing the point unnecessarily. If you have given adequate briefing and chosen your designer or landscaper properly, any problems should be ironed out between you.

Usually your designer/landscaper will present a concept plan then a completed plan. Alternatively they may deliver plans in stages, depending on the size of the garden and the design fee. The concept plan is a broad outline of the future garden and should reflect your brief and the designer's ideas. If you are unused to reading plans, the concept plan will be a good way to learn. The swirls and lines are confusing but once you establish where the house and drive are, the remainder soon becomes clear. Check that it meets your main requirements or that you like any variations the designer has introduced. Any changes should be made now.

The scalloped circles of various sizes represent the planting—the larger circles are trees and the smaller circles are shrubs (see page 14). Ground covers and very small planting are run together and quantities are determined by relating plan numbers to the accompanying planting schedule and/or the plan's scale. Precise planting details are generally not given until the plan (or plans) are produced after the concept plan has been accepted.

In most gardens the next plan will be completely detailed and final. It will be drawn to scale so that you or your landscaper can transfer it from paper to ground, placing the plants and all other design elements exactly where they are meant to be.

The designer will also be aware of many alternatives that may not occur to you. They may suggest retaining walls of brick, natural stone, sawn stone, or wood in a variety of forms (sleepers, logs, wharf timbers) laid lengthwise or standing upright. A slope calling for retaining walls may seem like a disadvantage to you, but to a designer the walls could become a handsome feature.

Paving is another area where the designer's

experience will prove valuable. They may either suggest several attractive possibilities and present you with a wide choice of materials, or simply provide one perfect finish, which you immediately recognise is right for the position.

In many low-maintenance gardens, paving is used to eliminate lawn mowing and plant maintenance. However, it must be attractive surfacing or it will irritate you and detract from the appeal of the house. It is easy to rush into inexpensive paving only to find that in the long-term it is unsatisfactory. Rely on your designer for a pleasing design and suggestions about materials. Brick laid in traditional patterns, sawn stone and granite setts are lovely in old gardens being renovated. In gardens around modern houses, a combination of pebbles and wood can work well. Slate, quarry tiles and tree rounds are other useful materials.

Pavers are available in a bewildering variety of finishes and styles. They are advertised as being so simple to put down that anyone can do it, which is not always correct. When you are going to do your own paving, make sure that your paving design is right for the materials you have chosen.

The designer will solve such problems as screening the neighbours and hiding the ugly bits and pieces that are part of any backyard (compost, garbage bins, work and storage areas). The solutions might involve simple inexpensive planting, beautiful screens, walls, or changes in level.

The designer will also be very conscious of the microclimate of your garden and might suggest extending the house into the garden with a simple pergola. It could be roofed in clear acrylic and placed on the western side of the house with a deciduous creeper growing over it, so that you have summer shade and winter sun. They may suggest a small conservatory on the north of the house, in reality a place for you to sit with a few large easy-care plants in the background to make it live up to its title.

These suggestions are all timesavers. The paved pergola or conservatory does not require any maintenance other than the odd sweeping.

Because they have taken up ground space, planting and work are both minimal.

Your designer understands and uses the lay of the land to its advantage. They will attempt to enhance the view, if you have one, or alternatively, plan an interesting inward-looking garden. If the land slopes, they will make the most of changes in levels by using steps and walls. You should expect your designer to have good ideas, experience, refined taste, and the ability to solve problems and to carry out your wishes.

THE DO-IT-YOURSELF APPROACH

If the prospect of drawing a plan is too daunting, collect a few hoses and use these to lay out the paths and beds of your garden. Hoses are useful because they allow good curves to be made. Once you are happy with the result, spade along the line of the hoses to establish garden and path edges. This approach works well on uncomplicated sites, that is, those that are flat or nearly so.

Planting can be simplified by measuring garden beds and selecting plants with your nursery specialist who will advise on planting distances. Also take along your garden photographs and collection of illustrations to help brief your adviser.

DRAWING YOUR OWN PLAN

To draw your own plan you will need a drawing board with a straight edge, a pair of compasses and a right-angled set square. Borrowing a drawing board is better than clearing the dining room table, as your drawing can then remain undisturbed on the board.

Begin by plotting in the essentials: paths, the drive, parking and/or turning areas, space to park the caravan or boat, utility or tool shed,

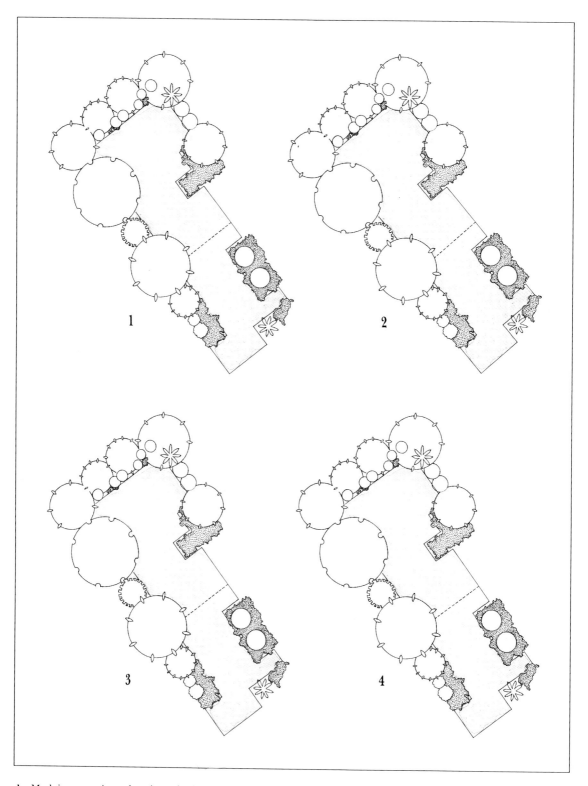

1 Mark in approximate locations of existing features.
2 Base your grid on a recurrent feature, such as fence posts, to achieve a sense of proportion.
3 Mark out the main outlines of the design.
4 Pencil in the detailed planting.

compost and garbage bins (screened from view and near the house but not so close that you will notice the decomposing vegetable smell), sand pit, clothes line, and a grassy play area for children. If possible, put the "living room" parts of the garden on the north side as this has the warmest and sunniest aspect.

Also plot in the telephone and electric light wires, street light posts, gas, water and sewer lines, oil-heater tank and drains. The utilities' servicemen must be able to reach the relevant meters with ease, so avoid planting in their path, or in the path of the hose used to fill the oil tank, or in the way of the wires or pipes that bring services to the house.

If neighbouring trees are likely to shade or overhang your garden, pencil in their likely perimeter to allow for suitable planting.

Shade, privacy and protection from road and noise pollution are essential in most gardens. In some gardens and in exposed areas, especially near the sea, a windbreak will also be called for. Sometimes thorny or spiney plants will be needed under windows to "burglar proof" bedrooms.

Each individual has their own needs in the garden. These could include a sitting-out area

that catches the winter sun, shady trees for a cool spot in summer, a barbeque and entertaining area, a vegetable or herb garden, space for a collection of favourite plants, a swimming pool and/or a spa. Fitting it all in will exercise your mind and use up lots of tracing paper! The grid under the tracing paper will help you keep everything in proportion.

Once the various areas are plotted in you can then begin to plan the planting. If you are following the "room principle", the areas can be divided from each other with screens of plants as an informal planting or a formal clipped hedge, though the latter requires annual trimming.

THE VALUE OF TREES

Trees are the most important element in the garden. Their large size puts the house in perspective and gives it an air of seclusion. They are very practical living air-conditioners that shade walls and reduce the amount of heat entering the house by more than 70 per cent. They will lower air temperature by 10°C and surface temperatures around the house by 25°Celsius. Research has shown that one strategically planted tree has the same cooling

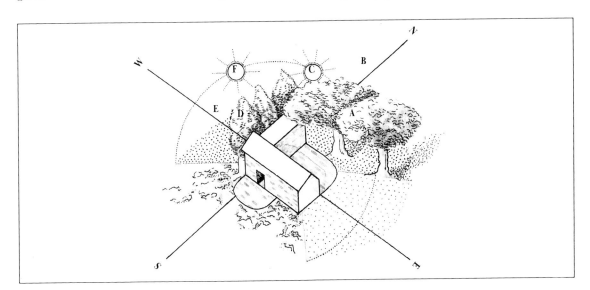

Trees will air-condition your house cheaply and efficiently. Large deciduous trees or high branching evergreens with large canopies (A) on the north side of the house (B) will shade it from summer sun (C). Screening shrubs or trees, or perhaps a pergola on the north-west (D) and west (E) will block out afternoon sun (F).

As the sun is in a lower position in winter, it will still warm the house.

effect as six domestic air-conditioners, and it does not pollute the atmosphere or make a noise!

To make your house cool in summer you will need large, wide-canopied trees on the north side. They could be deciduous or high branching evergreens, which would allow the warm winter sun to reach the house while protecting it from the high noon summer sun.

Screening trees on the north and north-west of the house will shelter it from the low afternoon sun. If there is no space for trees, try vines on a pergola—a grape is a good choice because it has delicious berries and it grows quickly.

MAKING THE MOST OF WINTER SUN

This will save you heating costs. Using deciduous trees or vines close to the house on the north side will allow the sun to reach the walls in winter because it follows a different path through the sky in winter. By keeping the walls warm, the house will be warmed and heating costs will be lowered. The same trees will provide cooling shade in summer.

If you want to have only native plants, the alternatives to deciduous trees are high-branching evergreens such as the taller eucalypts, for example, the lemon-scented gum (*Eucalyptus citriodora*). To achieve this warming effect in winter, make sure that on the northern side any low branching evergreen trees are placed well away from the house.

NATURAL BARRIERS

Privacy and protection from road and noise pollution are important factors to consider when planting. In large gardens, trees are used for this purpose, while in smaller areas it is better to use tall shrubs.

Noise barriers are necessities in most city gardens. Noise level can be reduced by a fence of some solid material—stone, brick or earth, or soil mounds—planted with tall growing grasses (not lawn). Mounds that are planted and heavily mulched are noise absorbent. If these are not feasible, your garden will seem to be less noisy when the noise source (road or whatever) is screened from view with planting. The best plants for this purpose are closely planted, bushy-to-the-ground and densely foliaged evergreens, which have large firm leaves.

The barrier will make the garden private, absorb pollutants from the air and protect the inner garden and the house from dust and dirt from the road.

This planting is your face to the world and your escape from it. Beautiful and practical, it can be a delight to passers-by and to all on the other side of its greenery.

Windbreaks "clothe" a garden and similarly can keep you warm in winter. Excessive wind can distort and damage plant growth and will reduce yield in fruits, especially citrus, which are intolerant of cold winds. When strong winds are combined with salt spray, cold or heat, foliage will be "burnt" and growth will be unsatisfactory.

Windbreaks insulate your home by preventing cold winds reaching the house; this could save up to 35 per cent on your heating bills. Plants slow windspeed by absorbing energy, as opposed to solid screens that deflect wind and increase its speed.

Three layers of planting make an effective windbreak. The first layer is placed closest to the wind source and consists of large wind-tolerant evergreens. Inside this (on the garden side) a second closely placed layer of two or three rows of smaller growing wind-tolerant plants is planted. The third layer may have one or two rows of closely placed, lower growing evergreen shrubs. In the confined space of a suburban block, a row or even a single tree may provide enough shelter from wind. In very large gardens, two or more graduated rows of planting (the lowest on the windward side) may be needed. Where space allows, the formula for a windbreak is based on its effectiveness being ten times the height of the trees; that is a tree gives shelter from wind for a distance of ten times its height.

In very windy seaside gardens, the windbreak may have to be established over two years—the tall layer first so that subsequent layers can be grown under its protection. Most suburban gardens away from the sea will not require this type of windbreak, because closely placed houses provide shelter and there is also not the same space.

Whatever the conditions, planted windbreaks answer the purpose more efficiently and more attractively than solid screens that deflect wind and increase its speed.

WHAT TO AVOID IN THE LOW-MAINTENANCE GARDEN

POT AND TUB PLANTS AND HANGING BASKETS

Especially those in hot sunny or windy positions. These need daily watering during hot weather and watering at least three times a week at other times. Exceptions are succulents such as agaves, yuccas, Jade Trees, geraniums, pelargoniums and hardy plants, for example, metrosideros (New Zealand Christmas Bush), agapanthus (Lily of the Nile), and abelia (see Plant Lists). Potted plants and baskets also need regular fertilising, re-potting every three or four years and many require trimming. The low-maintenance gardener will save time and effort by forgetting these!

ROCK GARDENS

Particularly avoid those adjacent to lawns. The problem here is that the grass finds its way between and under the rocks. Couch is a real pest in this way. Weeding a rock garden demands time and effort.

PLANTING UNDER THE EAVES

This is one of the most difficult positions in gardens. Eaves shelter soil for about two-thirds of their width. The soil within that shelter never receives dew or rain and is permanently dust dry. Even with assiduous watering or a watering system, plants in this location rarely receive enough to survive and their dry foliage becomes host to two-spotted mites. Azaleas, roses, hydrangeas, cypress and similar plants suffer very badly in this position. The solution is to plant 30 cm (12 in) beyond the eaves. Then plants will develop normally and hide the space, and the low-maintenance gardener will not be involved in time-consuming watering.

ROOT-CLINGING VINES

Root-clinging vines are very attractive, but they can escape and begin to grow where they are unwanted! Ivies, climbing fig (*Ficus* species), Boston Ivy and Virginian Creeper, to name but a few, will run amok through the garden, over the roof, in the drains, up the trees and into the living room through the ventilators! They can be kept in check by clipping, but the low-maintenance gardener is not looking for plants that need such maintenance.

LAWNS — LARGE OR SMALL

Of all the time-consuming garden activities, lawn-mowing is the worst. Lawns are advertised as time-savers by the manufacturers of lawn mowers, but they *demand* time on a weekly basis. If you fail to mow, the house looks as though you have skipped town! The mower consumes time too—rarely performing when expected to, forever in need of maintenance—and it is costly, noisy and in many cases air-polluting.

In the low-maintenance garden, lawn occupies minimal space—and then only while the children are young. Once they grow up it can be used for more interesting plantings—perhaps a bed of lavender, colourful perennials, or ground covers with a path running through to a small sitting-out area. Where a lawn cannot be avoided, a mixture of rough grass, weeds such as clover and the easy-to-get-along-with ground covers like native violets and alpine strawberries (see Plant Lists) are satisfactory alternatives, particularly in the shade. If the lawn is small, a pusher mower is kinder to the person mowing (it is exercise and there are no repair bills) the lawn, and to the neighbours because it is not noisy or smelly.

CORD-OPERATED EDGERS OR "SNIPPERS"

These are noisy and require constant maintenance. They are dangerous to the user and those nearby, and they also damage the base of trees. As lawn edgers they restrict plant growth at the edge of the bed for as much as 30 cm (12 in). Instead of allowing grass and garden to meet, they make an ugly broad division between the two. If the lawn is kept small—a wheel-operated edger will save time and effort. Grass around trees can be restrained by spraying with Zero® or Roundup®. Both courses require less maintenance than a cord-operated snipper.

HIGH-MAINTENANCE PLANTS

Some plants require more attention than others, especially if they are grown outside the climate to which they belong. They may need more frequent watering, covering against frost, pruning, frequent feeding and/or mulching, spraying for pests and diseases, and dead-heading. Hibiscus grown in a cold mountainous climate, for example, would need covering against frost; many roses need spraying and pruning; azaleas require spraying; hydrangeas need ample watering.

PLANTS THAT DO NOT SUIT THE CLIMATE

Plants and people are adaptable. They can be moved from their native climate to another most successfully when the new climate is comparable to the first. When it differs, the gardener will have to make special arrangements (which means extra work) to help the plants grow well. Garden plants that are grown in a climate to which they are suited can take care of themselves, except perhaps for watering in dry times.

"MEAN" HOLES AND/OR VERY DEEP HOLES

Planting holes can make or mar a garden. Deep holes that are sunk into the subsoil and filled with organic matter and manures become wells that fill with water from irrigation, rain or drainage. These holes are dug with the best of intentions, but digging into the hard subsoil leaves water with no place to go. The pathogens that cause root rot diseases multiply in badly drained soils and the plants slowly die.

"Mean" holes (only a little wider than the plant's container), which are dug into lawn, grass or hard soil, give the plant too much competition from the voracious grass roots and so the plant stagnates.

IGNORING PERENNIAL WEEDS

Nut grass, oxalis and onion grass keep returning. They can be eliminated by using Roundup® (for large areas) or Zero® (for small gardens), but one spraying will not be enough. The best time to apply these weedkillers is when the plants are flowering; then repeat applications as new growth appears. Once the weeds are more or less under control they can be covered with a mulching mat, preferably of the woven type. By excluding light but allowing air and water through, the mulching material prevents weed development, while still allowing shrubs and trees nearby to continue to grow. The mat can be hidden by overlaying it with a mulch of organic matter.

FORGETTING TO WATER

Once in the ground new plantings need daily watering in summer and at least twice weekly watering in winter. Generous soaking from a gently running hose is kept up until the depression around the plant is filled with water, which is then allowed to drain away before another application is made. Avoid using a nozzle, as these are too strong and harden surface soil. Water breakers deliver water more softly and are a good investment. Two or three months after planting summer watering can be reduced to two thorough weekly applications. Water is the life-blood of plants and if you forget to water, particularly during summer, the plant is likely to die.

PONDS AND FOUNTAINS

A pond is charming in the garden but trying to prevent the cat and birds eating the fish involves netting it. To prevent mosquito infestation, ponds need cleaning out at regular intervals, which is difficult if they are filled with fish and waterlilies. The latter are attractive to aphids and need spraying if the flowers are to open nicely. Most sprays kill fish, the exception being Rogor®. These chores mean maintenance though perhaps not much. Only you can decide whether you have the time or the inclination for this.

MISUNDERSTANDING GROUND COVERS

Ground covers in recent years have been hailed as the great work savers and everything with a spreading horizontal growth habit has been labelled a "ground cover". Perhaps they are, but not all should be welcomed in the low-maintenance garden because some actually shelter weeds. Thorny or spiky ground covers are too difficult to weed, so the weeds take over.

Violets are delightful ground covers, but not for the low-maintenance garden. They shelter voracious weedy growers such as honeysuckle, which runs through and under their leaves hiding itself from view until the weeding job is high maintenance. Others have thick stiff branches, like some of the cotoneasters. They let light in and up come the weeds!

Biennials that seed themselves and come up everywhere, and bushy dense ground covers are the best low-maintenance ground cover.

Creating your no-fuss garden

THE SOIL

Maintenance of a well thought out low-maintenance garden is hardly any trouble at all, but there are no ways to save time and effort when it comes to *creating* it! The preparation stage actually asks more, not less of you, because it is your intention to let the garden fend for itself in the years ahead and now is the time to spend time, effort and money on the basics.

The most basic part of the garden is its soil. This is going to feed the plants and hold them in place for the duration of the house despite you, climatic excesses and the inroads of people and animals.

An elementary knowledge of soil will help you to maintain your garden and to understand why some plants do well and others die. You will save money on water and fertilisers by not applying these unnecessarily, and your awareness of the relationship between the soil and plants will alert you to the needs of both.

Your aim is to develop a very fertile crumbly soil with a high organic matter content so that it receives and retains moisture well, drains effectively and is well aerated. Once you achieve this, most maintenance is done.

Soil is fascinatingly complex; it depends on its own structure and it alters whenever there is a change in that structure. It is made of particles of weathered rock that have been whittled away by the action of the climate over aeons of time. Soil types vary depending on the rock below, the steepness of the land and the length of time the climate has been working on the rock. Soil depth is also variable and its texture changes with depth. Usually there is more clay in the deeper layers. Some soils are shallow—that is, rock is found within a spade depth of the surface. Deep soils are at least 1 m (3 ft) deep.

Garden soils are usually divided into four main groups. To determine which group your soil falls into, dig a deep pit (soil "profile") at least 1 m (3 ft) deep and look at the layers (or "horizons") revealed.

Sandy throughout: These soils are found on recent (or old) beach sands, or on very steep sandstone slopes. They may or may not be shallow and very rocky. They reveal layers that are light to loamy sand on the surface with sandier or clayey sand deeper in the profile.

Loam to light clay through-out: These soils develop on shales, particularly thin shale beds that are intermixed with clay, volcanic rocks such as basalt and dacite, some mudstones, limestone and young alluvium. They have a well-drained crumbly loam at the surface; deeper into the profile they become more clayey but are still crumbly.

Loam to heavy clay at depth: The loamy, rather crumbly surface soil becomes heavy, blocky clay deeper down. It is hard in dry weather and gluggy in wet. Many mudstones and shales develop such soils.

Soils with a sharp change from sand to clay: These are known as duplex soils because they have an upper layer of sand or loamy sand that suddenly changes to one of heavy or sandy clay. These duplex soils are old mudstone and shale, sandstone and granite. Soil colour and acidity change with depth. Most gardeners regard dark soil as the ideal. Humus, the result of putting organic matter into the soil, darkens it. While colour is not important the best way to look after soil is to continually add humus, which does darken its surface. If your garden soil grows lighter with the years, it is in poor condition and needs the addition of humus.

Mulching is an effective way of adding humus to the soil in the low-maintenance garden. Allowing leaf and twig litter to fall from trees and shrubs and remain beneath their shelter to disintegrate and return to the soil, is another. You can see this happening on white sandy soils where, over the years, the combination of leaf-drop from the plants and mulching changes the soil colour to grey.

Most Australian soils are neutral to acid—a range that suits our natives and the majority of popular exotic shrubs. Lime decreases acidity and it is rarely necessary to add lime to our soils. Simple and inexpensive soil testing (or pH) kits are available and can be used if you suspect a soil problem. These kits measure the acidity or alkalinity of soil, and indicate the ability of plants to absorb soil nutrients. Below pH7 is acid and above is alkaline. Most plants like a slightly acid soil in the pH5.5-6.5 range. Below the ideal range, major elements such as calcium and phosphorus become less available with diminishing range and manganese may cause toxicity. Above pH7 minor trace elements such as manganese, boron, iron, copper and zinc, fall away quickly. The addition of lime increases pH, while the addition of sulphur diminishes it.

In most states the Department of Agriculture offers a home garden soil testing service. But unless things absolutely refuse to grow, you will probably manage by relying on observations. Hydrangeas are excellent indicators—flowering blue in acid soils and pink to deep red-pink in lightly limey to strongly limey soils respectively.

The soil is populated by both living microsopic soil organisms that help to break down organic matter to make nutrients available to plants, and by harmful plant pathogens, which may attack roots and cause plant death. Harmful pathogens build up when drainage is ineffective because the soil air spaces are waterlogged. On the other hand beneficial soil organisms multiply in well drained, nicely aerated soils and contribute to plant health by controlling the pathogens.

The term "well-drained soil" is used so often in gardening books and catalogues that some of its significance has been lost. When applied to a plant it means that in badly drained soils the plant could die as it is subject to root rot diseases that increase when soil air is excluded from the root zone.

This is an oversimplification, but perhaps it is enough to indicate that caring for soil is vital to the support of plant life. If you neglect the soil either through lack of water, poor drainage or insufficient humus from a lack of organic matter, plants will suffer from infertility and disease attack. When you care for the soil, the beneficial soil organisms dependent on soil air will help your garden to thrive.

SOIL IMPROVERS

Heavy clay and cracking soils: These can be improved by adding both gypsum and organic matter. On just moist (as opposed to wet) soil, gypsum is applied at 1-1.5kg (2-3lb) per m² together with a generous application of organic matter—at least 4 cm (1½ in) and up to 10 cm (4 in) deep. The organic matter helps the gypsum to work more effectively. The gypsum aggregates the clay particles into small lumps, which improves aeration and drainage.

Sandy soils: These can be water repellent and if this is the case, the plants will suffffer from lack of water. Adding organic matter increases the water-holding capacity of the soil. Organic matter can be worked in by light cultivation and also by laying it on the surface as a mulch. In time it filters into the soil.

Saline Soils: Near the sea where salt spray causes build-up, in flat areas where the water table is close to the surface, or in hilly locales that have a porous topsoil and a heavy clay base, the soil may be saline. In the worst cases the soil surface becomes white with salt (sodium chloride is unusual except by the sea). High concentrates of any salts will affect growth. Growing a wide variety of salt-tolerant species may lower the water table, and an application of fresh water will wash the salts away. Then, in time, less salt-tolerant species can be planted. Drainage can be improved to ensure quicker movement of excess water. Water by long weekly or twice weekly soakings. This deposits less salt on the foliage than frequent light sprinklings.

Too-alkaline soils: Very limey or calcareous soils (high in lime and calcium) register a high pH level and inhibit growth because they contain too much sodium. The trace elements such as zinc, iron and manganese may also be too low. Green crops can be grown for one or two years and ploughed in before any planting takes place. The addition of organic matter over the years will lower the pH slowly. To acidify the soil chemically, add elementary sulphur in powder form and aluminium sulphate—both in large quantities. The low-maintenance gardener, however, is unlikely to follow any of these courses. They should grow those plants that like calcareous soils.

Over-acidic soils: These have a pH of 5.5 or less and are treated with lime, which reduces their acidity and manganese or aluminium levels, and supplies deficient calcium. The forms used are: agricultural or garden lime, which is calcium carbonate; ground limestone; slaked lime or calcium hydroxide; or dolomite, a mixture of calcium and magnesium carbonates.

Of these, slaked lime is the most effective means of raising the pH, followed by lime and dolomite. Dolomite has the extra benefit of supplying magnesium. When soils are very acidic, the easiest solution is to choose plants that are known to thrive in acid soils, such as azaleas, camellias, pieris and rhododendrons. Even so, to make certain that calcium and magnesium are available to the plants, the careful addition of small amounts of lime or dolomite may be needed.

Even if you have no intention of amending your soil as a result of learning about its pH, you can garden happily and with minimal effort by planting species known to suit your environment. Adding organic matter to the soil not only in the early days of the garden but throughout its lifetime is, next to watering, the best care you can give your soil. Organic matter comprises such things as manures, compost, leaves, prunings, grass clippings, straw and spent hops. In heavy soils it improves the texture of the soil, increases air spaces and improves both drainage and water holding capacity.

In light soils organic matter aggregates soil particles and reduces air spaces so water holding capacity is increased. The living organisms of organic matter help nutrients become available to plants and keep plants in better health by controlling disease-causing, soil-borne pathogens. Organic matter also causes earthworm build-up, which improves soil aeration and nutrition. Adding a generous mulch of organic matter once or twice a year is therefore an easy and quick way to maintain or increase both soil fertility and plant health.

COMPOST

The low-maintenance garden affords the opportunity to re-cycle its litter as compost either by digging it in, or more usually as a mulch. Fallen leaves rot and return humus to the soil even if you simply leave them where they fall. In theory this sounds fine but it works only in part. Leaves that fall on paths or lawns eventually have to be gathered up or paths become slippery and dangerous, and grass yellows and dies. The answer to this is the compost heap.

Compost is the decomposed residue of animal or vegetable matter in any quantities, either alone or combined with several materials with or without the addition of chemical fertilisers. Animal manures, kitchen or garden refuse including vegetable peelings and leaves, grass clippings and prunings, and shredded paper, can be used in compost (avoid diseased plants or menace weeds such as onion weed, nutgrass and oxalis).

Burning or throwing out prunings or leaves is wasteful and depletes your garden of their valuable organic matter. Burning also causes air pollution. Even hard-to-break-down leaves such as eucalypts can be included in compost with the addition of a purchased "compost accelerator".

The simplest compost-making method is to pile the components in layers and cover the heap with plastic to keep it warm and humid, a condition that contributes to decomposition. It can also be left uncovered, but it will take longer to decompose. Compost-making bins, boxes and tumblers are available from nurseries. The best ones have air movement through the sides and no floor, which allows contact with the earth and encourages earthworms. Really keen compost-makers use three receptacles—one rotting down, one being filled and one in use.

The compost may be built up in layers of different materials, including one or more of soil, or be confined to one kind. A light sprinkling of lime and/or a sprinkling of compost accelerator is added to prevent the compost from smelling. A light dressing of fertiliser may also be sprinkled over one layer of the compost. Shade cloth or fine wire mesh may be used to cover the heap and contain compost flies. When lime is included, it is best not to use the resulting compost on lime-hating plants such as camellias and azaleas. The product is ready when the components have rotted down to the point where they are unrecognisable and the material is crumbly—usually 3–6 months, except for tumblers, which take only 14–21 days when full.

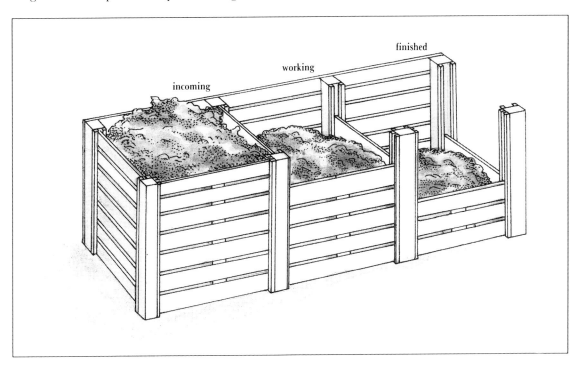

incoming   working   finished

This is one example of a compost bin. The first section holds new material, which is transferred to the second section after it rots. Well-rotted material from the second section can then be sifted into the third section, which acts as a storage bin until the material can be used. The bin is designed so that front and side boards slide out to make turning and removing material easy.

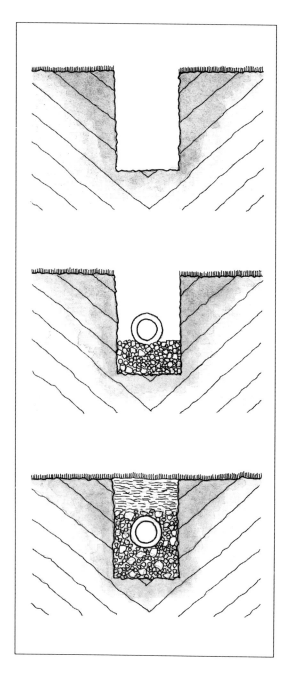

1 Dig a trench about 300 mm (11 in) wide by 450 mm (8 in) deep. Allow a fall of around 200 mm (8 in) over 20 m (65 ft) length.
2 Cover the base with broken tile and rough aggregate about 10-15 cm (4-6 in) deep. Sit the pipe on top. The top of the pipe should be 25-30 cm (10-12 in) below soil level.
3 Fill in around the pipe and to the top with aggregate. Place soil on top and restore soil level.

The low-maintenance gardener relies on soil conditioning to keep the garden in good health. Compost making is one of the easiest possible garden (and rubbish disposal) practices, and also helps to repair the damaged environment.

D R A I N A G E

In most gardening books you will find the expression "good drainage". Almost all plants are said to want it, but how do you know what "good drainage" is?

Good drainage is necessary because it prevents root rot and soil-borne diseases building up and debilitating or killing plants. Heavy clay soils are often poorly drained while sandy soils usually drain freely. If you suspect wet spots, dig a hole in each area—about 600 mm (23 in) deep—fill with water and check 24 hours later. If the drainage is satisfactory the water will have soaked away.

Digging, adding organic matter (especially bulky material) and the use of gypsum will all improve drainage. If these measures do not drain the soil well enough, you will need to put in drains in a pattern that picks up the water and takes it to an outlet. The conventional pattern is "herringbone". You may need only a single line of drainage or several lateral drains to bring the water to a central pipe and then to a soakaway.

Making a drain used to be heavy work because pipes were heavy, but now there are flexible slot drainage pipes that make this job easy to do. They are so light that one person can carry many metres, and drainage is now a do-it-yourself-job.

S I T E   P R E P A R A T I O N

With completed plan in hand you stand and survey the wilderness that hopefully will become your garden and ask "Where do I start?". The first step is to clean up, removing all surface and buried rubbish left by the builders or the previous owners.

The next step is to kill off all visible weed growth with one or more sprays of Zero® or Roundup® when the weeds are in flower. Allow new weed growth to emerge and then spray again. If the weeds are perennials, such as nut and onion grass and oxalis, weed killing could take a year or longer. Annual weeds may need only one or two applications.

If you are fortunate the site soil will be intact, though all too often grading has removed it. If you bring in garden soil, take care that it is loam and comes from a reputable supplier, otherwise sandy, clayey, or weed-infested soils may add to your problems.

Where the site soil is present, treat it with gypsum at the rate of 1–1.5 kg (2–3lb) per m³ then add an organic or "humus" mix or mushroom compost at three bags to the square metre. This will vary with the nature of the soil. Either fork this in, or hire a rotary hoe and scarifier. When the ground is heavy, ripping before you scarify and adding organic matter, will improve drainage.

Choose the organic matter with care. Mushroom compost certainly improves soil but it can also "burn" native plants. The "humus" or organic mixes available from nurseries and soil suppliers benefit all soil types. In very heavy soils, gypsum followed by a mix of sharp sand and humus mix is another approach.

In many organic mixes composted sawdust is the main ingredient. These mixes and mushroom compost or any organic materials improve drainage and aeration and give plants a good beginning. Time spent on preparing the soil saves maintenance time in the long run and ensures satisfactory growth. Avoid the temptation to take short cuts by planting into unprepared soil—it will mean poor growth and more work for you in the future.

LAYING OUT THE DESIGN

Transferring the design from paper to the garden relies on measurements. Use a tape measure and peg out the plan according to the scale of the drawing, which is usually 1 cm (⅓ in) to 1 m (3 ft). If measuring becomes too complicated, curves can be set out using the garden hose.

Plot the positions of large trees first and then stand back and take a good look at them to make certain they have room to grow. Check they are not under wires or too close to the house, paths, drains, or sewers.

Once you are satisfied with their positions, plant them and then put in the taller shrubs. Follow with the smaller shrubs and finally the ground covers and fill-in plants. Dig wide, shallow holes, not deep square ones, and plant with a damp soil ball into damp soil.

If you do not have a plan to follow, start by giving your garden the trees it needs and then plant a section at a time putting in the tallest shrubs first and working your way down to the ground covers and fill-in plants.

Choosing easy-care plants

A GUIDE TO PLANT BUYING

Planting is the most satisfying part of gardening. There is a conclusiveness about it— and a feeling of relief because all the debating about what goes where is over. Worry now gives place to expectation as you wait for the growth to begin.

However, people often find the actual size of plants disappointing, especially if their garden is brand new and plant-less. They want something *big*, because they see height as the solution to the problem of a new-looking garden.

This attitude is a mistake—at least for about 95 per cent of the plants in gardens. Plants such as natives and evergreen shrubs are rapid growers and in the advanced stage (200 mm (8 in) diameter container) are about 1–1.5 m (3–5 ft) high (except for dwarf varieties). This is an excellent size to buy—they are tall enough to be seen and come in containers small enough to make hole-digging easy.

Smaller native plants 10–30 cm (4–12 in) high in smaller containers would do just as well. The growth rate of most native and exotic trees and shrubs is 60 cm (24 in) to 1 m (3 ft) annually in their young stages. Health, not height, should be the standard when buying plants. Choose plants that look young, have healthy foliage and stems and are a nice height in relation to their container size. A few blemishes on foliage through pest attack is acceptable. Total freedom from pests and diseases is no longer feasible as nurseries and gardeners try to use less and less chemical means to control these.

Plants should be firmly anchored in the container without any movement at ground level. When the plant is not too tall for its container, this indicates that it is young and has a healthy root system. A few roots edging their way through the drainage hole of the pot are a further sign of health. They can be left on or cut off if they make removal of the container difficult.

However, if you want something large to give a settled effect to your garden, evergreens (except eucalypts, but including conifers) and deciduous trees are available in super-advanced stages and are worth buying to achieve shade in a hurry. Because the growth rate of many natives including eucalypts is so rapid, there is no reason to purchase these in super sizes. In any case, smaller plants anchor themselves more satisfactorily in the ground and cope with wind better than larger ones.

Most of us expect plants to be plump as well as tall. Our expectations are one thing—

plant growth habits are another. Some plants develop width first then put on height, while others become tall first and then thicken up. You can see this with camellia japonica varieties. Twenty different varieties, all the same age and growing side-by-side under nursery conditions, will show at least five different shapes—short and plump, plump and medium height, tall and fairly thick, tall and open and very tall and willowy.

Most people want to cut the willowy ones back to induce "bushiness". They are unable to accept that these plants are good value and a perfect shape for their variety. If they purchase the willowy ones it is with the intention of pruning to make them "bushy". However, these are usually by-passed in favour of varieties with a plump habit. The tragedy of this misconception is that many gardens miss out on beautiful plants because their owners— without any basis for thinking it—have decided that "plump is beautiful" and willowy is definitely doubtful!

Camellias, azaleas, hibiscus, rhododendrons, oleanders, crepe myrtles— plants that are available in a wide range of varieties—have a range of growth habits. They should be chosen for their flowers, or their habits, or both. Plump bushes are sometimes best in tubs while in other situations, willowy growth may look better. Shrubs and tree shapes are design elements in the garden as well as the shade patterns they cast on paving, lawn or walls. Willowy plants have more interesting shapes and shadows than plump ones, but both types have a place depending on the use to which they are being put.

Not all plants are straight! It is a mistake to insist that all trees and shrubs have perfectly straight main stems. Camellia sasanqua varieties, for example, may be either very erect, or inclined to lean first to one side, then to the other, so that the main stem is anything but straight. In nature, wattles, leptospermums, jacarandas, pepper trees, robinias, honey-locusts, some eucalypts, and gordonias do not have straight trunks, even though in nurseries they are often trained to a straight trunk.

Sometimes a bent trunk and/or low branches are far more attractive than an absolutely straight trunk. Again each has its place depending on space and the effect you seek to achieve; the garden will be characterless if you insist that all plants are plump and absolutely straight.

Marks on foliage or a few holes and occasional brown tips to leaves are minor pest and disease problems that can be ignored. In the interests of the environment, nursery specialists are using less toxic sprays or are not spraying as often to avoid further pollution of the atmosphere. This means that foliage does have some blemishes. Once nurseries depended on rigid pest and disease control measures that involved eradication of all insects. This upset the natural order by removing both the pest and its predator. The current approach is to keep the pests under control but not to the point where all useful predators are destroyed. Both gardeners and nursery specialists must accept minor pest and disease problems, otherwise the cost to the environment will be too great. Waxy scales (pink, white, brown, black) on a variety of plants should not be tolerated as they are easily checked with white or summer oil. Other problems that should not be tolerated include white markings on the stems of *Pittosporum eugenioides* 'Variegata', and gummy exudations on conifers, which are indicative of borers. Gumminess on stone fruit trees indicates the fungal disease brown rot. This and peach leaf curl, found on both fruiting and ornamental peaches, can be controlled quite easily with copper oxychloride sprays. Plants that "wobble" at ground level in their containers are probably suffering from root rot diseases. You should ask the nursery specialist to reassure you that they are in good health before purchasing them.

Yellowing or yellowed foliage on plants that are meant to be green can also be a sign of root rot, and is generally found on one side of the plant. It is most noticeable in autumn and winter. Some of the plants affected are lemons, daphne, rhododendrons, azaleas and luculia. The condition becomes obvious after prolonged periods of heavy rain, which causes waterlogging of the soil. Usually it cannot be cured and infected plants should be avoided.

Yellowing of the new growth of citrus can be the result of insect attack by sap-sucking insects, a problem which should have been cured in the nursery by spraying with Rogor® or Lebaycid®.

Some foliage problems are seasonal and may be caused by such factors as cold. Grapefruit is one of the most cold-sensitive citrus. Cold winter winds will cause its leaves to roll over, close up and yellow. Other citrus can be similarly affected, though to a lesser degree.

Some plants develop "symptoms" that are wrongly taken to be signs of a disease. The first corky bark on liquidambar is raised and cracked and only partly covers the smooth trunk and branches. It looks, however, as though some warty disease is infecting the plant. But by next year when all surfaces are covered the "disease" no longer causes concern.

The best way to get a good deal on your plants is to go to a reputable nursery where qualified advisers will help sort out your requirements and answer your queries with patience. Nurseries survive by fulfilling customers' needs; if they fail they know you will not be back and their income will suffer.

Even more reassuring for you is the fact that nursery specialists love plants. Most were hobbyists to begin with and often they are the second or third generations of their family to grow plants. They like their work and they are storehouses of information. Every day customers tell them of successes and failures, and they use this information to determine which plants the nursery will grow and which it will discard.

When you seek advice in a nursery listen to the young person who comes to your aid! He or she will either have, or be studying for, a Certificate or a Diploma of Horticulture—four years minimum of both practical and theoretical horitcultural knowledge that will work to your benefit.

Many gardeners discard this help quite thoughtlessly believing that some omnipotent, green-thumbed, overalled gardener will appear to solve their problems. The old-time nurseryman has disappeared and been replaced by a younger generation of equally keen but much better educated nursery specialists.

Similarly, women now dominate garden retailing. With a whole garden to plant you will need a friend in the business so make a friend of your nursery specialist. It is best to visit a nursery in the mornings or on a Saturday. These are the least busy times and the specialist will not be interrupted too much. Buy plants for one section of the garden at a time—put those in and come back for more the following week, looking up your specialist again because they now know your story and plans for the garden.

You could have everything delivered on the same day, but if planting is delayed you will have to water the plants at least daily in winter and twice daily in summer and protect them from damage by wind and animals.

HOLDING PLANTS AT HOME

Unfortunately it is possible to lose a percentage of your plants once you get them home because of the manner in which they are held until planting time.

In the nursery they were close together on a level water-absorbent site. Place yours about 4 or 5 cm (1½–2 in) apart on a level area of soil in light shade. If the pots are not level more water will reach one side of the plant or may escape too quickly. Concrete or any other hard, water-shedding surface is unsuitable because the water you apply runs through the pot too soon and away from it as run-off from the hard surface. On soil, watering wets both plant and soil, which keeps a nicely humid atmosphere around your plants. The plants were used to ample sunlight in the nursery. If you leave them in the boot of the car for a couple of days, in the garage, the dry shelter of the eaves, or under the stairs, they will be half dead within two

days. If your holding position faces west or north and has a heat reflecting brick or stone wall behind the plants, it may take only a morning (during summer) to kill your purchases.

Adequate watering, a level water-absorbent surface, humidity at ground level, light shade and the protection one affords the other when they are fairly closely spaced, are a must when keeping plants at home.

How you apply water also affects the plant's survival. Never apply water to container plants with a hose clad with a nozzle. It is much too severe and hardens the soil to the point where the top 2-3 cm (¾-1 in) looks wet but is dust dry below. Always use a hose with a water breaker.

An alternative to a water breaker is a *gently* running hose with your middle finger held lightly under the watering end of the hose to lift the water up and let it fall gently onto each container until it is filled to the rim. Allow this to drain away and then repeat it. Provided the standing surface drains sufficiently to avoid soggy conditions, and the drainage holes in the pots are working, you need not be afraid of overwatering container grown plants.

How long you hold plants depends on their size and that of their container. A very tall plant that blows over in every small breeze is obviously getting too large to be held for long periods. Most plants in 200 mm (8 in) diameter containers can be held for a year before repotting is necessary—the exception being any that grow quickly and become top-heavy and inclined to blow over. Checking for pests and diseases will be necessary as will a little light tip pruning of shrubs (not trees). From a low-maintenance viewpoint, it is preferable not to hold plants, but to buy them as needed, and plant either that day or the next, saving the bother of looking after potted plants.

AT THE NURSERY

When asked by the nursery specialist what height you want a plant to grow, be specific and reply in metres or feet. An answer such as "not too tall", is unenlightening. If you are not good with heights, measure the height between the ground and eaves of your house and use that as your scale. Similarly, the answer to the question "How wide is your garden bed" should be a definite measurement. "How much space is there between the fence and the pool?" is another vital measurement. "Not much" or "a lot" is inadequate from a planting viewpoint. When asked how old your plant is, express its age approximately in years. When you provide adequate information the right advice is given in return; insufficient or inaccurate information results in wrong advice.

Know where north is in your garden and always let the adviser know what aspect you are planting. Some plants are very fussy about their position and will only grow well on the sunny northern aspect or the cool southern side of the house. A long winded conference between you and your partner to establish this while the adviser waits (often with someone else waiting on them), frustrates everyone.

Define the wet spots in your garden as precisely as you can. Is it wet all year round, or wet only in the winter? How wet? Boggy wet all the time or just damp? If it dries out does the topsoil become hard and cracked? Which aspect does it face? What causes the wetness— low lying land, a septic tank, absence of drainage? Some plants will enjoy one or more of these positions but not all, so being specific helps to narrow the field of choice and ensure that you take the right plant home.

Also tell the adviser where you live, as many areas of a city have their own microclimate which is suitable for plants that would not grow in other parts of the same city. The Palm Beach peninsula in New South Wales, for example, grows tropical plants very well, but it is not suitable for the cold climate plants that do so well at Wahroonga, only 25 kilometres away. Your suburb can also be indicative of your soil type, another useful piece of information the adviser will apply when helping you.

It is also important to know the distances of your boundaries and the space between house and fences, the distances between electricity and other services and proposed planting, and the distance between that and any existing planting or features. Trees and shrubs can then be chosen to fit those dimensions and you will not buy more or less than is needed.

When you have cultural (plant health) problems, there is even greater need for specific replies. Responding to "How often do you water?" with "Not too often" is unhelpful. Say how much water you have given the plant (and whether you watered it daily or weekly), and estimate how long you have had the plant.

If there is a persistent pest or disease problem your adviser needs to know which spray was applied, how often it was used, and the time of day spraying took place. Where root problems are suspected, it helps to describe the depth and width of the planting hole, what else apart from soil went into it, how frequently the plant was watered and fertilised, how long it has been in the ground, and whether or not it is subject to wind.

Most of the problems mentioned can always be overcome by taking a photograph of your house with you when you visit a nursery. One glance and the specialist can be well-acquainted with your needs.

Alternative plants are often as good or better than the plants nominated on your plan so when a plant is unavailable, look at the alternatives and tell the adviser what other plants it will be growing near so that foliage, form and flowers will be compatible. Do not be afraid to change plants if you dislike those on the plan, but do take into account the fact that nursery-size plants are unprepossessing and many do not give much indication of their future handsome state at maturity. This is one of the hardest areas in garden making. You need faith in your designer/adviser in order to accept some plants in their young stages because they may look decidedly unappealing. If you are trying to make a decision about which trees to plant, it can help to walk around nearby suburbs or a botanic garden until you see a mature tree that you like.

PLANT HEIGHT

This can be confusing—labels will say one thing—books another—your designer/ adviser something else! In a sense all are correct. Plants respond to their environment and under good conditions in their ideal climate they could reach a greater height than they would in, for example, a windy situation in a less-than-ideal climate. The amount of care they receive may encourage or restrict growth. Competition will also affect height. Trees competing with each other for light and food in a forest tend to become tall and narrow, while those in an open garden will reach perhaps half their forest height and will grow wider than they would if growing among other trees. This is especially noticeable with tall varieties of eucalypts, which do not grow to their full height under garden conditions.

Trees are loosely classified as single trunked plants that grow more than 7 m (23 ft) tall, while shrubs are multi-stemmed plants over 7 m tall. There are of course exceptions, such as the multi-stemmed mallee eucalypts, which grow under that height, and the single-stemmed camellia sasanqua—some varieties of which can reach 10 m (33 ft) under ideal conditions.

Shrubs under 5 m (16 ft) high are easily controlled. If a shrub is listed as a metre taller than you want it to be, plant it anyway! When it reaches the desired height, you can restrict its growth by shearing it all over, just after flowering. Do this every couple of years or annually, depending on the growth rate. Most evergreen shrubs (except wattles), are improved by shearing so you will not be doing them harm and the work involved will be minimal.

Take given heights as a guide only. Most 2 m (6½ ft) high shrubs will grow to 3 m (10 ft) given the right conditions, and most 3 m high shrubs can be kept at 2 m by trimming. Time and disappointment will be saved if this is kept in mind.

ROOTS

These are another needless worry for many new gardeners. Poplars, ornamental figs (*Ficus* species) and willows may cause problems but few other plants should if planted 2-5 m (6½–16 ft) away from drains, foundations and paths. Two metres (6½ ft) away is sufficient for plants up to 7 m (23 ft) high; 3-5 m (10-16 ft) for those over 7 metres.

With age, tree roots rise above ground close to the base of the tree and act like buttresses to hold the tree firmly in the ground. Around 20 years, it may be necessary to lift paving for a metre or so around the tree to allow for this development. These roots are interesting and have a rugged beauty that complements the trunk. They should not be cut or covered with soil. Any alteration to the soil level at this stage will slowly kill the tree.

In new housing areas tree roots in sewer lines are rarely a problem because new and improved pipe material and the joins being used for the lines are not affected by roots. Old-fashioned pipes did allow tree roots to enter.

Plumbers and water supply bodies invariably blame tree roots for any problem that befalls pipes, but quite often the pipe was old and already leaking, which would encourage the roots to head in its direction. (Roots grow towards water.) Tablets such as Rootox can be put into the sewer on a monthly basis to discourage tree roots from growing.

You can also discourage roots from growing in the direction of the house, path or whatever, by applying more water on the opposite side.

Tree roots do not run under houses unless there is a leaky pipe or drainage problem, which makes that area wet. If this is the case then there is a much greater problem on hand than errant tree roots! The area under the house should be bone dry—a situation which is totally inhospitable to tree roots. Cracking foundations have been known to occur when roots dry out the area and destabilise foundations. During droughts or when large trees are removed or die, the roots are no longer taking up their accustomed amount of water and the soil

Many trees are often removed to allow for the building of a fence. A better solution is to have a break in the foundations to allow for tree roots.

To avoid root damage, the best place for wires is under the centre of a tree in a tunnel. The pipe and tunnel should extend for about 2 m (6½ ft) either side of the tree's centre.

shrinks, which causes movement in the foundation. This applies to giant trees with a voracious root system and huge roots such as *Ficus* species. Palms and the popular trees of gardens are not in this category when they are 2-5 m (6½-16 ft) away from the foundations (depending on their height).

Tree roots do take up whatever moisture they can from the ground and over the years this, combined with the shade from their canopy, will kill off the grass below. Plants that will grow in this area become restricted to ground covers such as the native violet, helxine (Soleirolia), clivias and some of the hardier spring flowering bulbs such as tritelia.

BRANCHES

Like tree roots, branches have to be considered, but if you have allowed roots room to spread, then the branches will have room too. A tall tree that is 5 m (16 ft) from your house means that it could (*need not* but *could*) be 10 m (33 ft) across at maturity and that is very large

indeed. If the tips of branches did reach the house in 20 years, they could be cut off fairly easily. Some trees lose their branches or parts of them readily. Many eucalypts and the Silky Oak, for example, are in this class and may need siting further from the house.

LEAVES

All plants lose leaves—most evergreens lose their leaves on a year round basis and a few at a time. Deciduous trees lose their leaves in autumn. Some finely textured leaves, such as those of the Chinese Tallow Wood and maples, fall to the ground and disintegrate rapidly. Others such as plane trees blow about and deteriorate very slowly. All leaves, however, are capable of filling gutters, blocking drains, making it difficult for the grass to grow, and also causing slippery paths. The low-maintenance gardener should site trees where these problems will be minimal and keep in mind that all fallen foliage is good for the soil as well as being a natural way of increasing soil fertility.

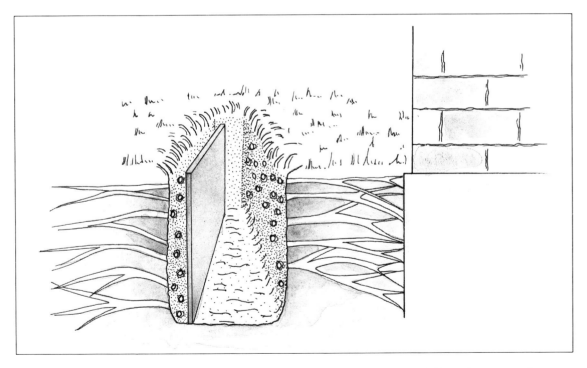

Root damage to foundations can be prevented with a solid barrier of fibro aluminium, or rigid plastic. The severed roots on the house side will die. The roots attached to the tree will live, but will not cross the barrier.

GARDENERS' LANGUAGE

PLANT NAMES

When you go shopping for plants, among the difficulties encountered are their names. They may render a non-plants person inarticulate trying to pronounce or spell them.

Plants are classified by botanists into an order that reflects similarities among the world's plant life. Botanists are concerned with every rank of the plant kingdom, which is the most inclusive of the natural kingdoms and is divided into division, class, order and the following groups:

Family Each plant belongs to a family, all members of which share certain characteristics. Most gardeners do not bother too much with the family rank of their plants, although an appreciation of this level frequently offers clues to the cultural requirements of others in the same family.

Genus A plant family is divided into closely related plant groups called genera (plural of genus). The first word in a plant's botanic name is the genus to which it belongs, for example, *Acacia* (wattles), *Rosa* (roses), *Liquidambar* (Sweet Gum).

Species There may be one or many species—each a particular kind of plant—within a genus. These are designated by specific names that are the second words in the botanic names of plants, for example, *Acacia floribunda; Rosa multiflora; Liquidambar styraciflua.*

Variety A third word in the botanic name indicates a variety (or subspecies), for example, *Liquidambar formosana monticola.* This denotes a plant that is growing wild or is in the garden, which differs in some way (flower colour or form, leaf size) from the species.

Horticultural variety (clone) is one that has been developed in cultivation and is not found in the wild. These plants may have a varietal name added to the generic and specific names, which is indicated by single quotes, for example, *Liquidambar styraciflua* 'Festerii'.

Hybrid is the result of a cross between two

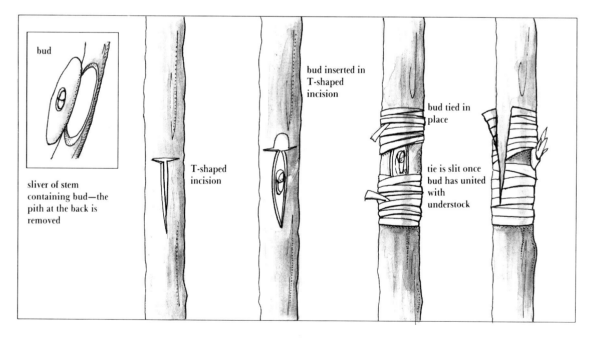

bud

sliver of stem containing bud—the pith at the back is removed

T-shaped incision

bud inserted in T-shaped incision

bud tied in place

tie is slit once bud has united with understock

The bud is found in the axil of the leaf. The leaf is removed. The bud is taken from the stem by cutting it out, taking only a sliver of wood about 1.75 cm (5/8 in) long (varies with the plant being budded). The pith at the back of the bud is removed. The bud is then inserted into a T-shaped incision in the understock, matching the cambium layers (the area of green below the outer covering) of both bud and stock. It is then tied in place. Once growth develops from the bud, the tie is cut off. The top of the stock is cut off when the bud develops into the new plant.

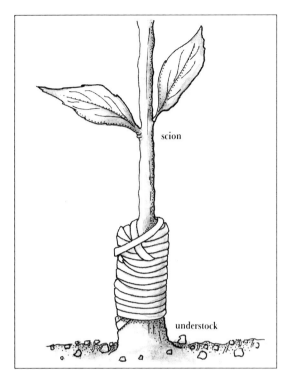

Hold the scion in place by tying with string. Painting the exposed area with a protective paint will help to seal the wound and prevent water reaching it.

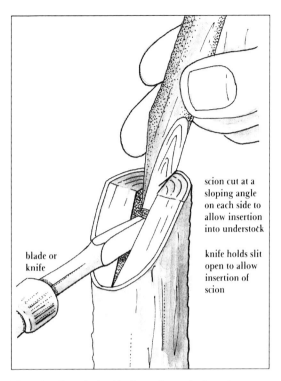

The scion is united with the understock, the robust root system of a closely related plant. This process is often used for deciduous and ornamental fruits.

species, two varieties, two strains, or two plants of different genera.

Strain is applied to mixtures or colour blends with similar characteristics but which are not sufficiently distinct to be separated out and given a horticultural variety name. Most gardeners encounter this term with annuals, seedlings (or bedding plants) and vegetables, but it is also applied to other plants.

Plant names are either derived from Latin or Greek or are "Latinised" to make the botanic language of plants international. They may commemorate a person or place or perhaps refer to some feature of the plant. Banksia, for example, is named after Sir Joseph Banks who was the first to collect these plants. Pyracantha (fire-thorn) comes from "pyr" meaning fire, and "acanthos" meaning thorn. The plant hunting story often involves the history, geography and politics of the age, plant properties—medicinal, culinary, poisonous—and of course their ornamental garden uses.

Other terms you will meet when purchasing plants are marketing or propagation terms:

Budding Roses and many deciduous and ornamental fruits including apples, peaches, cherries, plums, apricots and mulberries are grown by budding. This process unites a desirable plant, which is not a strong grower on its own roots, with the robust root system of a closely related plant, called the understock.

In summer a 'T'-shaped incision is made in the root stock. A bud is taken from the axil of the leaf of the desired plant and cut to a shield shape to fit into this incision. The wood behind the shield is removed to expose the green cambium layer, which is then matched with that in the cut on the understock. The two are tied together until they "knit", then the top growth on the understock is cut away leaving the bud to take over as a new plant on the root of the understock.

Bare-root refers to a plant that is sold in winter during its dormant or leafless period when deciduous plants can be lifted without soil and transplanted. They are classed as "bare-rooted", though the roots are usually packaged in a moisture retentive mix, which is discarded at planting. Roses, fruit trees and many ornamental trees are sold in this way.

Balled plants are dug from the field with a ball of soil surrounding the roots to avoid any root disturbance. This root ball is wrapped in hessian or other material, which is removed during transplanting. It is important that both bare root and balled plants are not allowed to dry out.

Grafting has a similar result to budding. It involves inserting a small section of one plant (the scion) into a branch or stem of another and matching their cambium layers. Once the graft "takes" the scion grows into a plant with the characteristics of the plant from which it was cut. Old fruit trees and camellias are often grafted to convert the plant to a better variety.

ANNUALS, BEDDING PLANTS, SEEDLINGS

These terms cover plants that live and die within a year. They also include many biennials, which, though capable of living for longer, are treated as annuals and dug up within the year. These are the colour-makers of our gardens. Vegetables are also annuals with a few exceptions such as asparagus, chokoes, globe artichokes, strawberries and rhubarb.

Colourful annuals are not used in low-maintenance gardens as much as they should be because of a widely held belief that they need a lot of attention. This used to be true but most modern varieties are highly disease resistant, very free flowering and quite undemanding, which makes them very suitable for the low-maintenance garden.

As long as they are watered in dry times and grown in fertile soil in a suitable aspect and climate, the following varieties will give colour without involving you in any effort other than planting. Those marked ■ will carry over from one year to another by self-sowing. Left

alone many will ramble through all the bare spots in the garden to make a lovely ground cover. They are not bothered too much by pest and disease problems. Viola and pansies will flower for up to 8 months.

- Alyssum (Sweet Alice)
- Impatiens (Busy Lizzie) (perennial)
  Petunia
  Chrysanthemums
- Marigolds (some varieties self-sow)
- Aquilegia (Columbine-Granny's Bonnets)
  Dahlias such as 'Hi-Dolly'
- Forget-me-not
- Honesty
  Helianthus (Sun Flowers)
  Mignonette
- Nasturtium
  Pansies
  Penstemons
- Primula
  Viola
- Bellis perennis
  Lobelia
  Ageratum
  Cosmos
- Salvia
  Phlox

Study their needs (see "Colourful fill-in plants") and plant these accordingly. Year round colour could be yours if you plan for it. You will not be obliged to spray or fertilise—just look and enjoy!

Herbaceous perennials live for three years or more and die down (or are cut down) to ground level in winter, coming into full new growth in spring. Examples are Michaelmas Daisies, Lavender Shower, Astilbes, Perennial Hibiscus, Perennial Phlox, Delphiniums (perennial types).

Perennials are soft wooded sub-shrubby plants, which last at least three years. Those popular in gardens are grown for their masses of flowers

or their colourful foliage. Some examples are Daisies (Marguerite, Shasta and Pyrethrum), Geraniums, Pelargoniums, Impatiens, Euryops, Acanthus, Chrysanthemum (may also be treated as an annual), Golden Rod (Solidago), Bergenia, Helleborus, Echium, Gazania, Nepeta, Cerastium, Rudbeckia.

Plants are sold by container size, which is measured by diameter. There is a multitude of sizes, shapes and materials. The most generally used terms are:

tube this may be long and slender, or short and wide with a diameter under 7.5 cm (3 in).

pot size is usually applied to pots with a diameter of:

    100 mm   (4 in)
    125 mm   (5 in)
    150 mm   (6 in)

advanced plant container diameter sizes are:

    175 mm   (7 in)
    200 mm   (8 in)
    250 mm   (10 in)
    300 mm   (12 in)

super advanced plant container diameter sizes are:

    400 mm   (14 in) and a variety of container sizes and shapes up to the semi-mature size.

semi-mature plants are grown in containers described by volume from:

    50 litre   (88 pints) upwards.

PLANT LISTINGS

Plants are listed in the following way:

Botanic Name The universally accepted scientific name for the plant is given first.

Common Name This follows the scientific name. One or several common names may be given to a plant by gardeners. These names may vary from one area to another and may be the same name for several different plants.

Climatic Zone Plants must be chosen to suit the climate for low-maintenance gardening.

Tropical T The temperatures are high throughout the year with heavy summer rains from December to March. The tropical zone covers north Queensland, the Northern Territory and some parts of Western Australia. Planting is mainly confined to tropical subjects, as those from dry climates succumb during the wet season.

Subtropical S An area of reliable summer rainfall with a dry mild winter. Humidity is high from November to March. Frosts are rare on the coast and common in highland and nearby inland areas. Plants include local species and adaptable species from both tropical and temperate areas. Dry climate plants may not stand the wet season and tropical subjects may be too slow growing in the cool winter.

Warm Temperate WT Characterised by a year-round rainfall with a winter maximum, high summer temperatures and fairly dependable sea breezes. The coast is salt laden, the winters are mild with light frost except on the coast, which is frost free. A wide range of plants from all climates can be grown within this zone.

Mediterranean M A maritime climate with hot dry summer temperatures moderated by sea breezes or aggravated by hot inland winds. Winters are cool with light to medium frosts becoming severe near the mountains, with cold, violent winter winds in the south and west sectors. Moderate rainfall is evenly distributed throughout the year. A wide variety of dry climate plants are grown plus adaptable species from cool climate areas.

Cool Temperate CT Low winter temperatures with frost likely in the colder months. Serious droughts and heatwaves are rare though hot, dry, northerly summer winds are common. Suitable for cool climate plants.

Cool Highland H The mountains or highland areas have mild dry temperatures and cooler nights. Most areas have long, cold winters with heavy frosts and some snowfalls on the higher parts. Variable winds are cold in winter or hot and dry in summer. Rainfall is variable. Plants grown are cold climate or cold resistant, local or introduced species.

Inland C Extremely high summer temperatures and a low rainfall. Variable dry winds and prolonged droughts are experienced. Lack of water is the limiting factor in plant growth.

Indigenous species are the least trouble to grow but exotic dry land plants do well where water is available.

Family Knowing a plant's family may be an indicator of its appearance and sometimes of plants to associate with it and/or suggest its needs when no other information is available.

Description A brief description of the plant follows including flower colour or other attraction.

SHADE TOLERANCE

Plants may be segregated into groups:

Sun lovers These need sun and do not grow well if given more than two hours shade daily.

Filtered light These need light shade but are tolerant of heavy shade or more than 5 hours shade a day in mid-winter.

Wind tolerance Wind tolerance accompanied by debilitating factors including lack of water, salt and reflected heat from walls or other hard surfaces, will scorch foliage and may kill plants. Bag or shade mesh screens are needed to protect young plants in windy sites during the establishment period.

Soil and Conditions Unless otherwise stated, the plants listed tolerate a wide range of soils and conditions. As long as water is available in drought times and plants are mulched and kept free of weeds, they will grow well in the climates nominated.

Frost Tolerance If plants are grown in the climates indicated, they will tolerate the frosts experienced in those areas.

Landscape Use Plants are listed according to their principal landscape use. As many plants have more than one use, they are described once and thereafter listed by name only in other sections.

HOW PLANTS GROW

Plants need light, air, water, nutrients and space to grow. Like humanity, land-growing green plants are made of protoplasm (mostly water and protein) and have a variety of tissues serving different functions. Both consume and store energy and are able to reproduce themselves. Plants also need root room. Another important difference is that plants are able to manufacture food from inorganic materials.

PLANT PARTS AND THEIR FUNCTIONS

THE ORGANISATION OF PLANT CELLS

The smallest single unit of a plant is the microscopic cell of living protoplasm, which is enclosed by a wall of cellulose. Cells group together to form tissues that are distinct parts or organs of the plant—the flower, fruit, leaf stem, seed and root. This applies to all garden plants. There are very simple forms of plant life, which are simply a collection of cells.

THE SEEDS

Beneath the protective coating that protects a seed is an embryonic plant and the stored food (starch, proteins, oils) it will need until it is able to manufacture its own food. Some seeds are edible, for example, grains, nuts and legumes. Seeds germinate under a variety of conditions, which vary with species.

Among factors that influence germination are high or low temperatures, moisture, absence or presence of light, a dormancy period to allow after-ripening and the cracking of the seed coat.

Germination begins as a rootlet grows downwards and a shoot grows upwards, carrying the seed leaves containing stored food. Most plants have two seed leaves except conifers, which have many, and grasses, irises and lilies, which only have one. The seed leaves are almost always different from the plant's mature leaves.

ROOTS

At the beginning of its life the plant is sustained by tiny white rootlets that absorb water and chemical nutrients from the soil. These are carried throughout the plant and if they were not available to it, the plant would die. In the presence of water, roots branch and change their function and appearance. Older roots develop a bark-like skin and become water and nutrient

THE STRUCTURE AND FUNCTION OF PLANTS

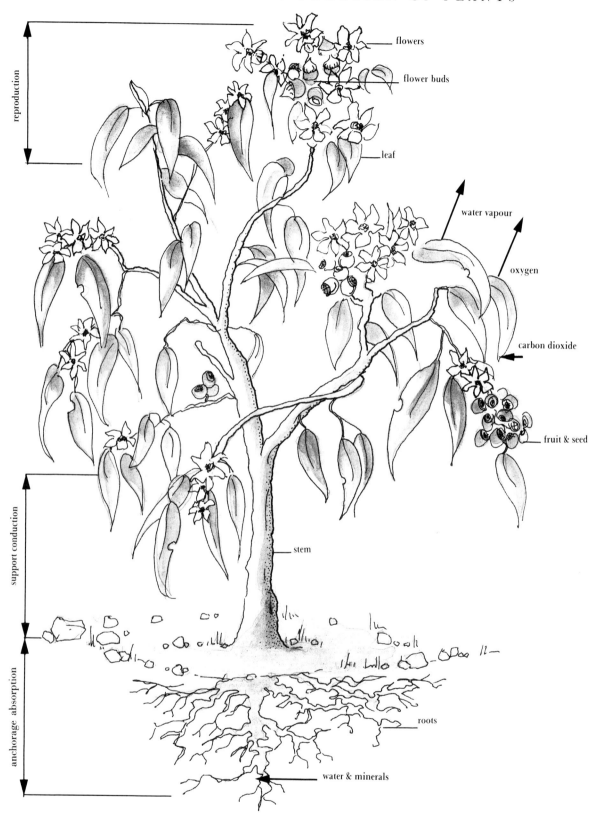

reproduction

flowers

flower buds

leaf

water vapour

oxygen

carbon dioxide

fruit & seed

support conduction

stem

anchorage absorption

roots

water & minerals

transporters or food storage vessels. The growing points that allow the plant to extend are at their tender root tips. The whole root system acts as an anchor. Just behind the root tip is the vital area of delicate root hairs that absorb water and chemicals from the soil. If these die, the plant will wilt until a new set develops. For this reason transplanting should be done carefully so that roots are not exposed to the drying effect of sun or wind.

LEAVES

These are the foodmaking area of the plant. This is where photosynthesis (manufacture of sugar and other carbohydrates) occurs. The plant uses the green chlorophyll in the leaves to change carbon dioxide, water, and energy from sunlight into carbohydrates and oxygen.

STEM

In between the seed leaves or inside a single leaf is the growing tip that becomes the stem. Along it buds will open and produce the first "true" leaves. Its terminal buds will take growth upwards and its lateral buds will take it outwards. When buds are removed, growth habit is altered, for example, with pruning or disbudding.

One function of the stem is to support the plant. In woody plants rigid stems gain strength from lignin and cellulose. With age, unused parts of the duct system become heartwood and hold the plant erect. Stems vary with plant type. Vines and creepers are anchored by twining or tendrils because their stems do not support them. Perennials and annuals may be too soft stemmed and will need staking. Bulbs, corms and tubers are modified stems that act as food storage organs in the dormant period and convert their stored food to sugar when growth commences.

The stem is the carrier of water and nutrients to the buds, leaves and flowers. It returns food as sugars, manufactured by the leaves, back to the roots. In the majority of plants the duct system is on either side of or very near the cambium layer, which is just inside the bark or outer covering of the stem.

The cambium layer is responsible for increases in plant growth and maintains the duct system. Ring-barking, mower damage, girdling of the stem by fencing wire or plant ties, or any other means including insect or animal attack, will damage and may kill the plant.

Water from the soil is conducted through the stem to the leaves where it meets carbon dioxide, which has entered the leaf through its breathing pores (stomata). To prevent dehydration in dry or windy weather (indicated by wilting), the stomata will close to keep the quantities of water necessary for foodmaking within the leaves. Leaves may be protected from dehydration by waxy, resinous, hairy or scaly leaf surfaces. Excess water vapour and oxygen leave the plant through the pores.

During winter deciduous plants become dormant and foodmaking stops; in evergreens it slows down. In both cases this reduces the demand for water, which makes winter a safe time for transplanting; even then though it is advisable to keep bare-rooted plants well covered against wind and sun until they are planted.

Container-grown plants, which have the roots protected by the soil in the container, can be planted year round provided water is available in the establishment period.

If leaves become coated with grime or dust or infected with disease as in black spot-ridden roses, this interferes with the foodmaking process and causes leaves to turn yellow and fall. Deciduous plants are used in city plantings because they lose their grimy leaves annually.

FLOWERS AND FRUIT

Most garden plants, except the spore bearing ferns, bear flowers. Most have male and female organs in the same flower on the one plant (bisexual or hermaphrodite plants). Unisexual plants have male and female organs in different

flowers. They are termed monoecious when both are on the one plant, and dioecious when they are on two different plants. Seeds are produced when the female sexual parts of a flower are fertilised by the male sexual cells or pollen. Seeds are capable of reproducing the plant, but they may vary widely from the parent.

Plants are propagated by seeds. In commercial undertakings, selection and breeding programmes are followed to produce trueness-to-type and uniformity especially with cereals, annual flowers and vegetables. Root, stem and leaf cuttings, tubers, corms, bulbs, divisions, budding and grafting, and layering are other propagation techniques used to ensure trueness-to-type.

CLIMATE ZONES

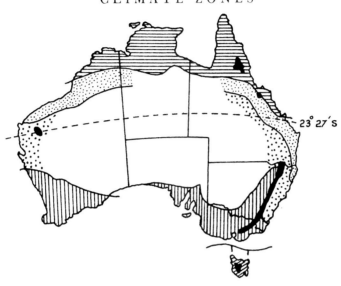

SYMBOL	MAP SYMBOL	CLIMATE	EXAMPLE
T.		Tropical	Darwin, Rockhampton
S.		Subtropical	Brisbane
W.T.		Warm Temperate	Sydney
M.		Mediterranean	Melbourne, Perth Adelaide
C.T.		Cool Temperate	Hobart
H.		Highland	see map
C		Arid	see map

KEY TO SYMBOLS IN PLANT LISTS

E EVERGREEN

* NATIVE

\# SHADE TOLERANT SPECIES

D DECIDUOUS

Shrubs and trees for privacy

These are easy-to-care for quick growers that tolerate cutting to shape and can be relied on to give privacy in a hurry.

Abelia x grandiflora
GLOSSY ABELIA

E

HEIGHT: 2 m (6½ ft)
CLIMATE: S., W.T., M., C.T., H.
FAMILY: Caprifoliaceae
DESCRIPTION: Pendulous branch tips give a pleasing outline to this glossy, dark green shrub that has mauve-white flower bells for about ten weeks in summer and autumn. Prune after flowering.

Acacia floribunda
WHITE SALLY; GOSSAMER WATTLE

E

HEIGHT: 4 m (13 ft)
CLIMATE: T., S., W.T., M.
FAMILY: Mimosaceae
DESCRIPTION: A tree-like shrub with pendulous branches and pointed, finely veined foliage. It has long cylinders of pale yellow flowers for 2 months during late winter and early spring. Among the hundreds of wattles, others to consider are *A. cardiophylla*. *A. podalyriifolia*, and *A. saligna*.

Aloysia triphylla
LEMON VERBENA

D

HEIGHT: 3 m (10 ft)
CLIMATE: T., S., W. T., M., C. T.
FAMILY: Verbenaceae
DESCRIPTION: Fast growing tree-like shrub with long, slightly rough, aromatic leaves and terminal panicles of tiny pale purple flowers. Regulate height by pruning. Grow near paths so that when brushed in passing, it will release a refreshing lemon scent.

Banksia ericifolia
HEATH-LEAVED BANKSIA

E

HEIGHT: 5-7 m (16-23 ft)
CLIMATE: S., W. T., M.
FAMILY: Proteaceae
DESCRIPTION: Compact, bushy shrub, lit up through autumn and winter by long orange-yellow flower spikes. First flowers appear in the second year. It is salt, wind and waterlogging tolerant.

'Port Wine' has rose-pink flower spikes, 'Golden Candles' has outsize flower spikes.

Banksia robur
SWAMP BANKSIA;
BROAD-LEAVED BANKSIA

E

HEIGHT: 2 m (6½ ft)
CLIMATE: W. T., M., C.T.
FAMILY: Proteaceae
DESCRIPTION: An open, branching shrub with large, dark green leaves in whorls towards the end of branches. New growth is vermilion and changes to russet red. It has blue-green flowers from late autumn to spring and is wind and waterlogging tolerant.

Others are: *B. victoriae*, *B. coccinea*, and *B. spinulosa*.

Banksia serrata
OLD MAN BANKSIA; SAW BANKSIA

E

HEIGHT: 6-10 m (19½-33 ft)
CLIMATE: S., W. T., M., C.T.
FAMILY: Proteaceae
DESCRIPTION: A small tree with a crooked grey trunk and branches covered with "cobblestone" bark. Flowers are large, green-grey cylinders, borne from late autumn to early spring and followed by grey seed cones—to give "Big Bad Banksia Men".

Berberis thunbergii
'Superba'
BIG LEAVED PURPLE BARBERRY

D

HEIGHT: 1.5-3.5 m (5-11½ ft)
CLIMATE: W. T., M., C.T., H
FAMILY: Berberidaceae
DESCRIPTION: Deep purple-plum coloured foliage. Height can be reduced by trimming lightly just after flowering. An easily grown specimen or hedge for sunny places. Others are: *B. thunbergii* 'Atropurpurea', which has smaller, lighter plum foliage; *B. thunbergii* 'Nana' is dwarf size.

Buxus microphylla var. *japonica*
JAPANESE BOX

E

HEIGHT: 1.3-2.5 m (4-8 ft)
CLIMATE: W. T., M., C.T., H
FAMILY: Buxaceae
DESCRIPTION: Gleaming light green foliage some of which turns soft orange in autumn, without falling. This sturdy dense shrub withstands light or heavy trimming. Attractive singly, as a hedge, or in tubs in sun or part shade.

Buxus sempervirens
ENGLISH BOX

E

HEIGHT: 60 cm-6 m (24 in-19½ ft)
CLIMATE: S., W. T., M., C.T., H
FAMILY: Buxaceae
DESCRIPTION: Hardy evergreen shrub with dark green foliage. Grown chiefly for clipping into formal shapes and delightful as a hedge, topiary or container plant. Suits sun or filtered shade.

Callistemon citrinus
'Endeavour'
ENDEAVOUR BOTTLEBRUSH

E

HEIGHT: 2-3 m (6½-10 ft)
CLIMATE: T., S., W.T., M., C.T.
FAMILY: Myrtaceae

DESCRIPTION: Crimson, silky soft brushes are highlighted by many gold tipped stamens in spring—the main season—and again in late summer to early autumn. It is a broad bushy shrub to 2 m (6½ ft) wide. Snip off spent flowers. Others are. *C. pallidus* (Lemon Bottlebrush); *C. phonoecius* (Fiery Bottlebrush). See "Trees for shade and windbreak" for *C. viminalis* and *C. salignus*.

Camellia japonica
CAMELLIA

E

HEIGHT: 2-5 m (6½-16½ ft)
CLIMATE: S., W.T., M., C.T., H
FAMILY: Theaceae
DESCRIPTION: The lovely winter blooms last well indoors. Colours are pink, white and red. Some are marbled, stippled or mottled. Height can be controlled by trimming. They need shade for half the day and ample water, well drained soil and mulched roots. Fertilise in spring with Camellia and Azalea plant food.

Camellia reticulata
CAMELLIA, RETICS

E

HEIGHT: 5 m (16 ft)
CLIMATE: W.T., M., C.T., H
FAMILY: Theaceae

DESCRIPTION: The open habit reveals the branch structure. These produce single and double pink, red or white blooms as much as 18 cm (7 in) across. They are long lived and stand sun. There are many varieties.

Camellia sasanqua
SASANQUA CAMELLIA

E

HEIGHT: 3-7 m (10-23 ft)
CLIMATE: S., W.T., M., C.T., H
FAMILY: Theaceae
DESCRIPTION: Superb evergreen shrubs with pink, white or red flowers. These can be kept as low as 1.3 m (4 ft) by occasional trimming. Some varieties may be left to become small trees. They can be kept narrow and so suit confined spaces. They also suit sun, shade or semi shade, tolerate wind, and bloom from April to October.

Cotoneaster lactea
COTONEASTER

E

HEIGHT: 3-5 m (10-16 ft)
CLIMATE: T., S., W.T., M., C.T., H
FAMILY: Rosaceae

DESCRIPTION: A salt and wind tolerant, fast growing, easily maintained shrub with large, oval, grey-green leaves showing a grey-white undersurface and pendulous clusters of bright red, late summer to winter berries. Others are *C. glaucophyllus*—habit and berry colour are similar to above; *C. franchetii*—sage-green foliage, orange-scarlet fruits, slender growth; *C. pannosus*—smaller foliage and fruits than *C. franchetti.*

Duranta repens
SKY FLOWER

E

HEIGHT: 3-5 m (10-16 ft)
CLIMATE: T., S., W.T., M., C.T., H
FAMILY: Vebenaceae
DESCRIPTION: A very fast growing, wind tolerant, bushy shrub with spiny, drooping branches of light green foliage and lilac flowers summer to autumn followed by yellow berries, which attract birds.

D. repens 'Alba' has white flowers.

Escallonia macrantha
ESCALLONIA

E

HEIGHT: 4-5 m (13-16 ft)
CLIMATE: T., S., W.T., M., C.T., H
FAMILY: Saxifracaceae
DESCRIPTION: A dense, bushy shrub that is much prettier when pruned to 2-3 m (6½-10 ft). It has clean looking, shiny dark green foliage and rose-crimson flowers. Others are available with pink or pinkish-white flowers.

Eupatorium megalophyllum
PURPLE MIST FLOWER

E

HEIGHT: 2-3 m (6½-10 ft)
CLIMATE: T., S., W.T., M.
FAMILY: Compositae
DESCRIPTION: This has 18 cm (7 in) or more heart-shaped, felty, olive-green leaves, veined purple and purplish stems, and lilac-mauve spring flower heads up to 18 cm (7 in) across. *E. sordidum* has lighter flowers and smaller foliage and is not as tall.

Gordonia axillaris

GORDONIA

E

HEIGHT: 2.5-4.5 m (8-15 ft)
CLIMATE: T., S., W.T., M., C.T.
FAMILY: Theaceae
DESCRIPTION: The single, white, camellia-like, autumn to spring flowers are 10 cm (4 in) across with a centre of gold tipped stamens. The foliage is dark green and glossy with an occasional orange leaf.

G. *yunnanense* has smaller leaves and flowers.

Grevillea banksii

BANKS' GREVILLEA

E ✳

HEIGHT: 3-5 m (10-16 ft)
CLIMATE: T., S., W.T., M., C.T., H.
FAMILY: Proteaceae
DESCRIPTION: A shrub or small tree with brushes of brilliant red spider flowers in summer. Likes full sun and moist soils. A light trimming just after flowering maintains shape and height required.

Hakea salicifolia

WILLOW-LEAVED HAKEA

E ✳

HEIGHT: 5 m (16 ft)
CLIMATE: W.T., M., C.T.
FAMILY: Proteaceae
DESCRIPTION: A tall shrub or small tree, which is usually multi-stemmed, with a deep crown extending almost to ground level, and bronze tinged foliage. Dense cream clusters of spring flowers are followed by persistent, woody, egg-shaped fruits.

Hibiscus rosa sinensis

'Surfrider'
HIBISCUS

HEIGHT: 2–3 m (6½–10 ft)
CLIMATE: T., S., W.T., M.
FAMILY: Malvaceae
DESCRIPTION: Lush, dark green, summer blooming shrubs with large trumpet flowers and prominent stamens. They need well drained soil in full sun or part shade. Fertilise in spring with a complete plant food. Trim lightly after flowering to maintain height and shape. Numerous double and single varieties in a wide range of colours and heights are available.

Ilex x altaclarensis
'J.C. Van Tol'
VAN TOL'S HOLLY

E

HEIGHT: 2–4 m (6½–13 ft)
CLIMATE: W. T., M., C.T., H.
FAMILY: Aquifoliaceae
DESCRIPTION: This has abundant, glossy crimson berries, dark lustrous green almost spineless leaves and purplish stems. Trim lightly after flowering to control height and width. Likes ample water, rich, organic soil and mulch to keep the roots cool. Suits sun or part shade.

Laurus nobilis
BAY TREE; LAUREL

E

HEIGHT: 2–14 m (6½–46 ft)
CLIMATE: T., S., W.T., M., C.T., H.
FAMILY: Lauraceae
DESCRIPTION: The salt and wind tolerant Laurel Wreath of the Greeks and Romans produces the leaves used in cooking. It has handsome, dark green glossy foliage, yellowish flowers and black or dark purple fruits, and tolerates cutting or trimming very well. A classic tub plant, shrub or small tree. There is a Willow-leaved Bay and a golden one and another with wavy margined leaves.

Leptospermum petersonii
LEMON SCENTED TEA TREE

E   *

HEIGHT: 5–7 m (16–23 ft)
CLIMATE: T., S., W.T., M., C.T.
FAMILY: Myrtaceae
DESCRIPTION: An Australian tree-like shrub with shining, scented foliage, a graceful pendulous habit and dainty open, white summer flowers. A light trimming just after flowering maintains a good shape. Grow in sun or part shade.

Melaleuca armillaris
BRACELET HONEY MYRTLE

E　✳

HEIGHT:　3–5 m (10–16 ft)
CLIMATE:　S., W.T., M., C.T.
FAMILY:　Myrtaceae
DESCRIPTION: Shining evergreen pine-like foliage is always fresh looking on this rapid grower with its white, brush-like summer flowers. An effective screen in sun or part shade. Trim lightly just after flowering to control height.

Melaleuca nesophila
SHOWY HONEY MYRTLE;
PURPLE PAPERBARK

E　✳

HEIGHT:　4 m (13 ft)
CLIMATE:　W.T., M., C.T.
FAMILY:　Myrtaceae
DESCRIPTION: A fast growing, large bushy shrub for screens or windbreaks, in sun or part shade. Trim lightly after flowering to control height and shape. Abundant pinkish-mauve pompom flowers during summer attract honeyeaters and are suitable for picking.

Metrosideros excelsa
NEW ZEALAND CHRISTMAS BUSH

E

HEIGHT:　2–5 m (6½–16 ft)
CLIMATE:　T., S., W.T., M., C.T.
FAMILY:　Myrtaceae
DESCRIPTION: A hardy, easily grown salt and wind tolerant tree-like shrub, usually 5 m (16 ft) high at 10 years, or as low as 2 m (6½ ft) with trimming. This has orange-red aerial roots, grey leaves with woolly undersurfaces and clusters of bright red early summer flowers. Others are *M. excelsa* 'Variegata'—grey and cream variegated foliage; *M. thomasii*—orange flowered.

Michelia figo
PORT WINE MAGNOLIA

E

HEIGHT:　3–5 m (10–16 ft)
CLIMATE:　T., S., W.T., M., C.T.
FAMILY:　Magnoliaceae
DESCRIPTION: A handsome shrub or screen for sun or shade, which may be trimmed to control height. Purple, heavily scented summer flowers are hidden under glossy foliage.

Murraya paniculata
COSMETIC BARK TREE

E ✳

HEIGHT: 2–3 m (6½–10 ft)
CLIMATE: T., S., W.T., M., C.T.
FAMILY: Rutaceae
DESCRIPTION: Sweetly scented, orange blossom-like summer flowers contrast with the deep green shining foliage on this bushy shrub. It stands trimming after flowering and is attractive singly or as a hedge in sun or part shade.

Nandina domestica
SACRED BAMBOO

E

HEIGHT: 2–5 m (6½–16 ft)
CLIMATE: T., S., W.T., M., C.T., H.
FAMILY: Berberidaceae
DESCRIPTION: A multi-stemmed, bamboo-like shrub, which is semi deciduous in cool climates The foliage changes to red in autumn and has white flowers followed by red berries. Suits tubs or garden in sun or shade.

Nerium oleander
'Monsieur Belaguier'
OLEANDER

HEIGHT: 3–5 m (10–16 ft)
CLIMATE: T., S., W.T., M.
FAMILY: Apocynaceae
DESCRIPTION: This salt and wind tolerant shrub can be kept pruned to as low as 2 m (6½ ft). It has single, clear pink, star-like flowers from late spring to autumn. Double and single white, pinks, salmon and single red varieties are also available.

Photinia x fraseri
'Red Robin'
RED ROBIN PHOTINIA

E

HEIGHT: 2–4.5 m (6½–15 ft)
CLIMATE: T., S., W.T., M., C.T., H
FAMILY: Rosaceae
DESCRIPTION: Young foliage is a bright coppery red and in spring is almost covered with attractive white blooms. This hedge or screen thrives on the frequent clipping that encourages

brilliant colour. Suits sun or part shade. *P. glabra* 'Rubens' has smaller red foliage; *P. glabra* 'Robusta' is similar with bronze foliage.

Plumbago auriculata
CAPE PLUMBAGO

E

HEIGHT: 2–3 m (6½–10 ft)
CLIMATE: T., S., W.T., M., C.T., H.
FAMILY: Plumbaginaceae
DESCRIPTION: Pale blue flowers in short spikes during spring and summer are pretty against the soft, light green foliage. It is semi climbing with long lax stems. Trim to maintain shape.

P. auriculata 'Alba' is another variety.

Pyracantha angustifolia
ORANGE FIRETHORN

E

HEIGHT: 1.3–5 m (4–16 ft)
CLIMATE: W., M., C.T., H.
FAMILY: Rosaceae
DESCRIPTION: Bright orange berries from mid summer to late winter cover this fast growing, colourful evergreen hedge or screen plant, which is enchanced by trimming to as low as 1.3 m. (4 ft).

Rhododendron
RHODODENDRON

E

HEIGHT: 2–6 m (6½–19½ ft)
CLIMATE: W.T., M., C.T., H.
FAMILY: Ericaceae
DESCRIPTION: Rhododendrons flower generously in late winter and spring and are notable for their red, pink, mauve, purple or yellow flowers.

There are more than 800 species of Rhododendrons plus many thousands of hybrids and varieties, including *R. vireya*, and tropical plants, which are suitable for M., W.T., S., and T climates.

Rondeletia amoena
PINK RONDELETIA

<blockquote>E</blockquote>

HEIGHT: 2-2.5 m (6½-8 ft)
CLIMATE: T., S., W.T., M.
FAMILY: Rubiaceae
DESCRIPTION: Masses of salmon pink flower heads through spring and summer are effective against broad, oval foliage. Control height by trimming lightly after flowering. Suits sun or part shade.

Juniperus x media
'Pfitzerana Aurea'
PFITZERS' GOLDEN JUNIPER

<blockquote>E</blockquote>

HEIGHT: 2 m (6½ ft)
CLIMATE: S., W. T., M., C.T., H
FAMILY: Cupressaceae
DESCRIPTION: A handsome shrub almost as broad as it is high. This has dark, grey-green foliage tipped with yellow. It suits sun and is easily grown. A privacy plant or a large scale ground cover.

Viburnum tinus
LAURUSTINUS

<blockquote>E</blockquote>

HEIGHT: 3 m (10 ft)
CLIMATE: T., S., W.T., M., C.T., H.
FAMILY: Caprifoliaceae
DESCRIPTION: A reliable, fast grower that stands sun or dense shade equally well and bears pink budded, scented, white flowers. Use as a shrub or screen. Trim lightly after flowering to maintain a good shape.

Xylosma japonicum
SHINY XYLOSMA

<blockquote>E</blockquote>

HEIGHT: 2-5 m (6½-16 ft)
CLIMATE: T., S., W.T., M., C.T.
FAMILY: Flacourtiaceae
DESCRIPTION: This shiny shrub thrives on trimming. It has orange and bronze tipped foliage and inconspicuous, fragrant yellow flowers. In tree or shrub form, it is a privacy plant for sun or part shade.

Foundation planting around the house

These are small attractive shrubs that add colour and charm to gardens and require nimimal effort from you.

Abutilon x frazeri
FLOWERING MAPLE;
CHINESE BELL FLOWER

E

HEIGHT: 2 m (6½ ft)
CLIMATE: S., W.T., M.
FAMILY: Malvaceae
DESCRIPTION: An evergreen shrub with pendulous, lantern-like flowers in summer and 3 or 5 lobed palmate foliage.

There are several kinds, a few with variegated foliage, such as *A. megapotamicum*, which has a trailing habit.

Acalypha wilkesiana
'Marginata'
FIRE BUSH, FIJIAN FIRE PLANT

E

HEIGHT: 1.5–2 m (5–6½ ft)
CLIMATE: T., S., W.T., M
FAMILY: Acanthaceae

DESCRIPTION: A very colourful, bushy shrub, which has bronze foliage flushed with red and marked with cream near the margins.

There are many varieties including those with crimped green and white foliage.

Acer palmatum
'Dissectum Atropurpurem'
RED WEEPING MAPLE;
CUT LEAF WEEPING MAPLE

D

HEIGHT: 1–2 m (3–6½ ft)
CLIMATE: W. T., M., C.T., H.
FAMILY: Aceraceae
DESCRIPTION: Delicate, yet capable of suffering poor growing conditions, this is a weeping plant with finely divided purple foliage that changes to fiery shades of red and gold in autumn before falling.

A. palmatum 'Dissectum' has green foliage. There are others in varying shades of red or green with variously dissected foliage.

Ardisia crenata

ARDISIA

E

HEIGHT: 1–2 m (3–6½ ft)
CLIMATE: T., S., W.T., M.
FAMILY: Myrsinaceae
DESCRIPTION: Usually 1 m (3 ft) high in clumps as the result of self-seeding. Shining dark green leaves about 18 cm (7 in) long are a foil for the bright red, long lasting berries carried in rings around the stem—one ring for each year of its life.

A. crispa is very similar; A. crenata 'Alba' has white berries.

Aucuba japonica

'Crotonifolia'
GOLD DUST SHRUB

E

HEIGHT: 2 m (6½ ft)
CLIMATE: T., S., W.T., M., C.T., H.
FAMILY: Cornaceae
DESCRIPTION: A compact, shade-loving shrub with serrated, shining foliage, boldly splashed and dotted with gold. Flowers are inconspicuous but the plant will bear scarlet berries if pollinated by a nearby male plant. There are several varieties including A. japonica 'Picturata' with green margined, gold-centred foliage and the male pollinator, which is plain green.

Azalea indica

'Splendens'
AZALEA SPLENDENS

E

HEIGHT: 1.5–2 m (5–6½ ft)
CLIMATE: S., W. T., M., C.T., H.
FAMILY: Ericaceae
DESCRIPTION: This forms a shapely mound with an irregular outline, covered in single, bell-shaped, salmon pink flowers for 6 weeks during spring. Suits light to full shade, tolerates sun. A. indica 'Mortii' or A. indica 'Alba Magna' are both white; A. indica 'Magnifica' is mauve.

Bauera rubioides

BAUER'S RIVER ROSE;
NATIVE DOG ROSE

E

HEIGHT: 1–2 m (3–6½ ft)
CLIMATE: S., W.T., M., C.T., H.
FAMILY: Baueraceae
DESCRIPTION: A fine foliaged shrub covered with six-petalled white to pink flowers in spring and summer. Wind and waterlogging tolerant. *B. sessiliflora* is a more compact shrub with stalkless flowers.

Bauhinia blakeana
DEEP PURPLE ORCHID TREE

HEIGHT: 7–12 m (23–39 ft)
CLIMATE: T., S., W.T.
FAMILY: Caesalpinaceae
DESCRIPTION: A handsome evergreen tree which may reach 12 m (39 ft) in tropical climates or 7 m (23 ft) elsewhere. Its fragrant purple flowers are carried in racemes up to 12 cm (5 in) across in summer. The grey-green foliage is made up of deeply lobed, butterfly-shaped leaves. In W.T. and M. climates foliage may thin out in winter. They need sunny positions and loam and light clay soils are the ideal though they will tolerate leaner conditions.

Others are: *B. variegata*, the Orchid Tree, with lighter coloured flowers and smaller leaves, and *B. variegata* 'Alba' with white flowers and similar habit. *B. galpinii* is an evergreen shrub, 5 m (16 ft), with brick-red summer flowers.

Bauhinia galpinii
RED BAUHINIA

E

HEIGHT: 3–5 m (10–16 ft)
CLIMATE: T., S., W.T.
FAMILY: Caesalpinaceae
DESCRIPTION: Brick red, orchid-like summer flowers cover this spreading cascading shrub with kidney-shaped grey-green leaves. It suits a warm, north-facing position against a wall or fence. It may lose some foliage in winter in W.T., and M. climates.

Begonia coccinea

TREE BEGONIA; BEGONIA;
ANGEL WING

E

HEIGHT: 1–2 m (3–6½ ft)
CLIMATE: T., S., W.T., M.
FAMILY: Begoniaceae
DESCRIPTION: They are evergreen with succulent leaves 18 cm (7 in) and more across, and equally wide pendulous racemes of rose-red flowers from spring to autumn. Begonias occupy only about 36 cm (14 in) of space and consist of about 4 slender stems. They need light to full shade. There are many named varieties.

Boronia heterophylla

PINK BORONIA

E

HEIGHT: 1–2 m (3–6½ ft)
CLIMATE: W.T., M., C.T.
FAMILY: Rutaceae
DESCRIPTION: Compact shrub with dark green leaves and plump, rose-pink, sweetly scented bell flowers from late winter to early spring. Needs light to filtered shade. *B. pinnata* is a robust shrub to 2 m (6½ ft) *B. serrulata*, the Native Rose, has a penetratingly sweet scent and toothed leaves, but is difficult to grow.

Boronia megastigma

BROWN BORONIA;
SCENTED BORONIA

E

HEIGHT: 1 m (3 ft)
CLIMATE: W.T., M., C.T.
FAMILY: Rutaceae
DESCRIPTION: Flowering from late winter to spring, this plant, esteemed for its rich scent, has a wide natural variation in flower colour, the most valued being rich velvety brown on the outside of the petals and gold on the inside. Varieties with deeper coloured flowers are sometimes available.

Brachysema lanceolatum
SWAN RIVER PEA

E

HEIGHT: 1 m (3 ft)
CLIMATE: S., W.T., M.
FAMILY: Papilionaceae
DESCRIPTION: Deep red pea-shaped summer flowers against olive-green, downy-backed foliage make a pleasing contrast. Stands light shade and is salt tolerant. *B. latifolium*, the Broad Leaved Swan River Pea, is a prostrate carpeting plant that roots as it spreads.

Brunfelsia australis
YESTERDAY, TODAY AND TOMORROW; NIGHT AND DAY FLOWER

E

HEIGHT: 2–3 m (6½–10 ft)
CLIMATE: T., S., W.T., M.
FAMILY: Solanaceae
DESCRIPTION: The purple summer flowers become mauve and then white with age, so there are 3 different colours on this bush at the one time. *B. calycina* var. *eximia* is more frost tolerant, though its foliage is not quite as pleasing.

Buddleia x davidii var. veitchiana 'Royal Red'
BUDDLEIA; POOR MAN'S LILAC; BUTTERFLY BUSH

E

HEIGHT: 2–3 m (6½–10 ft)
CLIMATE: T., S., W. T., M., C.T., H
FAMILY: Loganiaceae
DESCRIPTION: 20 cm (8 in) long, mauve, lilac-like, fragrant flower spikes on the ends of arching branches from late winter to early summer. *B. globosa*—heads of fragrant, orange summer flowers; *B. salvifolia*—handsome grey foliage and pale lilac flowers with orange throats.

Buxus microphylla var. *japonica*
JAPANESE BOX

E

HEIGHT: 1–2.5 m (3–8 ft)
CLIMATE: W.T., M., C.T., H.
FAMILY: Buxaceae
DESCRIPTION: See "Shrubs and trees for privacy".

Buxus microphylla var. *microphylla*
MINIATURE BOX

E

HEIGHT: 50–60 cm (20–24 in)
CLIMATE: W.T., M., C.T., H.
FAMILY: Buxaceae
DESCRIPTION: A small evergreen shrub used as a clipped edging to paths, entrances and formal flower beds or in tubs. It thrives in sun or shade and can be clipped to any shape or size. Trim lightly before spring growth begins.

Callistemon citrinus
'Endeavour'
ENDEAVOUR BOTTLEBRUSH

E

HEIGHT: 3 m (10 ft)
CLIMATE: T., S., W. T., M., C.T.
FAMILY: Myrtaceae
DESCRIPTION: See "Shrubs and trees for privacy".

Camellia japonica
CAMELLIA

E

HEIGHT: 2–5 m (6½–16 ft)
CLIMATE: S., W.T., M., C.T., H.
FAMILY: Theaceae
DESCRIPTION: See "Shrubs and trees for privacy".

Camellia reticulata
CAMELLIA

E

HEIGHT: 5 m (16 ft)
CLIMATE: W.T., M., C.T., H.
FAMILY: Theaceae
DESCRIPTION: See "Shrubs and trees for privacy".

Camellia sasanqua
SASANQUA

E

HEIGHT: 3–7 m (10–23 ft)
CLIMATE: S., W.T., M., C.T., H.
FAMILY: Theaceae
DESCRIPTION: See "Shrubs and trees for privacy".

Cassia fistula
GOLDEN SHOWER

E

HEIGHT: 3-5 m (10-16 ft)
CLIMATE: T., S., W.T.
FAMILY: Caesalpinaceae
DESCRIPTION: Spectacular in spring when 24-36 cm (9-14 in) long racemes of pendant, brilliant yellow flowers weep from leafless branches. This shrub can reach 10 m (33 ft) in tropical climates. *C. bicapsularis* is a brilliant yellow flowered shrub for T., S., and W.T. climates. Non-seeding varieties should be sought as otherwise this self-seeds to weed proportions. *C. artemisiodes*, evergreen 1 m (3 ft), and *C. eremophila* are Australian plants native to eastern and inland Australia respectively.

Ceanothus
'Blue Pacific'
CALIFORNIAN LILAC

E

HEIGHT: 2 m (6½ ft)
CLIMATE: T.,S., W.T., M., C.T., H
FAMILY: Rhamnaceae
DESCRIPTION: The summer flowers in panicles 8 cm (3 in) or so long make an arresting display of soft blue against bright shiny green foliage. There are many others including 'Marie Simon', 'x Edwardsii', 'Burkwoodi', and 'Veitchianus' all with pink or pinky-blue flowers.

Ceratopetalum gummiferum
NEW SOUTH WALES CHRISTMAS BUSH

E

HEIGHT: 3-5 m (10-16 ft)
CLIMATE: S., W.T., M.
FAMILY: Cunoniaceae
DESCRIPTION: In spring inconspicuous white flowers are followed by fruits surrounded by bright pink "flowers" (enlarged calyx lobes), which persist through summer. Selected forms with earlier or deeper coloured flowers are available.

Chaenomeles speciosa
'Rubra Grandiflora'
FLOWERING QUINCE;
JAPONICA

D

HEIGHT: 2 m (6½ ft)
CLIMATE: W. T., M., C.T., H
FAMILY: Rosaceae
DESCRIPTION: The first flowering fruits to bloom each year, these have saucer-shaped blossoms in mid winter against bare branches and among short, slender spines. A few gnarled quinces may appear. Both these and the flowers can be placed in vases. (The fruit is edible but unpleasant). Salt, wind and waterlogging tolerant.

Chamaecyparis obtusa
'Nana Aurea'
DWARF GOLDEN HINOKI CYPRESS

E

HEIGHT: 1 m (3 ft)
CLIMATE: W. T., M., C.T., H.
FAMILY: Cupressaceae
DESCRIPTION: A dense, compact, rounded evergreen shrub with golden tipped foliage arranged in small fan-like formations.

The Chamaecyparis genus includes hundreds of ornamental garden shrubs and small trees in dwarf to tall, grey-green to gold, blue and green forms.

Chamaelaucium uncinatum
GERALDTON WAX PLANT

E

HEIGHT: 3–5 m (10–16 ft)
CLIMATE: W.T., M.
FAMILY: Myrtaceae
DESCRIPTION: This is covered with many pale pink, star-shaped spring flowers against fine, almost needle-like foliage on a light and open bush. It is not long lived in heavy soils but is well worth trying.

Pink, deep pink, red ageing to purple, and white flowered forms are available. C. axillaris, 1 m (3 ft), is a dainty, little-known, white flowered species.

Choisya ternata
MEXICAN ORANGE BLOSSOM

E

HEIGHT: 1 m (3 ft)
CLIMATE: T., S., W.T., M., C.T., H.
FAMILY: Rutaceae
DESCRIPTION: A fresh looking evergreen shrub with a plump rounded shape and very scented, white, orange blossom-like flowers in spring and early summer.

Codiaeum
CROTON

E

HEIGHT: 1-2 m (3-6½ ft)
CLIMATE: T., S.
FAMILY: Euphorbiaceae
DESCRIPTION: Shrubs with colourful, ornamental foliage, which may be splashed or dotted, or margined with red, gold or green, some with differently coloured veins. Named varieties are numerous.

Coleonema pulchrum
DIOSMA

E

HEIGHT: 1.5 m (5 ft)
CLIMATE: S., W.T., M., C.T., H.
FAMILY: Rutaceae
DESCRIPTION: A mid-green shrub with tiny aromatic leaves and very small, pink, starry flowers from late winter to spring.

A "red" form (cerise pink) is a tall untidy grower unless pruned. A compact or 'Nana' form with pink flowers has the neatest growth habit. 'Sunset Gold' has golden foliage.

Coprosma repens
'Marble Queen'
MARBLE QUEEN COPROSMA

E

HEIGHT: 1-2 m (3-6½ ft)
CLIMATE: T., S., W. T., M.
FAMILY: Rubiaceae
DESCRIPTION: Grown for its green and white foliage and neat mound shape, this is a representative of a large genus of useful New Zealand garden subjects. *C. baueri*, the Looking Glass Plant, has glossy, rich green foliage and black berries. Responds to cutting and makes an excellent hedge or screen in sandy soils in windswept coastal locations. There is a golden form. *C. repens*, Kirkii, a spreading evergreen 30 cm (12 in) high and 75 cm (30 in) across, is a first class ground cover. All are salt and wind tolerant.

Correa reflexa
NATIVE FUCHSIA; CORREA

E

HEIGHT: 1.5 m (5 ft)
CLIMATE: W.T., M., C.T.
FAMILY: Rutaceae
DESCRIPTION: Small shrub with dark green, rough-surfaced leaves with pale undersides and spring flowers with long green-and-red bells vaguely resembling Fuchsia. *C. alba* is salt tolerant, with soft grey-green leaves and white star flowers; *C. pulchella* has scarlet bell flowers; and *C. lawrenciana* has rusty, hairy leaves; grass green bell flowers.

Cotoneaster conspicuus
'Decorus'
LOW GROWING COTONEASTER

E

HEIGHT: 45 cm (18 in)
CLIMATE: T., S., W. T., M., C.T., H.
FAMILY: Rosaceae
DESCRIPTION: A representative of a large genus. This spreads as much as 1 m (3 ft). In summer the leaves are nearly obscured by the white flowers which form bright red fruits in the same generous way during late summer.

These are held into winter. *C. horizontalis* is semi-evergreen with pinkish-white flowers and red berries. *C. horizontalis* 'Hodginsii' has daintier, smaller foliage and berries than the others. *C. horizontalis* 'Variegata' has cream variegated foliage blushed with red. *C. microphyllus* has glossy foliage and red berries.

Cryptomeria japonica
'Elegans Nana'
DWARF JAPANESE CEDAR

E

HEIGHT: 2–3 m (6½–10 ft)
CLIMATE: W. T., M., C.T., H.
FAMILY: Taxodiaceae
DESCRIPTION: A bright green shrub with a precise round shape, which combined with the distinctive foliage gives definition to shrubbery and garden.

Cyathea cooperi
TREE FERN,
ROUGH BARKED TREE FERN

E

HEIGHT: 5-6 m (16-17 ft) in gardens; more in the wild.
CLIMATE: T., S., W.T., M.
FAMILY: Cyatheaceae
DESCRIPTION: A superb, fast-growing tree fern from Queensland and New South Wales, with large much-divided fronds up to 4 m (13 ft) in length. Dead fronds are shed cleanly from the single trunk, leaving a pattern of egg-shaped, elongated depressions. Long whiskery pale fawn and red scales clothe the base of the fronds. It prefers filtered shade but stands sun. For cooler climates *C. australis* with persistent frond bases, or *C. leichhardtiana* with purplish-black fronds rachides are more suitable.

Cycas revoluta
SAGO PALM,
JAPANESE SAGE PALM

E

HEIGHT: 3.5 m (11 ft)
CLIMATE: T., S., W.T., M.
FAMILY: Cycadaceae
DESCRIPTION: Stiff, evergreen, palm-like plants that may develop a woody trunk. Radiating from the trunk is curved, stiff pinnate foliage forming a rosette at ground level or a crown on a trunk, which may be 3.5 m (11 ft) high. The plants are either male or female and both bear interesting cones, the female cones being larger. It is very slow growing though always a delight even as a tiny plant. They suit most loamy soils and some shade. Others are: *C. media*, Australian Nut palm, trunk to 6 m (17 ft) high, not easy to find commercially; *C. rumphii*, similar to *C. media*, another rare species; *C. circinalis*, the Sago Palm, a fern palm to 7 m (23 ft) high with leaves 2.5 m (8 ft) long.

Daphne odora
'Rubra'
DAPHNE

E

HEIGHT: 1-2 m (3-6½ ft)
CLIMATE: W. T., M., C.T., H.
FAMILY: Thymelaeaceae
DESCRIPTION: Difficult to grow, Daphne is a continuing challenge to many gardeners because of its sweet scent. During winter rose-pink buds open to glistening white flowers tinged with pink. Suits semi-shade. A variegated form has gold margined leaves.

Deutzia scabra
'Candidissima'
WEDDING BELLS

D

HEIGHT: 2-3 m (6½-10 ft)
CLIMATE: W. T., M., C.T., H.
FAMILY: Philadelphaceae
DESCRIPTION: Very free flowering shrub, which is a mass of pure white double flowers in spring. Numerous forms available with white or pink-to-white flowers.

Dicksonia antarctica
SOFT TREE FERN

E

HEIGHT: 4.5 m (15 ft)
CLIMATE: S., W.T., M., C.T., H.
FAMILY: Cyatheaceae
DESCRIPTION: A tree fern native to
Queensland, New South Wales, Victoria,
Tasmania and South Australia, this is able to
grow in sheltered situations even in a highland
climate. Trunk is 4.5 m (15 ft) high with large,
much divided fronds up to 3 m (10 ft) in length.
The fronds bases are persistent, but become
matted in a dense fibrous mass of brown roots
which clothe the trunk. Needs a shaded position.

Drejerella guttata
PRAWN OR MEXICAN
SHRIMP BUSH

E

HEIGHT: 1 m (3 ft)
CLIMATE: T., S., W.T., M.
FAMILY: Acanthaceae
DESCRIPTION: Almost always carrying its
strange shrimp flowers, though summer is the
main season, this becomes a clump of stems clad
with soft, hairy, pale green foliage and drooping
flower spikes. It is tenacious and long-lived.
D. guttata 'Lutea' has chartreuse-green bracts.

Eriostemon myoporoides
LONG LEAF WAXFLOWER

E

HEIGHT: 1-2 m (3-6½ ft)
CLIMATE: T., S., W.T., M., C.T., H.
FAMILY: Rutaceae
DESCRIPTION: This is beautiful from winter
to spring when pink buds along the stems open
to white star-shaped flowers against blue-green
foliage. *E. australasius* has thick leaves, large
pink waxy flowers; *E. verrucosus* 'Stardust' has
pink-budded white flowers.

Euonymus japonicus
'Ovatus Aureus'
EUONYMUS

E

HEIGHT: 1-2 m (3-6½ ft)
CLIMATE: S., W. T., M., C.T., H.
FAMILY: Celastraceae
DESCRIPTION: A plump, rounded, wind tolerant shrub up to 2 m (6½ ft) high or 1 m (3 ft) if pruned, with green foliage heavily margined and suffused with gold. There are taller and shorter shrubs and several ground covering forms. Foliage colours are variations of cream and gold with green.

Euphorbia milii
CROWN OF THORNS,
CHRIST PLANT, CHRIST THORN

E

HEIGHT: 75 cm–1 m (30 in–3 ft)
CLIMATE: T., S., W.T., M.
FAMILY: Euphorbiaceae
DESCRIPTION: An almost leafless plant with horizontal habit and foliage on young growth only which is armed with many ugly-looking spines. The stems and thorns are grey and the flowers are wind tolerant. Stands hot positions. Useful man and animal deterrent. *E. wulfenii* is a perennial to 1 m (3 ft) with small yellow bracts.

Euphorbia pulcherrima
'Henrietta Eck'
POINSETTIA

D

HEIGHT: 2-3 m (6½-10 ft)
CLIMATE: T., S., W.T., M.
FAMILY: Euphorbiaceae
DESCRIPTION: A flamboyant shrub, which glows in winter with brilliant scarlet bracts up to 18 cm (7 in) across surrounding small yellow flowers.
  E. pulcherrima 'Annette Hegg' is a dwarf indoor plant that lasts for 8-10 weeks indoors, and can then be planted in the garden. Similar cream, red and pink forms are available.

Fatsia japonica
ARALIA

E

HEIGHT: 2 m (6½ ft)
CLIMATE: T., S., W.T., M., C.T., H.
FAMILY: Araliaceae
DESCRIPTION: Glossy, maple-like foliage is a feature of this dense bushy shrub on which rather insignificant white flowers are followed by decorative black berries.

C. japonica 'Variegata' has creamy-white margined leaves.

Forsythia viridissima
GOLDEN BELLS

E

HEIGHT: 2–5 m (6½–16 ft)
CLIMATE: W.T., M., C.T., H.
FAMILY: Oleaceae
DESCRIPTION: Shrubs with long arching branches covered in yellow, bell-shaped flowers in mid-winter before the leaves appear.

Several varieties are available, all with similar bright yellow flowers.

Fortunella japonica
MARUMI KUMQUAT,
CUMQUAT

E

HEIGHT: 2–5 m (6½–16 ft)
CLIMATE: T., S., W.T., M.
FAMILY: Rutaceae
DESCRIPTION: These popular tub-plants produce white, orange, blossom-like spring flowers followed by edible, round, orange fruits, which (though bitter) may be eaten raw, made into liqueurs or preserves, or dried. Height can be regulated; control by trimming.

See "Trees for fruit and foliage".

Fraxinus oxycarpa
'Raywoodii'
CLARET ASH

D

HEIGHT: 10 m (33 ft)
CLIMATE: W.T., M., C.T., H.
FAMILY: Oleaceae
DESCRIPTION: A splendid, rapid-growing tree with pinnate foliage that becomes claret-coloured in autumn before falling. It is tolerant of most soils and conditions and is easy to maintain. Others are: *F. oxycarpa*—fast growing, sturdy deciduous shade tree; *F. ornus*—the Flowering or Manna Ash, rapid growing, hardy shade tree for tough conditions, with white fragrant flowers.

Gardenia augusta
'Florida'
GARDENIA

E

HEIGHT: 1–1.5 m (3–5 ft)
CLIMATE: T., S., W.T., M.
FAMILY: Rubiaceae
DESCRIPTION: An evergreen with pure white, headily scented flowers, approximately 10–12 cm (4–5 in) across in summer. It needs light to full shade.
  G. augusta 'Magnifica' is 1–2m (3–6½ ft) high, flowers 12–14 cm (5–6 in) across; *G. augusta* 'Radicans' is 45 cm (18 in) across with a prostrate ground-covering habit and smaller flowers and foliage.

Fuchsia x hybrida
FUCHSIA

E

HEIGHT: 1–3 m (3–10 ft)
CLIMATE: T., S., W.T., M., C.T., H.
FAMILY: Onagraceae
DESCRIPTION: These are usually kept between 2 and 3 m (6½ and 10 ft) high by trimming. They are laden in spring and summer with pendulous flowers like drop earrings. They are usually in two colours. There are thousands of hybrids to choose from.

Grevillea hookerana
HOOKER'S GREVILLEA

HEIGHT: 2–3.5 m (6½–11 ft)
CLIMATE: T., S., W.T., M., H.
FAMILY: Proteaceae
DESCRIPTION: There are more than 250 species of Grevilleas and as many hybridise readily, the number of garden forms is growing rapidly. They range from prostrate ground-covers to low, medium and tall shrubs, and trees. Many are adaptable and some of those from Western Australia settle happily in the more humid eastern States. *G. hookerana*, from Western Australia has dark green lustrous foliage deeply divided into almost fern-like segments. The year-round, bird attracting flowers have their main flowering season in spring and are two shades of red. It tolerates wet, heavy soils well and is long lived; 20 years is common.

Grevillea x 'Robyn Gordon'
ROBYN GORDON GREVILLEA

E

HEIGHT: 1.5–2 m (5–6½ ft)
CLIMATE: T., S., W.T., M., C.T., H.
FAMILY: Proteaceae
DESCRIPTION: This blooms every day of the year! It is a home for honey-eaters. A grey, horizontal bush about 1 m (3 ft) wide with pendulous racemes of bright red flowers. Others are 'Clearview Robin', 'Clearview David', 'Dargan Hill', 'Pink Pearl', 'Poorinda Constance', 'Poorinda Leane', 'Audrey', 'Canberra Gem', 'Desert Flame', 'Glen pearl', 'Jenkinsii', 'Poorinda Elegance', 'Poorinda Hula', 'Rhondeau' and 'White Wings'.

Grevillea 'Misty Pink'
MISTY PINK

E

HEIGHT: 1.5–2 m (5–6½ ft)
CLIMATE: T.S., W.T., M.
FAMILY: Proteaceae
DESCRIPTION: Spectacular rich pink and cream 15 cm (6 in) long flower brushes are carried all year on this bushy, greyish shrub with lobed leaves. A bird attracting shrub.
    See Grevillea 'Robyn Gordon'.

Grevillea x 'Royal Mantle'
GREVILLEA ROYAL MANTLE

E

HEIGHT: 45 cm (18 in) x 1 m (3 ft) wide
CLIMATE: S., W.T., M., C.T.
FAMILY: Proteaceae
DESCRIPTION: A ground-cover with deeply divided, olive-green foliage, purple-red when new and deep, purple-red toothbrush shaped flowers. Grows 45 cm high and as much as 1 m wide.

Hebe diosmifolia
DWARF HEBE

☒
HEIGHT: 45 cm (18 in)
CLIMATE: T., S., W.T., M., C.T., H.
FAMILY: Scrophulariaceae
DESCRIPTION: A rounded shrub with small, box-like, dark green foliage and lavender-white, 4–5 cm (1–2 in) long, summer flower spikes for 2 months. Salt tolerant. There are many species, all worthwhile garden plants.

Hebe speciosa
VERONICA

☒
HEIGHT: 1.5 m (5 ft)
CLIMATE: T., S., W.T., M., C.T., H.
FAMILY: Scrophulariaceae
DESCRIPTION: A rounded shrub grown for its glossy foliage and year-round, amaranth-red flowers. Light pruning after flowering retains shape and promotes flowering. H. 'Blue Gem' is light green with blue flowers. It is salt and wind tolerant. *H. speciosa* 'La Seduisante' has crimson flowers.

Hibbertia stricta
GUINEA FLOWER

☒
HEIGHT: 60 cm (24 in)
CLIMATE: S., W.T., M., C.T., H.
FAMILY: Dilleniaceae
DESCRIPTION: A fine-leafed, rounded shrub with brilliant yellow, 5-petalled, mid-winter to late-spring flowers. Salt tolerant. Others are: *H. candens*—golden, guinea-sized flowers on rampant salt-tolerant vine; *H. serphyllifolia*—has tiny flowers on a prostrate or decumbent shrub; *H. stellaris*—is prostrate and smothered with flowers.

Hibiscus rosa-sinensis
HIBISCUS

See "Shrubs and trees for privacy".

Hibiscus syriacus
ROSE OF SHARON

☒
HEIGHT: 2–3 m (6½–10 ft)
See "Shrubs and trees for privacy".

Juniperus conferta
JUNIPER, SHORE JUNIPER

E

HEIGHT: 20 cm (9 in) high x 1 m (3 ft) wide
CLIMATE: W.T., M., C.T., H.
FAMILY: Cupressaceae
DESCRIPTION: A pale green, spreading, evergreen ground-cover, which is salt and wind tolerant. It covers rocks and soil or, as a spill-over, drapes itself prettily over walls. There are many Junipers including ground-covers, low, medium and tall shrubs.

Kolkwitzia ambilis
CHINESE BEAUTY BUSH

D

HEIGHT: 2-3 m (6½-10 ft)
CLIMATE: W.T., M., C.T., H.
FAMILY: Caprifoliaceae
DESCRIPTION: Usually kept at above height by pruning, this is capable of reaching 5 m (16 ft) in very cold climates. Long lax branches, which give a weeping effect, are clothed in late spring with yellow-throated pink bells.

Lagerstroemia indicia eavesii
CREPE MYRTLE

D

HEIGHT: 5-7 m (16-23 ft)
CLIMATE: T., S., W.T., M., C.T., H.
FAMILY: Lythraceae
DESCRIPTION: An easily grown shrub that can tolerate all kinds of neglect and still be laden with trusses of papery, pale mauve, 2 cm (¾ in) wide flowers, weighing down the ends of the branches during summer. If pruned severely it can be kept at 3 m (10 ft) high and will be covered in erect stems of bloom. If left unpruned, except for shaping, it will become an attractive small tree, 5-7 m (16-23 ft) tall.

Lantana montevidensis
TRAILING LANTANA

E

HEIGHT: 1 m (3 ft)
CLIMATE: T., S., W.T., M., C.T.
FAMILY: Verbenaceae
DESCRIPTION: Rosy-lilac flower heads for 9 months of the year make this shrub a useful ground cover in inaccessible areas. Though related to the weedy Lantana it does not share its bad habits. Bushy 1 m (3 ft) high hybrids include red, pink, white, yellow and red, and yellow on the one bush.

Lepidozamia peroffskyana

ZAMIA, SAMIA PALMS

E

HEIGHT: 1–2 m (3–6½ ft)
6 m (19½ ft) in 40–50 years
CLIMATE: T., S., W.T., M.
FAMILY: Zamiaceae
DESCRIPTION: A beautiful, evergreen, Australian palm-like tree with pinnately divided leaves radiating from a woody trunk. Leaves may be from 1.5–3 m (5–10 ft) long according to age. They are dark green and lustrous. Male and female plants are separate. The male cones are twisted and up to 0.5 m (1½ ft) long; female cones are 75 cm (29 in) long, 24 cm (9 in) in diameter and orange-red when ripe.

Leptospermum x lambethii

LAMBETH TEA TREE, MANUKA

E

HEIGHT: 2 m (6½ ft)
CLIMATE: T., S., W.T., M., C.T.
FAMILY: Myrtaceae
DESCRIPTION: Open starry winter flowers are red, pink and white on this shrub with fine coppery new growth.

Many named varieties include dark red, double flowered 'Red Damask', and double pink and white flowered 'Gaiety Girl'.

Leptospermum 'Pacific Beauty'

PACIFIC BEAUTY TEA TREE

E

HEIGHT: 1.5–2 m (5–6½ ft)
CLIMATE: T., S., W.T., M., C.T.
FAMILY: Myrtaceae
DESCRIPTION: A shrub covered in winter and spring with starry white flowers with pale green centres. New growth is pink, the foliage fine and lacey. It forms a mound of cascading branches. Salt tolerant.

Lonicera nitida

'Aurea'
HONEYSUCKLE,
GOLDEN BOX HONEYSUCKLE

E

HEIGHT: 1–2 m (3–6½ ft)
CLIMATE: T., S., W. T., M., C.T., H.
FAMILY: Caprifoliaceae
DESCRIPTION: A neat, golden shrub with compact habit and fine small foliage. In cold climates it carries small creamy-white flowers and amethyst berries. It responds to trimming and is wind and salt tolerant. L. nitida has green foliage.

Loropetalum chinense

FRINGE FLOWER

E

HEIGHT: 3-4 m (10-13 ft)
CLIMATE: T., S., W.T., M., C.T., H.
FAMILY: Hamamelidaceae
DESCRIPTION: A rounded shrub with horizontal branches curving downwards at their tips and covered with creamy-yellow, strap-like winter flowers.

Luculia gratissima

LUCULIA

E

HEIGHT: 3-4 m (10-13 ft)
CLIMATE: T., S., W.T., M., C.T.
FAMILY: Rubiaceae
DESCRIPTION: This forms a wide but not dense shrub with sweetly fragrant, pink tubular winter flowers in big heads up to 16 cm (6 in) across. *L. grandiflora* from Bhutan has larger, white, scented flowers.

Macrozamia communis

BURRAWANG

HEIGHT: 2 m (6½ ft)
CLIMATE: T., S., W.T., M.
FAMILY: Zamiaceae
DESCRIPTION: An ornamental native from New South Wales, very like a palm because its foliage rises in a spiral arrangement from the tops of its thick woody stem, which is usually underground but can become 2 m (6½ ft) high. The leaves are dark green and shiny, divided into 70-100 pinnae. The male and female cones are borne on different plants; both cones are cylindrical and 36 cm (14 in) long. Moist conditions in semi-shade are needed. Others are: *M. morrei*, *M. fawcettii*, *M. diplomea*, *M. spiralis* from New South Wales and Queensland, and *M. riedlei* from Western Australia.

Magnolia x soulangiana
PINK TULIP, OR
JAPANESE MAGNOLIA

D

HEIGHT: 5 m (16 ft)
CLIMATE: S., W.T., M., C.T., H.
FAMILY: Magnoliaceae
DESCRIPTION: This is a tall, bushy, several-stemmed shrub. When mature it is 5 m (16 ft) or more high and 2 m (6½ ft) wide. The tulip-shaped flowers are purplish-pink outside and white inside, and approximately 12–14 cm (5–6½ in) across. It is the first Magnolia to flower. There are many variations in form, flower colour and time of flowering. Some have goblet, star or lily, rather than tulip-shaped flowers, all of which are followed by curious contorted fruits.

Melaleuca thymifolia
THYME-LEAVED HONEY MYRTLE

E

HEIGHT: 1.5 m (5 ft)
CLIMATE: W.T., M., C.T.
FAMILY: Myrtaceae
DESCRIPTION: A shrub with showy lilac flowers in summer, grey-green foliage and corky bark. *M. lateritia*—is a brilliant red-flowered shrub to 1.5 m (5 ft), which favours clay soils.

Michelia figo
PORT WINE MAGNOLIA

See "Shrubs and trees for privacy".

Murraya paniculata
COSMETIC BARK TREE

See "Shrubs and trees for privacy".

Nandina domestica
SACRED BAMBOO,
HEAVENLY BAMBOO

E

HEIGHT: 2.5 m (8 ft)
CLIMATE: T., S., W.T., M., C.T., H.
FAMILY: Berberidaceae
DESCRIPTION: See "Shrubs and trees for privacy".

Philadelphus x *virginalis*

MOCK ORANGE

D

HEIGHT: 1–3 m (4–10 ft)
CLIMATE: S., W.T., M., C.T., H.
FAMILY: Philadelphaceae
DESCRIPTION: White, scented spring flowers, each about 5 cm (2 in) wide cover a strong-growing shrub with light green foliage.
Several varieties are available, all with white, scented flowers of varying size and shape.

Phormium tenax

'Atropurpurea'
RED NEW ZEALAND FLAX

E

HEIGHT: 1–3 m (3–10 ft)
CLIMATE: S., W. T., M., C.T., H
FAMILY: Agavaceae
DESCRIPTION: This forms a clump of bronze-purple, sword-like foliage. There are several varieties and heights. Foliage may be erect and stiff or slightly bent in some kinds, including several variegated forms in heights from 1–2 m (3–6½ ft). The curious flowers of Phormium are in 1 m (3 ft) long panicles held above the foliage from mid-summer to autumn.

Pieris japonica

'Bert Chandler'
CHANDLER'S LILY OF THE
VALLEY BUSH; ANDROMEDA

E

HEIGHT: 1–1.3 m (3–4 ft)
CLIMATE: W. T., M., C.T., H
FAMILY: Ericaceae
DESCRIPTION: This dainty shrub has white lily-of-the-valley type spring flowers and colourful new growth, which changes from salmon pink to cream, white and then rich green. It suits shade or semi-shade. Others are *P. japonica* 'Christmas Cheer—pink flowers; *P. japonica*—green foliage and *P. japonica* 'Variegata'—creamy-white margined leaves, both of which have white flowers.

Pimelea ferruginea

PINK RICE FLOWER

E

HEIGHT: 1 m (3 ft)
CLIMATE: W.T., M., C.T.
FAMILY: Thymelaeaceae
DESCRIPTION: A dense, rich green shrub with prolific white-to-pink terminal flower heads from early spring to autumn.

P. linifolia is salt-tolerant, and white-flowered *P. rosea* has deep pink flowers.

Pinus mugo
MOUNTAIN PINE

E

HEIGHT: 60 cm (24 in) x 1 m (3 ft) wide
CLIMATE: W.T., M., C.T., H.
FAMILY: Pinaceae
DESCRIPTION: The dark green, shining, needle-like foliage sits stiffly on short, curved branchlets arising from its base. The effect is that of a windswept bonsai tree. Wind tolerant.

Platycladus orientalis
'Aurea Nana'
DWARF GOLDEN BOOKLEAF PINE

E

HEIGHT: 1 m (3 ft)
CLIMATE: S., W. T., M., C.T., H
FAMILY: Cupressaceae
DESCRIPTION: A tidy, bright little conifer, which is bun-shaped with flattened sprays of dark green foliage edged with gleaming yellow. The colour intensifies in spring and summer. *P. orientalis* 'Filiformis' has drooping thread-like branches, dwarf; *P. orientalis* 'Meldensis'— dwarf, blue-green.

Platycerium bifurcatum
ELKHORN

E

HEIGHT: 1 m (3 ft)
CLIMATE: T., S., W.T., M.
FAMILY: Polypodiaceae
DESCRIPTION: Large bracket-epiphyte with two kinds of fronds: sterile fronds that form a humus-collecting bracket against their support; and fertile fronds that are forked and stand out from the sheathing base like elkhorns from a trophy head. Spores occur in large brown patches on their undersurface. They need a shady situation, ample water and should be fed with leaf litter, tea leaves, banana skins, etc. put into the sheathing leaf cup. *P. grande,* the Staghorn, has more finely divided fertile fronds.

Plumbago auriculata
CAPE PLUMBAGO

E

HEIGHT: 2–3 m (6½–10 ft)
CLIMATE: T.S., W.T., M., C.T., H.
FAMILY: Plumbaginaceae
DESCRIPTION: See "Shrubs and trees for privacy".

Plumeria rubra
RED FRANGIPANI

D

HEIGHT: 5 m (16 ft)
CLIMATE: T., S., W.T., M.
FAMILY: Apocynaceae
DESCRIPTION: Scented, rose-red, salver-form summer flowers 12 cm (5 in) wide are carried in a broad inflorescence. Their scent is heady and pervasive. The shrub tolerates neglect and city pollution. *P. acutifolia* is fragrant, yellow-centred, and has white flowers.

Polygala myrtifolia
SWEET PEA SHRUB

E

HEIGHT: 1.5-2 m (5-6½ ft)
CLIMATE: T., S., W.T., M., C.T.
FAMILY: Polygalaceae
DESCRIPTION: This dense shrub blooms throughout most of the year, most heavily from winter to spring. It has light green, myrtle-like leaves and rich, reddish-purple flowers.

Prostanthera ovalifolia
PURPLE MINT BUSH

E

HEIGHT: 2-3 m (6½-10 ft)
CLIMATE: W.T., M., C.T.
FAMILY: Labiatae
DESCRIPTION: A dense, bushy native shrub bearing masses of mauve flowers in spring. The foliage is aromatic and adds fragrance to the air. Others are: *P. nivea*—with snow-white flowers; *P. caerulea*—bluish-mauve flowers; *P. cuneata*—dark lilac flowers.

Prunus serrulata
'James H. Veitch'

D

HEIGHT: 5-7 m (16-23 ft)
CLIMATE: W.T., M., C.T., H.
FAMILY: Rosaceae
DESCRIPTION: It is densely branched with graceful habit, a beautiful trunk and branches and clouds of double pink spring flowers. It suits cool, moist soils in a cool climate best. Others are: *P.* 'Ukon'—semi-double, almost chartreuse-yellow flowers; *P.* 'Amanogawa'—fragrant, semi-double, shell-pink flowers, columnar habit; *P.* 'Mt. Fuji' ('Shirotae')—snow-white, semi-double, campanulata—single red.

Punica granatum
'Nana'
DWARF POMEGRANATE

HEIGHT: 1.5-2 m (5-6½ ft)
CLIMATE: T.,S., W.T., M., C.T., H.
FAMILY: Punicaceae
DESCRIPTION: A scaled-down, semi evergreen, small pomegranate with light green shiny foliage. It needs a long hot summer to ripen the fruit and has a spring-to-autumn flowering and fruiting season (see "Trees for fruit and foliage"). *P. granatum* 'Andre Leroy' has double flowers.

Raphiolepis x *delacourii*
PINK INDIAN HAWTHORN

E

HEIGHT: 1 m (3 ft)
CLIMATE: T., S., W.T., M.
FAMILY: Rosaceae
DESCRIPTION: A small, broad shrub with glossy leathery leaves, panicles of rose-pink summer flowers and dark blue berries in autumn and winter. Salt and wind tolerant.

R. indica, the Indian Hawthorn, and *R. umbellata* have white flowers, blue berries, and are 2-4 m (5-13 ft) high.

Reinwardtia indica
LINUM

E

HEIGHT: 1 m (3 ft)
CLIMATE: T., S., W.T., M.
FAMILY: Linaceae
DESCRIPTION: This spreads by its roots and bears dainty, pure yellow flower bells throughout winter. It may sucker too freely but the suckers are easily removed. Shade tolerant.

Rhododendron
RHODODENDRON

See "Shrubs and trees for privacy".

Rondeletia amoena
PINK RONDELETIA

E

HEIGHT: 2-4 m (6½-13 ft)
CLIMATE: T., S., W.T., M.
FAMILY: Rubiaceae
DESCRIPTION: See "Shrubs and trees for privacy".

Rosa
'Hybrid Tea Roses'
ROSE, HYBRID TEA OR
BUSH ROSE

D

HEIGHT: 45 cm –3 m (18 in–10 ft)
CLIMATE: S., W. T., M., C.T., H.
FAMILY: Rosaceae
DESCRIPTION: In the southern hemisphere, modern roses are almost evergreen, losing their leaves for only about a month in late June and July and, depending on the weather, breaking into foliage again from mid-July onwards. In C.T. and M. climates the deciduous period may be 3 months.

Rosa
FLORIBUNDA ROSES

D

HEIGHT: 45 cm –1.75 m (18 in–5½ ft)
CLIMATE: S., W.T., M., C.T., H.
FAMILY: Rosaceae
DESCRIPTION: Floribunda roses are often erroneously referred to as 'Polyantha Roses'. The flowers of Floribunda roses have a hybrid tea shape but are smaller with 25–35 blooms in a truss.

They flower abundantly from spring to autumn.

Rosa
STANDARD ROSES

D

HEIGHT: 75 cm–2 m (30 in–6½ ft)
CLIMATE: S., W.T., M., C.T., H.
FAMILY: Rosaceae
DESCRIPTION: Standard roses are roses of any type grafted onto a single stem well above ground so that their branches will arise at the grafting point rather than at ground level. Usually hybrid bush roses with neat tidy heads and medium-height growth habits are chosen and are grafted at about 75 cm (30 in) from the ground. The effect is tree-like.

Rosa
MINIATURE ROSES

D

HEIGHT: 45–60 cm (18–24 in)
CLIMATE: S., W.T., M., C.T., H.
FAMILY: Rosaceae

DESCRIPTION: Useful low-growing roses 45 cm (18 in) high or less, in some, a little taller in others. The bushes are neat and rounded with double, semi-double or single flowers throughout spring, summer and autumn in red, yellow, mauve, white, pink and variants of these.

Rosmarinus officinalis
ROSEMARY

E

HEIGHT: 0.5-1 m (1½-3 ft)
CLIMATE: T., S., W.T., M., C.T., H.
FAMILY: Labiatae
DESCRIPTION: A shrub with olive-green, shiny, aromatic foliage and pale lavender spring and summer flowers.

R. lavandulaceus is a pretty ground cover, rock garden or spill-over plant.

Russelia equisetiformis
'Coral Plant'

E

HEIGHT: 1-1.5 m (3-5 ft)
CLIMATE: T.,S., W.T., M.
FAMILY: Scrophulariaceae
DESCRIPTION: A rush-like plant, which rises in a central cluster of long rush-like weeping stems carrying whorls of small leaves. The branches are continuously covered by clusters of 3-6 tubular coral-red bells.

Sabina vulgaris
SAVIN JUNIPER

E

HEIGHT: 45 cm (18 in)
CLIMATE: S., W.T., M., C.T., H.
FAMILY: Cupressaceae
DESCRIPTION: A spreading, grey-green, ground-hugging, wind tolerant conifer. It is long-lived and stands harsh conditions. The foliage is juniper scented. Prostrate ground covers are: *S. horizontalis* 'Douglasii'—plum-coloured winter foliage, 0.6 m (2 ft) high, 1 m (3 ft) wide; *S. virginiana* 'Prostrata Glauca'—silvery-blue foliage, 0.3 m (1 ft) high, 1 m (3 ft) wide.

Spartium junceum
SPANISH BROOM

E

HEIGHT: 3.5 m (12 ft)
CLIMATE: T., S., W.T., M., C.T., H.
FAMILY: Leguminosae
DESCRIPTION: A salt and wind tolerant plant with fragrant, yellow, pea-shaped flowers in spring. It is rush-like and appears to be leafless.

Spiraea cantoniensis
'Lanceata'
DOUBLE WHITE MAY

D

HEIGHT: 1.75-2 m (6-6½ ft)
CLIMATE: S., W. T., M., C.T., H
FAMILY: Rosaceae
DESCRIPTION: Long arching branches are literally weighed down in spring with small white flowers in dainty corymbs, 5 cm (2 in) across.

S. *cantoniensis* has single white flowers; S. x *bumalda* 'Anthony Waterer' has crimson flowers; and S. *thunbergii* has single, very small white flowers.

Strelitzia reginae
BIRD-OF-PARADISE

HEIGHT: 1.5 m (5 ft)
CLIMATE: T., S., W.T., M.
FAMILY: Musaceae
DESCRIPTION: Forms clusters of shapely grey-green blade-like foliage up to 36 cm (14 in) long and 12 cm (5 in) wide rather like a miniature banana. In young plants these may be 1 m (3 ft) high. With age, 30 years or more, they can be 2–3 m (6½–10 ft) across and still only 1.5 m (5 ft) high. The green flower bracts are edged with purple or red and are 16 cm (6 in) long, sheltering similar-sized orange or yellow flowers with dark blue tongue. Indoors these may last up to 10 days. In the garden they need a sunny, well drained position. Others are: S. *alba (S. augusta)*, which has a "trunk" to 6 m (19½ ft) with white flowers and is often mistaken for a banana. It can be better value than a banana if effect, not fruit, is the reason for planting, as it is not as easily damaged by wind. S. *reginae* var. *juncea* has rush-like leaves.

Streptosolen jamesonii
ORANGE BROWALLIA,
MARMALADE BUSH

E

HEIGHT: 1-2 m (3-6½ ft)
CLIMATE: T., S., W.T., M.
FAMILY: Solanaceae
DESCRIPTION: A shrub with many flexible soft branches rising from its centre and bearing clusters of orange-red and yellow flowers in early spring and summer.

Strobilanthes anisophyllus
GOLDFUSSIA

E

HEIGHT: 1.3–1.5 m (4–5 ft)
CLIMATE: T., S., W.T., M.
FAMILY: Acanthaceae
DESCRIPTION: A shrub valued for its purple-black foliage and 2 cm (¾ in) long, lavender flowers at the ends of its branches in autumn. *S. dyeranus* (The Persian Shield) has purple foliage and is grown indoors.

Syringa vulgaris
LILAC

D

HEIGHT: 4.5 m (15 ft)
CLIMATE: W.T., M., C.T., H.
FAMILY: Oleaceae
DESCRIPTION: Tall, long-lived, tree-like, hardy shrubs suited only to cold winter climates. Their magically fragrant, single or double, late spring flower spikes can be up to 24 cm (9 in) long.

Telopea speciosissima
NEW SOUTH
WALES WARATAH

E

HEIGHT: 3 m (10 ft)
CLIMATE: W.T., M.
FAMILY: Proteaceae
DESCRIPTION: The flame red flowers of this open shrub light up the bush or a mixed shrubbery in spring. Broad, toothed, leathery leaves on long stems support each flower head, which is followed by a group of curved woody seed "pods".

T. *truncata*, the Victorian Waratah, suits richer, moister, shadier sites in C.T. & M. climates.

Thryptomene saxicola

THRYPTOMENE PINK
ROCK MYRTLE

E

HEIGHT: 1 m (3 ft)
CLIMATE: T., S., W.T., M., C.T.
FAMILY: Myrtaceae
DESCRIPTION: A delicate, shapely, native shrub 1 m (3 ft) high, and 1 m (3 ft) wide with small, flat, oblong aromatic leaves. Graceful, low-spreading, arching branches bear tiny soft-pink flowers from mid-winter to spring.

Thuja occidentalis
'Rheingold'
RHEINGOLD

E

HEIGHT: 1 m (3 ft)
CLIMATE: S., W. T., M., C.T., H.
FAMILY: Cupressaceae
DESCRIPTION: This carries 2 types of foliage: the juvenile form is soft and plume-like, the adult sprays are lacey and firm. It is golden-yellow for most of the year, changing to bronze in winter.

T. *occidentalis* 'Little Gem' is globular; *T. orientalis* 'Meldensis' has sea-green foliage, turning plum-purple in winter.

Tibouchina granulosa
PURPLE SPRAY BUSH,
PRINCESS FLOWER

E

HEIGHT: 2-3 m (6½-10 ft)
CLIMATE: T., S., W.T., M.
FAMILY: Melastomaceae
DESCRIPTION: This rapidly reaches 2 m (6½ ft) and can be pruned to that height or allowed to reach 3 m (10 ft). Its rose-purple to purple-violet winter flowers are carried in long sprays.

T. *macrantha*, Lasiandra, has deep rose-purple flowers, and is an evergreen shrub, 2-3 m (6½-10 ft).

T. *bicolor* has lavender and white flowers on the one bush.

Vibrunum opulus

'Sterile'
SNOWBALL,
GUELDER ROSE

D

HEIGHT: 3-4 m (10-13 ft)
CLIMATE: W. T., M., C.T., H.
FAMILY: Caprifoliaceae
DESCRIPTION: A spring-flowering shrub with 3-5 lobed, lightly hairy foliage and white flowers in 10 cm (4 in) wide cymes so heavy and numerous that the branches become pendulous with their weight. Foliage colours richly in autumn. *V. opulus* has translucent orange-red berries.

Viburnum tinus

LAURUSTINUS

E

HEIGHT: 3 m (10 ft)
CLIMATE: T., S., W.T., M., C.T., H.
FAMILY: Caprifoliaceae
DESCRIPTION: See "Shrubs and trees for privacy".

Weigela florida

'Variegata'
WEIGELIA
VARIEGATED DIERVILLA

D

HEIGHT: 1.5-2 m
CLIMATE: W. T., M., C.T., H.
FAMILY: Caprifoliaceae
DESCRIPTION: A free-flowering shrub with arching canes covered in spring with pink flower bells and yellow and green variegated foliage. Others are: *W.* 'Abel Carriere'—rose-carmine; *W.* 'Bristol Ruby'—ruby-red; *W.* 'Conquette'—large deep rose-pink; *W.* 'Eva Rathke'—bright crimson, compact growth; *W.* 'Newport Red'—large light red.

Westringia fruticosa

COAST ROSEMARY

E

HEIGHT: 1-1.5 m (3-5 ft)
CLIMATE: T., S., W.T., M., C.T., H.
FAMILY: Labiatae
DESCRIPTION: A dense, twiggy native shrub with grey-green, leathery, rosemary-like leaves and white to pale mauve flowers from late winter to summer.

W. glabra has lavender flowers, while *W. floribunda* has white flowers.

Xanthorrhoea australis

GRASS TREE OR
BLACK BOY

HEIGHT: 2-3 m (6½-10 ft)
CLIMATE: S., W.T., M.
FAMILY: Xanthorrhoeaceae
DESCRIPTION: A long-lived native plant bearing a skirt of grass-like leaves crowning a trunk up to 2 m (6½ ft) high. At maturity it bears numerous small creamy flowers on a tall spike in spring. Attractive specimen plant for tubs and rockeries. Likes a well drained, sunny position.

Trees for shade and windbreak

Heights given are approximate under garden conditions in a suitable climate. (In forests the same trees may be taller and more narrow). Selection has been limited to long-lived, easy-to-care-for trees, so some beautiful trees such as wattles are missing either because they have problems that involve maintenance, they are short-lived, or they have voracious root systems. All suit sunny positions.Windbreak species are marked by (W) . In this context "Windbreak" means small scale shelter from wind.

Acer negundo
THE BOX ELDER

[D]

HEIGHT: 6–9 m (19½–29½ ft)
CLIMATE: W.T., M., C.T., H.
FAMILY: Aceraceae
DESCRIPTION: Green maple-like foliage turns gold in autumn on this fast, round-headed shade tree with two handsome variegated forms: *A. negundo* 'Variegatum', has white edges; while *A. negundo* 'Aureo Variegatum', has gold edges.

Acer palmatum
THE JAPANESE MAPLE

[D]   [#]

HEIGHT: 4–6 m (13–19½ ft)
CLIMATE: W.T., M., C.T., H.
FAMILY: Aceraceae
DESCRIPTION: Dainty light-green spring and summer foliage colours brilliantly in autumn. Other maples (all shade tolerant) are:
A. palmatum 'Atropurpureum' (Bloodleaf); *A. senkaki* (Coral Bark); *A. japonicum* (also called "Japanese"); *A. davidii* (Snake Bark).

Acmena smithii
LILLY PILLY

E ✳

HEIGHT: 10–15 m (33–49 ft)
CLIMATE: T., S., W.T., M., C.T.
FAMILY: Myrtaceae
DESCRIPTION: Clusters of creamy-white fringed summer flowers are followed by white to purple edible berries in late summer. Glossy foliage is bronze tipped when new. May be cut to hedge height. Shade tolerant. (W)

Agonis flexuosa
WEEPING MYRTLE;
PEPPERMINT TREE

E ✳

HEIGHT: 8–12 m (26–39 ft)
CLIMATE: T., S., W.T., M.
FAMILY: Myrtaceae
DESCRIPTION: Has pendulous, willow-like, peppermint-scented foliage on a wide, flat-topped tree with flexuous zig-zag branchlets and a dark brown trunk and branches. _A. flexuosa_ 'Variegata', has green and cream foliage.

Archontophoenix cunninghamiana
BANGALOW PALM

E ✳ #

HEIGHT: 3–6 m (10–19½ ft)
CLIMATE: T., S., W.T., M.
FAMILY: Palmae
DESCRIPTION: Graceful native palm with 3–4 m (10–13ft) pinnately divided leaves, cascades of tiny lilac flowers and coral-red fruits. Leaves fall off cleanly leaving a smooth trunk. A companion palm is _A. Alexandrae_ (Alexandra Palm). Tolerates shade.

Arecastrum romanzoffianum
PLUME PALM, QUEEN PALM

E　#

HEIGHT:　6 m (19½ ft)
CLIMATE:　T., S., W.T., M.
FAMILY:　Palmae
DESCRIPTION:　A smooth slim trunk is topped by ribbon-like, shiny foliage hanging from arching mid-ribs of leaves 3–4 m (10–13 ft) long. Old fronds drop off cleanly. Creamy flowers are followed by edible orange fruits. Shade tolerant.

Backhousia citriodora
LEMON SCENTED MYRTLE

E　#　*

HEIGHT:　6–8 m (19½–26 ft)
CLIMATE:　T., S., W.T., M., C.T.
FAMILY:　Myrtaceae
DESCRIPTION:　The lemon-scented, 8–9 cm (3–3½ in) long lanceolate leaves yield a commercial oil. Fringed white flowers appear in summer. *B. aniseta* has creamy-white anise scented flowers. # *B. myrtifolia* is a tall shrub or small tree. Both are shade tolerant native plants.

Betula pendula
SILVER BIRCH

D

HEIGHT:　10 m (33 ft)
CLIMATE:　M., C.T., H
FAMILY:　Betulaceae
DESCRIPTION:　The white trunk is marked with the black scars of fallen branches; pendulous foliage turns gold in autumn. Others are: *B. pendula* 'Dalecarlica' (Swedish Birch); *B. pendula* 'Youngii, (Weeping Birch); *B. papyrifera* (Canoe or North American Birch).

Brachychiton acerifolium
ILLAWARRA FLAME TREE

E　*

HEIGHT:　10 m (33 ft)
CLIMATE:　T., S., W.T.
FAMILY:　Sterculiaceae
DESCRIPTION:　Scarlet, late spring to mid-summer flowers follow dry winters and leaf shedding. Often grown with Jacaranda. Others are: *B. discolor*—furry brown bells with icing pink interiors; *B. populneum* (Kurrajong), can withstand drought. All Ⓦ .

Butia capitata
WINE PALM

E

HEIGHT: 4.5-6 m (15-19½ ft)
CLIMATE: T., S., W.T., M
FAMILY: Palmae
DESCRIPTION: Distinctive grey foliage curves towards the ground and is cut off at trunk when spent. Creamy flowers are followed by grape-like clusters of yellow to red fruits. Shade tolerant.

Callistemon salignus
WHITE OR WILLOW BOTTLEBRUSH

E ✳

HEIGHT: 5-10 m (16-33 ft)
CLIMATE: T., S., W.T., M., H.
FAMILY: Myrtaceae
DESCRIPTION: New spring growth is pink against grey-green foliage and white bottlebrush flowers. Fast growing native in wet, dry or salty conditions. There is a rare, red-flowered form. Ⓦ .

Callistemon viminalis
'Hannah Ray'
HANNAH RAY
WEEPING BOTTLEBRUSH

E ✳

HEIGHT: 5 m (16 ft)
CLIMATE: T., S., W.T., M., H.
FAMILY: Myrtaceae
DESCRIPTION: Weeping branches and weeping pink new growth offset clear red bottlebrush flowers on this native tree . Tolerates wind and waterlogging and is very fast growing. Ⓦ .

Callitris rhomboidea
PORT JACKSON PINE

⊡

HEIGHT: 4.5–6 m (15–19½ ft)
CLIMATE: S., W.T., M., H.
FAMILY: Cupressaceae
DESCRIPTION: Graceful deep green pencil-form native conifer, which becomes pyramidal in old age. Fast growing, salt and shade tolerant. Others are: *C. columellaris* (Coast Cypress); *C. huegelii* (Murray River Pine). All Ⓦ .

Calodendrum capense
CAPE CHESTNUT

E

HEIGHT: 6–10 m (19½–33 ft)
CLIMATE: T., S., W.T., M., H.
FAMILY: Rutaceae
DESCRIPTION: Large, round-headed tree, covered in flesh-coloured, orchid-like summer flowers. Grafted plants flower earlier than seedlings. Ⓦ .

Casuarina torulosa
FOREST OAK, BULL OAK

E   ⊡

HEIGHT: 10 m (33 ft)
CLIMATE: W.T., M., C.T.
FAMILY: Casuarinaceae
DESCRIPTION: Drooping branchlets produce clouds of pollen on males and tiny reddish flowers and woody fruits on females. Others are: *C. littoralis* (Black She-Oak); *C. glauca* (Swamp Oak); *C. cunninghamiana* (River Oak); *C. stricta* (Drooping She-Oak). All Ⓦ .

Cedrus atlantica
'Glauca'
BLUE ATLAS CEDAR

E

HEIGHT: 8 m (26 ft)
CLIMATE: S., W.T., M., C.T., H.
FAMILY: Pinaceae
DESCRIPTION: A handsome blue foliaged tree with pendulous branches and black wood, this becomes pyramidal in old age. It is a popular lawn tree. Others are: *C. atlantica* 'Aurea', golden tipped foliage; *C. atlantica* 'Glauca Pendula', weeping blue foliage. Ⓦ .

Cedrus deodara

DEODAR, HIMALAYAN CEDAR

E

HEIGHT: 10 m (33 ft)
CLIMATE: S., W.T., M., C.T., H.
FAMILY: Pinaceae
DESCRIPTION: Soft, grey-green pyramid becomes almost blue-grey when new spring foliage appears. It becomes a pyramid 5–8 m (16–26 ft) wide at the base and 10 m (33 ft) tall. *C. deodara* 'Aurea' is golden yellow in spring. There is also a weeping form, *C. deodara* 'Aurea Pendula'. Both (W) .

Chamaecyparis obtusa

'Crippsii'
FALSE CYPRESS

E

HEIGHT: 4–5 m (13–16 ft)
CLIMATE: S., W.T., M., C.T., H.
FAMILY: Cupressaceae
DESCRIPTION: A golden foliaged conifer with flattened fan-shaped sprays of foliage. Many hundreds of dwarf and tall forms exist. (W) . *C. lawsoniiana* and forms suit cold climates only, the others tolerate the range above. (W) .

Clethra arborea
LILY OF THE VALLEY TREE

E   #

HEIGHT: 6-8 m (19½-26 ft)
CLIMATE: W.T., M., C.T., H.
FAMILY: Clethraceae
DESCRIPTION: Bears long panicles of white Lily-of-the-Valley type summer to autumn flowers, and has long, elliptic foliage. It is a nice shade or background plant for Azaleas. Shade tolerant.

Crataegus phaenopyrum
WASHINGTON THORN

D

HEIGHT: 6-8 m (19½-26 ft)
CLIMATE: W.T., M., C.T., H.
FAMILY: Rosaceae
DESCRIPTION: Has shiny, heart-shaped serrated foliage, white spring flowers and bright red autumn fruits. Others are: *C. crus-galli* (Cockspur Thorn), red berries; *C. oxycantha* var. *rosea plena*, double rose pink flowers (no berries).

Cupressus sempervirens
'Swane's Golden'
SWANE'S GOLDEN PENCIL PINE

E   #

HEIGHT: 6-8 m (19½-26 ft)
CLIMATE: T., S., W.T., M., C.T., H.
FAMILY: Cupressaceae
DESCRIPTION: A slender, golden soldierly conifer popular as a narrow screen and as a specimen. E *Cupressus sempervirens*, the green Pencil Pine, 6-8 m (19½-26 ft) high, is used in the same way. Both Ⓦ .

Elaeocarpus reticulatus
BLUEBERRY ASH

▣ ▦ ✳

HEIGHT: 6–10 m (19½–33 ft)
CLIMATE: T., S., W.T., M.
FAMILY: Elaeocarpaceae
DESCRIPTION: Shiny serrated foliage and white fringed flowers followed by blue fruits. Shape is pyramidal while young, later more rounded. There is a pink flowered form. Shade tolerant.

Eucalyptus ficifolia
RED FLOWERING GUM

▣ ✳

HEIGHT: 10 m (33 ft)
CLIMATE: M
FAMILY: Myrtaceae
DESCRIPTION: The flowers vary from white to red (on different trees). Actual colour is unknown until flowering takes place.
E. sideroxylon (Pink Flowered Ironbark) is more reliable (though a softer pink) in W.T. areas.

Eucalyptus haemastoma
SCRIBBLY, WHITE OR SAPPY GUM

▣ ✳

HEIGHT: 10–20 m (33–65½ ft)
CLIMATE: W.T., M., C.T.
FAMILY: Myrtaceae
DESCRIPTION: A spreading tree with white bark, which is shed in flakes and scribbled by insect larva. Other white trunked species include: *E. scoparia* (The Willow Peppermint); *E. salignus* (River Red Gum); and *E. citriodora* (Lemon-scented Gum).

Eucalyptus nicholli
NARROW-LEAVED
BLACK PEPPERMINT

⊞

HEIGHT: 12 m (39 ft)
CLIMATE: W.T., M., C.T.
FAMILY: Myrtaceae
DESCRIPTION: This has a light grey-green weeping crown, brown fibrous bark, masses of creamy autumn flowers and peppermint-scented foliage. There are more than 600 Eucalypts, many of which are specific to their area. Seek specialist advice when choosing Eucalypts. Ⓦ

Eucalyptus polyanthemus
RED BOX

Ⓔ ⊞

HEIGHT: 10 m (33 ft)
CLIMATE: W.T., M., C.T., H.
FAMILY: Myrtaceae
DESCRIPTION: Excellent honey is made from the white spring and summer flowers of this large, grey-green, round headed, short-boled tree. Other box are: *E. melliodora* (Yellow Box)—M. W.T., S., C.T; *E. bauerana* (Blue box)—M. and W.T. *E. moluccana* (Grey Box)—W.T. and S. All Ⓦ .

Eucalyptus sideroxylon
RED IRONBARK, MUGGA,
PINK-FLOWERING IRONBARK

⊞

HEIGHT: 7-10 , (23-33 ft)
CLIMATE: W.T., M., C.T.
FAMILY: Myrtaceae
DESCRIPTION: Black deeply furrowed, persistent bark contrasts with the cream to rose-pink flowers (on different plants). Usually slender and single-trunked. Ⓦ .

Fagus sylvatica
BEECH

Ⓓ

HEIGHT: 15 m (49 ft)
CLIMATE: W.T., M., C.T., H.
FAMILY: Fagaceae
DESCRIPTION: Shiny green foliage becomes reddish-brown in autumn. It is valued by flower arrangers. A straight, tidy pyramidal tree. All are shade tolerant. Others are:
F. sylvatica 'Atropurpurea', (Copper Beech); *F. sylvatica* 'Pendula', weeping branches and green foliage; *F. sylvatica* 'Laciniata', (Cut Leaf Beech); *F. sylvatica* 'Tricolor', white and pink. All Ⓦ .

Ficus benjamina
WEEPING FIG

E # *

HEIGHT: 20 m (65½ ft)
CLIMATE: T., S., W.T.
FAMILY: Moraceae
DESCRIPTION: A weeping habit and pendulous leaves make this popular indoors, in pots and as a shade tree. (W) .Others are: # *F. elastica* 'Decora' (Rubber Tree), not suitable for gardens; # *F.microcarpa* 'Hillii', tolerates T., S., W.T., and M. climates. (W) .

Fraxinus excelsior
'Aurea'
GOLDEN ASH

D

HEIGHT: 10 m (33 ft)
CLIMATE: W.T., M., C.T., H.
FAMILY: Oleaceae
DESCRIPTION: This has deep golden stems, blackish buds and bright lemon-yellow summer foliage becoming gold in autumn. *F. excelsior* 'Aurea Pendula' has pendulous branchlets.

Ginkgo biloba
MAIDENHAIR TREE

D

HEIGHT: 10 m (33 ft)
CLIMATE: W.T., M., C.T., H.
FAMILY: Ginkgoaceae
DESCRIPTION: Pollution tolerant tree with thick fan-shaped leaves turning yellow in autumn. Yellow plum-shaped fruits produce ginkgo "nuts".

Gleditsia triacanthos
'Sunburst'
GOLDEN HONEY LOCUST

D

HEIGHT: 7-9 m (23-29½ ft)
CLIMATE: S., W.T., M., C.T., H.
FAMILY: Leguminosae
DESCRIPTION: This fast growing tree casts light shade, has an irregular outline and is golden tipped, becoming deeper gold in spring. The foliage disintegrates quickly and improves soil. (W) .

Jacaranda mimosifolia
JACARANDA

D

HEIGHT: 10 m (33 ft)
CLIMATE: T., S., W.T., M.
FAMILY: Bignoniaceae
DESCRIPTION: Jacaranda bears masses of lavender-blue, bell-shaped summer flowers and has delicate, pinnate foliage, giving a light fern-like effect.

Koelreuteria paniculata
GOLDEN RAIN TREE

D

HEIGHT: 10 m (33 ft)
CLIMATE: W.T., M., C.T., H.
FAMILY: Sapindaceae
DESCRIPTION: The very large terminal panicles of golden yellow flowers do suggest "Golden Rain". It is a handsome tree with pinnate foliage and pinkish new growth.

Lagunaria patersonia
NORFOLK ISLAND HIBISCUS

E ✳

HEIGHT: 7–8 m (23–26 ft)
CLIMATE: T., S., W.T., M.
FAMILY: Malvaceae
DESCRIPTION: Pink, hibiscus-like summer and autumn flowers are pretty against dark, grey-green foliage with undersurfaces of grey. It is wind and salt tolerant, and is excellent by the coast. Ⓦ .

Liquidambar styraciflua
LIQUIDAMBAR

D

HEIGHT: 9–15 m (29½–49 ft)
CLIMATE: S., W.T., M., C.T., H.
FAMILY: Hamamelidaceae
DESCRIPTION: A corky barked tree with yellow, claret, gold and purple foliage in autumn. Others are *L. styraciflua* 'Festeri', orange-red foliage is retained into winter. *L. styraciflua* 'Burgundy', purple foliage remains into winter; *L. styraciflua* 'Canberra Gem', grows to 7 m (23 ft) columnar habit, autumn colours. *L. styraciflua* 'Palo Alto', fiery scarlet and orange, 7 m (23 ft). All Ⓦ .

Livistona australis
CABBAGE TREE PALM

E # ✳

HEIGHT: 7–10 m (23–33 ft)
CLIMATE: T., S., M., C.T., M.
FAMILY: Palmae
DESCRIPTION: A handsome, fibrous-trunked Australian palm with dark green lustrous fan-shaped foliage about 2.2 m (7 ft) wide. Another fine palm is *L. chinensis* (The Chinese Fountain Palm) with pendulous "fingers" of foliage. Both are shade tolerant.

Magnolia grandiflora
WHITE MAGNOLIA

E   #

HEIGHT: 7-10 m (23-33 ft)
CLIMATE: T., S., W.T., M., C.T., H.
FAMILY: Magnoliaceae
DESCRIPTION: Fragrant summer flowers are creamy-white, waxy textured and large; up to 18 cm (7 in) across. Foliage is shiny with a brown undersurface. A long-lived, trouble free tree. Shade tolerant.

Malus floribunda
JAPANESE CRAB APPLE

D

HEIGHT: 5-8 m (16-26 ft)
CLIMATE: W.T., M., C.T., H.
FAMILY: Rosaceae
DESCRIPTION: Long arching branches covered in crimson buds open to white or pale pink flowers in spring, followed by red and yellow fruits. There are many others, all flowering, some non-fruiting.

Melaleuca quinquenervia
PAPER BARK

E   *

HEIGHT: 10 m (33 ft)
CLIMATE: T., S., W.T., M., C.T.
FAMILY: Myrtaceae
DESCRIPTION: A neat hardy tree with handsome white papery bark and cream early winter bottlebrush flowers. Tolerates drought, wind, waterlogging and is moderately salt tolerant. Others are:
M. bracteata (The Bracelet Honey Myrtle), 5-6 m (16-19½ ft)—dark green; E *M. steedmanii* 10 m (33 ft)—dark green foliage.

Nyssa sylvatica
TUPELO

D

HEIGHT: 10 m (33 ft)
CLIMATE: W.T., M., C.T., H.
FAMILY: Nyssaceae
DESCRIPTION: A magnificent tree with drooping horizontal branches and brilliant autumn foliage. Black berries follow inconspicuous flowers. Tolerates wet conditions well. (W) .

Olea europaea
FRUITING OLIVE

E #

HEIGHT: 8 m (26 ft)
CLIMATE: S., W.T., M., H.
FAMILY: Oleaceae
DESCRIPTION: Weeping silvery foliage is offset by a silver trunk and an attractive growth habit. It may be pruned to 3 m (10 ft). The green summer fruits are picked in autumn. Another olive is *O. africana* (Wild Olive), a handsome clipped hedge up to 2 m (6½ ft), or a small tree to 6 m (19½ ft). Both (W) .

Parrotia persica
PERSIAN WITCH HAZEL

D

HEIGHT: 7 m (23 ft)
CLIMATE: S., W.T., M., C.T.
FAMILY: Hamamelidaceae
DESCRIPTION: Spreading, tidy tree with lovely beech-like leaves that colour red and gold in autumn. It retains the brown papery foliage into winter. (W) .

Phoenix canariensis
CANARY ISLAND
DATE PALM

E

HEIGHT: 15 m (49 ft)
CLIMATE: T., S., W.T., M., C.T.
FAMILY: Palmae
DESCRIPTION: A stately, long-lived, hardy palm with foliage up to 7 m (23 ft) long and large clusters of bright yellow to orange fruits. The following are equally worthwhile and shade tolerant: *P. dactylifera*, true Date Palm, bears edible dates; *P. rupicola* (Indian Date Palm), green, slender to 7 m (23 ft); *P. reclinata* (Senegal Date Palm), has a cluster of stems to 7 m (23 ft); *P. roebelenii* (Miniature or Pygmy Date Palm), 3–5 m (10–16 ft).

Picea pungens
'Koster'
KOSTER'S BLUE SPRUCE

E

HEIGHT: 7-10 m (23-33 ft)
CLIMATE: W.T., M., C.T., H.
FAMILY: Pinaceae
DESCRIPTION: Powder-blue spring growth becomes deep blue on this neat pyramidal conifer. A slow growing, but very hardy long-lived tree when grown in rich soil.

Pistacia chinensis
CHINESE PISTACHIO

D

HEIGHT: 7-10 m (23-33 ft)
CLIMATE: W.T., M., H.
FAMILY: Anarcardiaceae

DESCRIPTION: A fast growing tree with pinnate foliage changing colour spectacularly in autumn. The form is neat and rounded. Fallen leaves disintegrate readily.

Pittosporum rhombifolium
ORANGE-BERRIED PITTOSPORUM

E   #   ✳

HEIGHT: 7 m (23 ft)
CLIMATE: T., S., W.T., M., C.T., H.
FAMILY: Pittosporaceae
DESCRIPTION: A neat densely furnished tree with clusters of bright orange berries in autumn. It is shade tolerant. Ⓦ . Others are:
E *P. crassifolium*, long leathery foliage, whitish undersurfaces; 5 m (16 ft); E ✳ *P. undulatum* (Night-scented Daphne), 8 m (26 ft); E *P. tenuifolium* 'Garnetti', rounded green and white leaves, 5 m (16 ft); E *P. tenuifolium* 'James Stirling', blackish stems, dainty silvery green foliage, 5-7 m (16-23 ft). All Ⓦ .

Platanus orientalis
ORIENTAL PLANE TREE

D

HEIGHT: 9–15 m (29½–49 ft)
CLIMATE: W.T., M., C.T., H.
FAMILY: Platanaceae
DESCRIPTION: Giant maple-like foliage colours gold in autumn. Rounded bristly fruits remain after leaf-fall. A fast growing wind and pollution tolerant tree, which stands heavy pruning. Ⓦ . *P. x hybrida*, The London Plane, has larger leaves and is taller. It stands heavy pruning. Ⓦ .

Podocarpus elatus
ILLAWARRA PLUM, PLUM PINE, BROWN PINE

E   ✳

HEIGHT: 6 m (19½ ft)
CLIMATE: T., S., W.T., M., H.
FAMILY: Podocarpaceae
DESCRIPTION: Dense, dark green, thick glossy foliage makes this an excellent screen. It carries blue-black, plum-like fruits. Others of similar dimensions and habit are *P. falcatus*, the Plum-fruited Yew; *P. macrophyllus*, the Japanese Yew. All Ⓦ .

Prunus x blireiana
DOUBLE PINK FLOWERING PLUM

D

HEIGHT: 4.5 m (15 ft)
CLIMATE: W.T., M., C.T., H.
FAMILY: Rosaceae
DESCRIPTION: This is covered in spring with slightly fragrant double pink blossom against black trunk and branches. Summer foliage is coppery. Others are: *P. cerasifera* 'Nigra', single pale pink with deep purple foliage; *P. campanulata* (Taiwan or Bell Cherry) , green foliage colours in autumn—winter flowers are single, claret and bell-like; *P. serrulata*, the flowering cherries, varieties are easy to grow in cold climates.

Quercus palustris
PIN OAK

D

HEIGHT: 8 m (26 ft)
CLIMATE: W.T., M., C.T., H.
FAMILY: Fagaceae
DESCRIPTION: Drooping branches carry deeply lobed leaves, which turn red and gold in autumn and remain on the tree in a papery state in winter. Others are:
D *Q. coccinea* (Scarlet Oak), 8 m (26 ft);
E *Q. ilex* (Holm or Holly Oak), 8-10 m (26-33ft); *Q. robur* (English Oak), only problem free in cold climates.

Sabina chinensis
'Keteleeri'
KETELEER'S JUNIPER

E

HEIGHT: 6-8 m (19½-26 ft)
CLIMATE: S., W.T., M., C.T., H.
FAMILY: Cupressaceae
DESCRIPTION: Lively deep green colour, dense foliage and an irregular peaked outline are the attractions on this tidy reliable screen or specimen conifer. Ⓦ .

Rothmannia globosa
TREE GARDENIA

E

HEIGHT: 5-7 m (16-23 ft)
CLIMATE: S., W.T., M.
FAMILY: Rubiaceae
DESCRIPTION: Scented creamy white bells cover this neat, small tree in spring and are followed by large black seed pods. It is long-lived and very hardy. Shade tolerant.

Salix matsudana

'Tortuosa'
CORKSCREW WILLOW

D

HEIGHT: 6-10 m (19½-33 ft)
CLIMATE: W.T., M., C.T., H.
FAMILY: Salicaceae
DESCRIPTION: Fast growing paddock tree with contorted stems and weeping foliage give the effect of a giant bonsai. Others are:
D *S. alba* var. *vitellina* (Golden Willow), 12 m (39 ft); D *S. babylonica* (Weeping Willow), 12 m (39 ft); D *S. caprea* (Pussy Willow), 6 m (39 ft).

Sapium sebiferum

CHINESE TALLOW TREE

D

HEIGHT: 6 m (19½ ft)
CLIMATE: T., S., W.T., M.
FAMILY: Euphorbiaceae
DESCRIPTION: This is a very fast growing, pretty tree with heart-shaped leaves turning deep red and gold in autumn. The fatty seed covering is used in making soap and candles.

Schefflera actinophylla

UMBRELLA TREE

E ✳

HEIGHT: 6-13 m (19½-43 ft)
CLIMATE: T., S., W.T., M.
FAMILY: Araliaceace
DESCRIPTION: Slender and single-stemmed at first, this native tree becomes broad and tall in old age. Long leaflets are arranged umbrella fashion. All (W) . E *S. elliptica* has yellow flowers and grows to 2-5 m (6½-16 ft).

Schinus molle
PEPPERCORN TREE

E

HEIGHT: 6 m (19½ ft)
CLIMATE: T., S., W.T., M., H.
FAMILY: Anarcardiaceae
DESCRIPTION: Fast growing, grey-green tree with shiny pinnate foliage against rough bark, which gives it an appearance of age. Female trees carry pendant clusters of red berries. (W) .

Sorbus aucuparia
ROWAN TREE

D

HEIGHT: 7–10 m (23–33 ft)
CLIMATE: W.T., M., C.T., H.
FAMILY: Rosaceae
DESCRIPTION: The much divided fresh green foliage highlights woolly inflorescences, which are followed by brilliant scarlet fruits. These are acid and can be used in preserves.

Stenocarpus sinuatus
FIREWHEEL TREE

E   ✳

HEIGHT: 7–14 m (23–46 ft)
CLIMATE: T., S., W.T.
FAMILY: Proteaceae
DESCRIPTION: Bright red, wheel-like flowers may extend from mid-summer to autumn and can take up to 10 years to appear. The beautiful lobed foliage is deep green and shining. Shade tolerant.

Tamarix ramosissima
FLOWERING CYPRESS

D

HEIGHT: 5–6 m (16–19½ ft)
CLIMATE: T., S., W.T., M., C.T., H.
FAMILY: Tamaricaceae
DESCRIPTION: A spreading tree with feathery greyish foliage and rose pink flowers in long racemes during late summer. Others are:
D *T. aphylla* (The Athel Tree), pale pink, 6–10 m (19½–33 ft); D *T. parvifolia*, deep pink, 3–5 m (10–16 ft).

Thuya plicata
'Zebrina'
ZEBRINA THUYA

E

HEIGHT: 4–6 m (13–19½ ft)
CLIMATE: S., W.T., M., C.T., H.
FAMILY: Cupressaceae
DESCRIPTION: This robust conifer with shining bright green foliage banded with yellow and arranged in book leaf pattern makes a dense screen. They stand clipping. Others are: E *T. plicata* (Western Red Cedar), 5 m (16 ft), rich green; E *T. plicata* 'Aureo-variegata', 5 m (16 ft), golden yellow. All Ⓦ .

Trachycarpus fortunei
WINDMILL OR CHINESE
WINDMILL PALM

E   #

HEIGHT: 10–15 m (33–49 ft)
CLIMATE: T., S., W.T., M., C.T.
FAMILY: Palmae
DESCRIPTION: A tall, slender palm with a dense clump of drooping, much-segmented foliage atop a trunk that is black and hairy in youth and free of fibre in old age. Shade tolerant.

Tristaniopsis conferta
BRUSH BOX

E   #   *

HEIGHT: 7–10 m (23–33 ft)
CLIMATE: T., S., W.T., M.
FAMILY: Myrtaceae
DESCRIPTION: Hardy, adaptable rainforest tree with green foliage and a smooth tan trunk. It is round headed but can be pruned to any shape and dimension. Shade tolerant. (W) .

E *T. conferta* 'Variegata', 7–10 m (23-33 ft), has a pinky-tan bark and green and gold variegated foliage. Unsuitable for shade. (W) .

Ulmus glabra
'Lutescens'
GOLDEN ELM

D

HEIGHT: 7.6–12 m (25–39 ft)
CLIMATE: W.T., M., C.T., H.
FAMILY: Ulmaceae
DESCRIPTION: Lemon spring foliage becomes chartreuse through summer and deep gold in autumn. The light canopy produces light shade which allows other plants to grow beneath it. (W) .

D *U. procera* 'Picturata', 10 m (33 ft), the Silver or Picture Elm, has green and white variegated foliage. (W) .

Ulmus parvifolia
CHINESE ELM

D

HEIGHT: 8–10 m (26–33 ft)
CLIMATE: T., S., W.T., M., C.T., H.
FAMILY: Ulmaceae
DESCRIPTION: Fine weeping head is made up of small, serrated, shiny green leaves against a mottled grey trunk. It has a weeping habit and a very short deciduous period.

Climbers

These will all require a support on which to climb. A wall or a fence to lean on will be needed for *Monstera deliciosa*, wires or posts will suffice for the others. Most are sun lovers. Where shade tolerance is a feature, it is mentioned in the description. All suit average soil except Clematis, Stephanotis, Mandevillea, Dipladenia and Hoya, which grow better in soils rich in organic matter.

Root-clinging climbers, such as Parthenocissus (Boston Ivy), Ficus (Creeping Fig) and Ivies (Hedera) have NOT been included on the grounds that they are too rampant. To keep these in check requires severe pruning and therefore high maintenance.

Akebia quinata
FIVE-LEAFED AKEBIA

□D
CLIMATE: W.T., M., C.T.
FAMILY: Lardizabalaceae
DESCRIPTION: Sweetly scented, chocolate purplish spring flowers and shiny green 5-part leaves make this an attractive climber. It is fast growing and wind tolerant.

Allamanda cathartica
'Hendersonii'
ALLAMANDA

□E
CLIMATE: T., S., W.T.
FAMILY: Apocynaceae
DESCRIPTION: A 2–3 m (6½–10 ft) high warm climate climber with superb butter-gold trumpet flowers in late spring and through summer. It may be grown as a shrub by pinching back the long wavy shoots. Others are: *A. neriifolia*, a shrubby vine with yellow flowers; *A. violacea* has reddish-purple flowers and suits tropical or frost-free areas only.

Antigonon leptopus
MEXICAN CREEPER, CORAL VINE,
LOVE'S CHAIN

E D

CLIMATE: T., S., W.T.
FAMILY: Polygonaceae
DESCRIPTION: Evergreen in warm climates, deciduous in cooler areas, this lovely vine has heart-shaped grass green leaves and long drops of coral pink late summer and autum flowers. It suits a sunny position.

Aristolochia elegans
DUTCHMAN'S PIPE

E

CLIMATE: T., S., W.T., M.
FAMILY: Aristolochiaceae
DESCRIPTION: The flowers change from a U-shaped tube to an inverted heart shape and are a velvety red-brown, stippled green and up to 5 cm (2 in) wide. The bush has light green shovel-shaped leaves.

Bougainvillea glabra
'Trailli'
BOUGAINVILLEA

E

CLIMATE: T., S., W.T.
FAMILY: Nyctaginaceae
DESCRIPTION: Bougainvilleas are evergreen rampant vines with strong woody canes and can be trained as a shrub, or a standard, or kept in a pot. This one is purple and so large that it suits only big gardens. There are numerous named kinds with less rampant habits for smaller gardens. Bougainvillea are wind tolerant.

Campsis grandiflora

TRUMPET VINE

D

CLIMATE: T., S., W.T., M.
FAMILY: Bignoniaceae
DESCRIPTION: A deciduous climbing vine to
5 m, which has glossy green leaves and large, soft,
orange, bell-shaped flowers during summer and
autumn. It is wind tolerant and fast growing.

Clematis x jackmani

'Nellie Moser'
LARGE FLOWERED
GARDEN CLEMATIS

D

CLIMATE: W.T., M., C.T.
FAMILY: Ranunculaceae
DESCRIPTION: A spectacular deciduous
climber, 3-4 m (10-13 ft) high with pinnate
leaves and large pale, mauve-pink flowers, each
sepal with a carmine bar. There are numerous
hybrids in a variety of colours including white,
blue, pink and red. They need a cool, moist,
limed soil with the top of the vine in the sun.
Renews itself each spring.

Clematis montana

'Rubens'
PINK CLEMATIS, VIRGIN'S BOWER,
TRAVELLER'S JOY

D

CLIMATE: W.T., M., C.T., H.
FAMILY: Ranunculaceae
DESCRIPTION: Four-petalled, pale pink, star-
like flowers cover this delicate vine in spring.
The trifoliate foliage is bronze when young. It
is fast growing and easily maintained.

Clytostoma callistegiodes

VIOLET TRUMPET VINE

E

CLIMATE: S., W.T., M.
FAMILY: Bignoniaceae
DESCRIPTION: A fast climber about 3 m (10 ft) needing minimal support except on bare walls. Has lilac and yellow flowers in profusion in spring and summer.

Gelsemium sempervirens
CAROLINA JASMINE,
FALSE JASMINE

E

CLIMATE: T., S., W.T., M., C.T.
FAMILY: Loganiaceae
DESCRIPTION: A sweetly scented dainty vine to 3 m (10 ft) with prolific golden bell flowers in spring and early summer and again in autumn. It has shiny leaves.

Hardenbergia violacea
SARSAPARILLA VINE

E ✳

CLIMATE: W.T., M., C.T.
FAMILY: Papilionaceae
DESCRIPTION: This is covered by violet pea flowers in late winter. It is a tough, wind tolerant, fast growing vine to 3 m (10 ft).

Hoya carnosa
WAX FLOWER

E ✳

CLIMATE: S., W.T., M., C.T.
FAMILY: Asclepiadaceae
DESCRIPTION: Sweetly scented, waxy pink, red-centred flowers against thick, glossy, smooth edged foliage account for the popularity of this as either a pot plant or a mild growing vine in light to filtered shade. Many Australian species are now available.

Jasminum polyanthum
SWEET-SCENTED JASMINE

E

CLIMATE: W.T., M., C.T.
FAMILY: Oleaceae
DESCRIPTION: A strong climber with long pink tubes opening to white starry, sweetly scented flowers in spring. It is inclined to pop up everywhere in warm climates. Other jasmines are *J. officinale* 'Grandiflorum'— almost year round, with white flowers; *J. nudiflorum*—mid-winter, lemon-yellow blooms.

Kennedia rubicunda
DUSKY CORAL PEA

E *

CLIMATE: W.T., M., C.T.
FAMILY: Papilionaceae
DESCRIPTION: A strong rambling vine with red spring flowers followed by furry brown seed pods. It scrambles rather than climbs to 3 m (10 ft). Others are *K. nigricans*—has black flowers; *K. coccinea*—has red flowers; *K. prostrata*, (Running Postman), has brick-red flowers.

Lonicera x brownii
'Firecracker'
HONEYSUCKLE, RED HONEYSUCKLE

E

CLIMATE: W.T., M., C.T.
FAMILY: Caprifoliaceae
DESCRIPTION: Vigorous, evergreen vine about 4 m (13 ft) high with claret red, spring and autumn flowers. It stands light shade and is fast growing. In the worst frost climates it may be deciduous.

Macfadyena unguis-cati
CAT'S PAW CREEPER

[E]

CLIMATE: T., S., W.T., M.
FAMILY: Bignoniaceae
DESCRIPTION: Orange-veined golden trumpet spring flowers are spectacular on this glossy evergreen vine, which reaches 3-4 m (10-13 ft). It is fast growing.

Mandevilla laxa
CHILEAN JASMINE

[E]

CLIMATE: T., S., W.T., M., C.T.
FAMILY: Apocynaceae
DESCRIPTION: Masses of Gardenia-scented white summer flowers are lovely against the glossy light green leaves of this 5 m (16 ft) high climber. *M.* 'Alice du Pont' has large rose pink flowers. Others like 'Red Riding Hood' are sold under the name Dipladenia

Monstera deliciosa
FRUIT SALAD PLANT

[E]

CLIMATE: T., S., W.T., M.
FAMILY: Araceae
DESCRIPTION: Happy outdoors or in, Monstera has large glossy perforated foliage and produces pleasant tasting green/yellow fruit. It climbs by aerial roots.

Pandorea pandorana
WONGA WONGA VINE

[E] [✳]

CLIMATE: S., W.T., M., C.T.
FAMILY: Bignoniaceae
DESCRIPTION: A vigorous climber to 6 m (19½ ft) with shining dark green compound leaves and long clusters of creamy white spring flowers spotted with mauve inside.

Phaedranthus buccinatorius

MEXICAN BLOOD TRUMPET

E

CLIMATE: T., S., W.T., M.
FAMILY: Bignoniaceae
DESCRIPTION: Cascades of tubular, frilled, blood-red flowers spill over the foliage in late spring. This climbs by tendrils and soon reaches 3 m (10 ft).

Phaseolus caracalla

SNAIL FLOWER

E   D

CLIMATE: T., S., W.T., M.
FAMILY: Papilionaceae
DESCRIPTION: Inclined to be deciduous in cold climates, this has trifoliate leaves and is covered in summer with large fleshy flowers, which are purplish, shaded yellow, and curled rather like a snail but more handsome. Reaches 3 m (10 ft).

Pyrostegia ignea

FLAME VINE

E

CLIMATE: T., S., W.T., M.
FAMILY: Bignoniaceae
DESCRIPTION: This carries brilliant red/gold clusters of winter flowers. It suits a northerly position. A very rapid grower, which covers 2 m (6½ ft) square.

Rosa
CLIMBING ROSE

D

CLIMATE: S., W.T., M., C.T., H.

FAMILY: Rosaceae

DESCRIPTION: There are many climbing roses that, given reasonable soil conditions, will grow satisfactorily without spraying for fungal diseases. A few are listed below:

Altissimo Large, single red and lightly fragrant with variable cupped to flat blooms.

Blackboy A fragrant deep-crimson rose.

Bloomfield Courage Clusters of single, deep-red, white centred, wide flowers.

Dorothy Perkins Small double rose pink, slightly fragrant flowers in spring and early summer.

Paul's Scarlet Clusters of vivid scarlet, semi-double blooms.

Queen Elizabeth Rich pastel pink in clusters or singly.

Rosa banksiae
'Lutea'
BANKS' ROSE

D

CLIMATE: S., W.T., M., C.T., H.

FAMILY: Rosaceae

DESCRIPTION: A nearly thornless climber with fine foliage and masses of sweetly scented lemon yellow flowers in spring. It can reach 4–6 m (13–19½ ft) and does not require spraying for fungal diseases. A double white form is available.

Solandra maxima
CUP OF GOLD, CHALICE VINE, HONOLULU LILY

E

CLIMATE: T., S., W.T., M.

FAMILY: Solanaceae

DESCRIPTION: Large, glossy green foliage is a foil for the giant chalice-shaped golden summer flowers. It is a very rapid grower and is wind and salt tolerant.

Sollya heterophylla
BLUEBELL CREEPER

E ✱

CLIMATE: W.T., M.

FAMILY: Pittosporaceae

DESCRIPTION: Pale and dark blue summer flower bells are followed by purple berries in autumn on this dainty climber with slender, oval, pale green foliage.

Stephanotis floribunda
CLUSTERED WAX FLOWER,
MADAGASCAR JASMINE

E

CLIMATE: T., S., W.T., M.

FAMILY: Asclepiadaceae

DESCRIPTION: The waxy, sweetly scented white summer flowers of this vine are used in bridal bouquets. The foliage is shiny and deep green. It needs light to filtered shade in a warm position.

Stigmaphyllon ciliatum
BRAZILIAN GOLDEN VINE,
BUTTERFLY VINE

E

CLIMATE: T., S., W.T., M., C.T.

FAMILY: Malpighiaceae

DESCRIPTION: Clear, golden yellow flowers with fringed petals are produced in groups of 3 to 6 and almost cover the 3 m (10 ft) high vine. It suits a sunny position.

Thunbergia alata
BLACK-EYED SUSAN, ORANGE CLOCK VINE, GOLDEN GLORY VINE

E
CLIMATE: T., S., W.T., M., C.T.
FAMILY: Acanthaceae
DESCRIPTION: Golden orange flowers with jet black, velvety centres are carried throughout the year in warm climates or in summer only in cold climates. In the latter it behaves as an annual. Others are: *T. gibsonii,*—with solid gold flowers; *T. grandiflora,*—with periwinkle blue flowers.

Trachelospermum jasminoides
STAR JASMINE

E
CLIMATE: T., S., W.T., M., C.T.
FAMILY: Apocynaceae
DESCRIPTION: This has sweetly scented star-like flowers in late spring. The leaves are dark green and glossy. It suits sun or shade and can be grown as a ground cover or hedge. As a vine it may reach 2 m (6½ ft).

Vitis vinifera
'Alicante Bouchet'
ORNAMENTAL GRAPE

D
CLIMATE: W.T., M., C.T.
FAMILY: Vitaceae
DESCRIPTION: The handsome grape foliage changes to brilliant reds and golds in autumn. It is fruitless and therefore does not create a problem with fruit on paths. It needs a sunny position.

Wisteria sinensis
CHINESE WISTERIA

D
CLIMATE: S., W.T., M., C.T., H.
FAMILY: Papilionaceae
DESCRIPTION: Wisterias bear pendant racemes of sweetly scented, lilac-blue flowers on the almost bare vine in late winter/spring. They are rampant growers and will strangle trees. They can be grown as a standard or tub plant. Others are *W. sinensis* 'Alba'—white; *W. sinensis* 'Plena'—double blue' *W. floribunda*— (Japanese Wisteria)—blue.

Trees for fruit and foliage

Growing your own fruit does involve maintenance but when minimal pest and disease controls are practised, *AT THE RIGHT TIME*, and the plants are fertilised and mulched annually and kept watered, the rewards are the beauty of the trees and the delicious fresh fruit. You also have the comfort of knowing what the tree was sprayed with, and when. This is important since the interval between spraying with chemicals and harvest should be 7 days (in most cases). There are organic means to control pests and disease. You *do not have* to use chemicals to grow fruit, though often the results will be better if you do, provided you follow the directions and take the precautions outlined in "Pests and Diseases".

Fruit trees are worth growing for their appearance alone, Citrus, loquats and mangoes make handsome screen plants, hiding fences with their beautiful foliage and bringing birds, bees, butterflies and possums to the garden. Mangoes, avocadoes and lychees, in tropical climates, and deciduous fruits elsewhere make elegant shade trees—especially during spring when most deciduous fruits are covered in exquisite blossoms.

All you need to grow fruit trees is an open sunny position in well drained, fertile soil, satisfactory year round watering, annual fertilising and mulching and a willingness to control pests and diseases. Home gardeners can forget pruning except in the initial stages when forming a "head" (3 or 4 main branches near each other and about 45cm (17½ in) above ground level) is necessary. This is done in the first and second years after planting (if it was not already done in the nursery). This will save branch and fruit loss later on because the stronger branches will be well able to carry the weight of fruit. In developed trees removal of crossing or dead branches will be an occasional, optional occupation. With or without that,

trees will go on bearing fruit! Orchardists practise pruning to increase size and fruit quality, but home gardeners will receive more fruit than they can eat without pruning. Three to 4 metres apart is the desired spacing for most fruits but it is not essential. They produce and look attractive even when they grow into each other.

All respond to cutting back and, as a screen, shearing will restrain them from growing wider. Only those few mentioned in the listing need male and female plants to ensure cross-pollination and fruit production. Where this is the case, for example, Chinese Goosberries and Japanese Plums, 2 different varieties can be planted in the same hole, or 2 or even 3 kinds can be grafted onto the one root system. Examples are Santa Rosa and Wilson Plums on one tree. The Santa Rosa is the pollinator, without it the Wilson would bear few, if any, fruit. Another example is 2 peaches and an apricot on the one tree. Here pollination is not a factor, but 3 varieties on the one tree is a space-saver and for small families prevents a surplus of fruit because the different types spread their fruit over an extended period.

If you decide to grow fruit, choose varieties that suit your climate, otherwise the result will not be worth the effort. Deciduous kinds have a chill factor, which means they must have a certain number of cold days called the "Chilling Requirement" before they start to grow again. This is based on the total number of hours below 10°C that each variety requires. It varies within a species. The best way to get the right variety for your climate is to ask for kinds known to suit the area.

With only minimal care—mostly in the pest and disease control area—most fruit trees could be grown successfully in the low-maintenance garden. However, evergreens, mangoes, lychees, star fruit, jack fruit, guavas, and loquats are the opposite and need warm climates. Their success south of Brisbane depends on finding a suitably warm, almost tropical or subtropical micro-climate.

EVERGREEN FRUIT TREES

These evergreens are Australia's most popular fruit. They thrive in all climates except cold mountainous and extremely frosty climates. However, even in some of these climates lemons (the most cold tolerant) manage to exist against warm northern walls under the protection of overhanging eavees. To enjoy fruit without excessive labour, low-maintenance gardeners should choose varieties suited to their climate and follow the care outlined below. Citrus are not normally double or treble grafted and only one tree is planted per hole.

CITRUS

T., S., W.T., M., C.T.
The best varieties of these winter fruits are:

Oranges Late Valencia and the various forms of Valencia are grown for juice, though they are also nice to eat. There are "seedless" forms containing fewer seeds than earlier varieties. Valencias tolerate poorer soils than navel oranges. Navel oranges, especially the Washington Navel and its various forms, are the best eating oranges. These suit well drained soils, rich in organic matter.

Lemons Eureka (Sweet Rind), which has a thin skin and bears fruit almost year round, is a favourite but is subject to root rot in coastal and humid areas. Lisbon and its various strains, including the Prior Lisbon are better than Eureka when grafted onto the root

stock trifoliata, which is not susceptible to root rot diseases and is therefore more reliable. Its fruit is as good as that of Eureka but the tree carries more thorns (small birds appreciate these as protection from cats). Meyer lemons are the most cold tolerant, but not as "lemony" tasting.

Mandarins These require ample water and organic matter to produce sweet fruit. Ellendale is a late maturing variety thought to be a hybrid between a mandarin and an orange. It has large flattened, smooth, bright orange fruit with a thin skin. Imperial bears early with a pale orange skin and has a distinctive mandarin flavour. Kara matures late. It is bright orange and large with a tangy flavour. Emperor is large, though not as big as Kara. It has loose orange skin and a delicious taste.

Grapefruit Marsh's Seedless is almost seedless with pale yellow skin and pale yellow flesh. The flavour depends on location and care. Its skin thickness is greater in cooler areas. Wheeny is more cold tolerant but contains more seeds. It is the best choice in cool and coastal climates. Pink-fleshed grapefruit such as Ruby and Thompson only develop their colour in hot, dry climates north of the Tropic of Capricorn.

Tangelo This is a hybrid between a mandarin and grapefruit, and does best in hot conditions. Minneola fruits mid-to-late season and has bright orange, thin, smooth, adherent skin and orange-like flesh with a tangy flavour, plenty of juice and few seeds. Orlando has a smooth orange skin and is flattened at both ends. It is more cold tolerant. Both will produce more fruit if cross-pollinated with Seminole. On its own, Seminole fruits well and has slightly pebbled, deep orange rind. It is richly flavoured, though seedy.

Limes These are more cold sensitive and less vigorous than lemons and their fruit does not hang on the tree for as long. The most usual lime in Australia is Tahiti or Persian lime, a seedlesss fruit about half the size of a large lemon. This is more vigorous and cold tolerant but not as strongly flavoured or as scented as the West Indian Lime. Its fruit is small, thin-skinned and lime green in the tropics and pale lemon when produced elsewhere. The flesh is apple green and seedy and its juice is more acid and has less vitamin C than a lemon.

Kumquats (or Cumquats) are grown mostly as tub plants but are attractive screens. The Nagami or Teardrop kumquat has oval fruit with a sweet skin and can be eaten whole. Marumi is the round fruited kumquat with sweeter skin and bitter flesh. Calamondin are kumquat-like trees, usually sold as Kumquats. The fruit is round and slightly larger than Marumi but very bitter; it makes excellent marmalade.

CITRUS CARE

On fungal diseases on fruit and foliage use Copper Oxychloride sprays; on scale, white or summer oil; on fruit fly and other citrus pests, spray with Rogor® or Lebaycid®.

OTHER EVERGREEN FRUIT TREES

Carica papaya
PAW PAW

CLIMATE: T., S., W.T. (in frost protected positions)
DESCRIPTION: Female plants require pollination by a male plant. Male plants have long funnel-shaped flowers on branched flower stalks; female flowers are close to the trunk and are large with fleshy petals. Plants with bisexual flowers are self-pollinating and are the best for home gardeners. Paw Paws are site specific, which means they adapt to their environment. Seeds saved from a tree fruiting satisfactorily in your garden will give a good result. Sow several and thin out the excess males once flowering occurs. Life span is usually 3 to 5 years.
CARE: Minor pest and disease problems.

Cyphomandra betacea
TAMARILLO, TREE TOMATO

CLIMATE: S., W.T.
DESCRIPTION: The egg-shaped fruits mature from autumn onwards and may be red or yellow according to variety. They grow readily from seed and will begin bearing within 3 months, with one tree producing up to 30kg (66 lbs) of fruit. Height is about 3 m (10 ft).

CARE: Spray for fruit fly, aphids and caterpillars.

Eriobotrya japonica
LOQUAT

CLIMATE: T., S., W.T., M., C.T.
DESCRIPTION: These trees have handsome foliage and attractive form and make pleasant shade trees. They flower in autumn and winter and fruit in spring. Herd's Mammoth is early—its large brown fruit has deep yellow flesh: Chatsworth Victory has large high quality fruits and cream flesh; Enormity is late with large pear shaped deep yellow to orange flesh.
CARE: Though early fruiting, they will be attacked by fruit fly.

Fragaria spp.
STRAWBERRIES

CLIMATE: T., S., W.T., M., C.T., H.
DESCRIPTION: Spreading plants on bushes 20 cm (8 in) tall, these radiate from a central crown and form horizontal runners, which become new plants. Runners from fruiting plants should not be used as propagating stock as they may carry virus diseases.
CARE: Various fungal diseases of fruit and foliage. Birds, aphids, mites and weevils can be a problem.

Litchi chinensis
LYCHEE

CLIMATE: T., S., W.T.
DESCRIPTION: The lychee may live to 400 years. It carries strawberry-like fruits that have a hard, rough, thin shell covering the jelly-like, sweet, slightly acidic fruit.
CARE: Minimal pest and disease problems.

Macadamia integrifolia
MACADAMIA NUT

CLIMATE: S., W.T., T.
DESCRIPTION: Nut bearing begins at 5 or 6 years of age. It is advisable to purchase a grafted tree as they are produced from trees with a known fruiting performance, whereas seedlings are very variable. *M. tetraphylla* is a tall tree
CARE: Most problems are caused by leaf or flower eating insects. Once established the tree bears without input from the grower, at least on the home garden scale.

Mangifera indica
MANGO

CLIMATE: T., S., W.T.
DESCRIPTION: Highly ornamental trees, which may take up to 7 years to fruit and may be grown from seed. They do not tolerate frost.
CARE: May be affected by fruit fly and tip borers and is susceptible to Black Spot.

Musa sapientum
BANANA

CLIMATE: T., S., W.T.

DESCRIPTION: Giant herbs that reproduce themselves from suckers developed from their tuberous underground stems. Bananas will flower and fruit 12 months after planting. They are subject to virus diseases and their movement out of banana growing areas is restricted.

CARE: Leaf spotting and speckle diseases will need spraying with Mancozeb or Maneb and white or summer oil.

Olea europaea
OLIVE

CLIMATE: M., W.T., C.T.

DESCRIPTION: The most popular varieties are:

Barouni—very large;

Manzanillo—smaller than the above, early maturing;

Sevillano—large mid-season fruit, suits cold areas best;

U.C.13.A.6—a selection from the University of California, this has the largest fruits and a small stone.

CARE: Spraying against scale insects will be necessary.

Passiflora species
PASSIONFRUIT

CLIMATE: W.T., S., M.

DESCRIPTION: The purple passionfruit *P. edulis* is more frost tolerant than the Banana Passionfruit *(P. mollissima)*. They are self-fertile but may not produce fruit if pollination is affected by rain. Virus diseases make it necessary to replace purple passionfruit every 2 or 3 years and to destroy the old ones once they appear unthrifty.

CARE: Control fungal disease of fruit and foliage with a fungicide.

Persea americana
AVOCADO

CLIMATE: T., S., W.T., M.

DESCRIPTION: Silvery barked, broad, spreading shade tree, which tolerates being pruned (though they need not be) to within a metre of the ground. Many varieties are cold tolerant. Fuerte bears without a pollinator, though in orchards all varieties are planted with another for cross-pollination.

CARE: Seedling-raised avocadoes are slow to fruit. Grafted plants are preferable. Check for thrips, fruit fly and aphids.

Psidium spp
GUAVAS

CLIMATE: T., S., W.T.

DESCRIPTION: Guavas are noted for their high vitamin C content. *P. guajava*, the Yellow Guava, has pear-like light yellow fruits with pink to red flesh inside. The Cherry or Strawberry Guava *(P. litorrale)* has plum-sized yellow to red fruit, not strongly scented as the above.

CARE: Fruit fly control will be necessary.

DECIDUOUS FRUITS
Actinidia chinesis
KIWI FRUIT

CLIMATE: S., W.T.

DESCRIPTION: These vines require a male and female plant to produce fruit and they need a support on which to climb. They bear at 4 to 5 years.

CARE: Pest and disease problems are few but removal of lateral growth in winter is necessary.

Carya illinoensis
PECAN NUT

CLIMATE: M., W.T.

DESCRIPTION: Some varieites are self-pollinating; others require a pollinator. Western Schley and Pabst are two self-pollinating types. Pecan trees are attractive shade trees.

CARE: Checking for the fungal disease Scab and spraying for fruit-spotting bug and the larvae of the yellow peach moth will be necessary as will netting against birds.

Cydonia oblonga
QUINCE

CLIMATE: S., W.T., M., C.T.
DESCRIPTION: Portugal is a mid-season variety with medium pear shape and near orange colour. Champion has small fruit, mild flavour and tender flesh.
CARE: Spray with Bordeaux at bud burst against Quince Fleck and with lime sulphur before the blossoms open and when the tree is in foliage.

Diospyros kaki
JAPANESE PERSIMMON

CLIMATE: S., W.T., M., C.T., H.
DESCRIPTION: Astringent and non-astringent varities are available in flat, rounded or domed shapes. Persimmon foliage changes colour spectacularly in autumn.
CARE: Though attacked by fruit fly the maggots do not develop until the fruit is ripe, so early picking will avoid fly damage.

Juglans regia
WALNUT

CLIMATE: H., C.T., M.
DESCRIPTION: A good-looking shade tree with silvery trunk and branches and delicious nuts appreciated by birds and possums.
CARE: Moist, free-draining soil in a suitable climate is the main care.

Malus domestica
THE APPLE

CLIMATE: W.T., M., C.T., H.
DESCRIPTION: There are now apple varieties to suit all Australian climates, though apples from cold winter climates are still the best-tasting. Choose varieties to suit your climate. Some are self-fertile, others need another flowering at the same time for cross pollination. Double and triple-grafted trees overcome space problems.
CARE: Control pests—aphids, bugs, mites, moths, fruit fly, weevils and woolly aphids. Diseases are Target Spot, Powdery Mildew, Scab and Collar Rot.

Morus
THE MULBERRY

CLIMATE: S., W.T., M., C.T., H.
DESCRIPTION: Both black and white fruited mulberries make effective shade trees. Hick's Fancy is the best black for warm climates. Black English suits cold areas. Both have a nicer taste than white mulberries.
CARE: Minimal, apart from bird problems.

Prunus amygdalus
THE ALMOND

CLIMATE: M., C.T.
DESCRIPTION: Two varieties that cross-pollinate and a hot dry climate are necessary to produce good almonds. Choose from "Soft", "Paper" and "Hard Shelled" varieties.
CARE: Protect from birds, control mites, wood-boring beetles and spray for fungal diseases.

Prunus armeniaca
APRICOT

CLIMATE: W.T., M., C.T.
DESCRIPTION: Plant late varieties in cold climates to avoid frost damage to flowers; mid-season and early kinds in warm climates.
CARE: See *P. persica*.

Prunus domestica
PLUM

CLIMATE: S., W.T., M., C.T., H.
DESCRIPTION: English or European plums suit climates with frosty winters; both Japanese and English Plums require a pollinator, except for Santa Rosa (Japanese) and Prune d'Agen

(English). Seek local knowledge for best varieties for your area.
CARE: See *P. persica*

Prunus persica
PEACH, NECTARINE

CLIMATE: T., S., W.T., M., C.T.
DESCRIPTION: Late varieties suit climates with long cold winters; early varieties are suitable for other climates. Dozens of varieties are available. It is best to choose those known to suit your area.
CARE: Control aphids, mites, peach-tip moth, fruit fly and pear and cherry slugs. Disease problems are peach leaf curl, brown rot and bacterial gummosis. See "Pests and Diseases".

Prunus avium
CHERRIES

CLIMATE: H., C.T.
DESCRIPTION: Cherries require two to ensure cross pollination. They grow only in a limited climatic range.
CARE: Bacterial canker is a problem; other care as for *P. persica*.

Pyrus communis
PEAR

CLIMATE: W.T., M., C.T., H.
DESCRIPTION: Pears suit climates with a long cold winter. Two plants that cross pollinate each other are necessary to ensure fruit. Choose from brown or yellow-skinned varieties. Also consider the Asian or Nashi pears, which tolerate W.T. climates better than the above and have crisp apple-like flesh and brown skin.
CARE: Pest and disease problems similar to those of apples.

Punica granatum
POMEGRANATE

CLIMATE: T., S., W.T., M., C.T.
DESCRIPTION: Pomegranates are grown for fruit, as a hedge, as tub plants and as a component of a screen.
CARE: Minimal; they can be attacked by fruit fly.

BERRY FRUITS

Ribes nigrum and R. rubrum
BLACK AND RED CURRANTS

Rubus species
BLACKBERRIES

R. idaeus
RASPBERRIES

R. grossularia
GOOSBERRIES

DESCRIPTION: Can all be grown with minimal effort in W.T., M., C.T., & H. They do best in the colder areas, except for blackberries, which adapt to many others. Berries are planted about 1 m (3 ft) apart and grow about 1 m (3 ft) high.
CARE: Spray to control mites and fungal diseases.

Vaccinium corymbosum
BLUEBERRIES

CLIMATE: W.T., M., C.T., H.
DESCRIPTION: Warm climate and cold climate varieties are available. Two that cross pollinate ensure a better crop and would produce enough for an average family.
CARE: Protect from birds; spray for fungal diseases and light brown apple moth and caterpillars.

Vitis vinifera
GRAPES

CLIMATE: W.T., M., C.T., H.
DESCRIPTION: One grape will be sufficient for a family. A wide range of varieties is available to suit a range of climates.
CARE: Protect from birds, spray to control mites and caterpillars and foliage and fruit diseases. Prune annually.

Colourful plants to fill-in the corners

The low-maintenance garden needs colour ranging from the soft greens of ferns to the vibrant flowers of many easily grown bulbs and perennials.

Many of these colourful plants are trouble free and require minimal space. They fit in between shrubs or in odd corners. You plant and forget them, and annually they will cover more space by multiplying underground or by self-sowing. Covering space minimises work by controlling weeds and, when the right plants are chosen, adds colour and interest to your garden.

This is a select list of evergreen and herbaceous (die down in winter and renew themselves in spring) perennials, bulbous or cormous plants and subshrubs. All suit sunny positions unless shade is indicated.

Almost all are trouble free. The few that do have problems (for example, fungal diseases on Pelargoniums) still look attractive when given a suitable aspect and climate, and most of their problems can be overcome with a good pruning.

Acanthus mollis
OYSTER PLANT, OAK LEAF

E

HEIGHT: 45 cm–1 m (18 in –3 ft)
CLIMATE: W.T., M., C.T., H.
FAMILY: Acanthaceae

DESCRIPTION: Dark green, deeply indented, shiny foliage radiates from a central point with mid-summer, mauve-tinged white flowers closely packed on a tall spike 50 cm (20 in) or more above the leaves. It is waterlogging tolerant and stands sun or shade. Oak Leaf has more finely toothed foliage. There is a variegated form.

Actinotus helianthi
SYDNEY FLANNEL FLOWER

E ✳

HEIGHT: 50 cm (20 in)
CLIMATE: S., W.T., M., C.T.
FAMILY: Apiaceae
DESCRIPTION: This has 5-8 cm (2-3 in) diameter starry white flowers with soft flannel-like bracts in spring and summer. They are wind-tolerant biennials with silver-grey, much divided soft foliage. They grow readily from seed as well as self-sow.

Adiantum aethiopicum
MAIDENHAIR FERN

E *

HEIGHT: 45 cm (18 in)
CLIMATE: T., S., W.T., M., C.T.
FAMILY: Adiantiaceae
DESCRIPTION: Long, delicate, black-stemmed fronds support masses of tiny cuneate leaflets, which dance in every breeze. It suits light to full shade. There are many varieties, ranging in overall frond size and fineness of the leaflets.

Agapanthus orientalis
LILY OF THE NILE

E

HEIGHT: 50-75 cm (20-29 in)
CLIMATE: T., S., W.T., M., C.T., H.
FAMILY: Liliaceae
DESCRIPTION: A clump-forming salt and wind tolerant plant with arching, strap-shaped leaves about 50 cm (20 in) long and 5 cm (2 in) wide, above which rises a 60 cm (24 in) high stalk carrying a giant umbel of 100–200 sky blue or white, tubular flowers from November to February. *A. africanus* and hybrids reach 45 cm (18 in) with blue or white flowers.

Agave attenuata
AGAVE

E

HEIGHT: 1-1.5 m (3-5 ft)
CLIMATE: T., S., W.T., M., C.T.
FAMILY: Agavaceae
DESCRIPTION: The rosette shape is created by soft, fleshy, grey-green, pointed foliage. The flowers are creamy-white bells carried on 2–3 m (6½–10 ft) high spikes. It is salt and wind tolerant and stands sun or shade. *A. americana* and its varieties are close, spiny relatives.

Ajuga reptans
BLUE BUGLE;
CARPET BUGLE

E

HEIGHT: 10-15 cm (4-6 in)
CLIMATE: S., W.T., M., C.T., H.
FAMILY: Lamiaceae
DESCRIPTION: Ajuga is a marvellous ground-cover, spreading quickly with oval, dark-green leaves and high spikes of blue spring flowers. *A. reptans* 'Multicolour' has variegated, cream, pink and burgundy leaves and pale blue flowers. *A. reptans* 'Alba' has white flowers. *A. reptans* 'Jungle Beauty' has outsized green leaves and flower spikes up to 30 cm (12 in) long.

Amaryllis belladonna

BELLADONNA LILY, NAKED LILY,
MARCH LILY

BULB: 60-75 cm (24-29 in)
CLIMATE: T.S., W.T., M., C.T., H.
FAMILY: Amaryllidaceae
DESCRIPTION: Hippeastrum-like scented flowers between January and March are followed by strap-like leaves during the winter. Flower stems are more striking because of the absence of foliage. White and shades of pink are available.

Anemone x hybrida

(syn. Anemone hupehensis 'Japonica')
JAPANESE AMEMONE,
JAPANESE WINDFLOWER

E

HEIGHT: 1-2 m (3-6½ ft)
CLIMATE: W.T., M., C.T., H.
FAMILY: Ranunculaceae
DESCRIPTION: Clump-forming plants with a tall, branching flower stem carrying white-mauve or rose-coloured poppy-like flowers in autumn. It suits light shade. Others are usually chosen by colour not name. *A. blanda* has circular flowers with a black centre, usually white though other colours are available.

Aquilegia vulgaris

COLUMBINE, GRANNY'S BONNETS

E

HEIGHT: 45-60 cm (18-24 in)
CLIMATE: W.T., M., C.T., H.
FAMILY: Ranunculaceae
DESCRIPTION: Perennial plants, usually grown as annuals. Single or semi-double flowers are funnel-shaped and carry a spur. Colours may be white, cream, pink, yellow, lavender or purple and shades of those, or two colours. Numerous strains are available.

Asplenium australasicum

BIRD'S NEST FERN

E   *

HEIGHT: 1-3 m (3-10 ft)
CLIMATE: T., S., W.T., M.
FAMILY: Aspleniaceae
DESCRIPTION: A handsome epiphytic fern that consists of a circle of very stiff light green shiny fronds around an open centre. It suits light shade or sun. Others are *A. bulbiferum*, the Mother Spleenwort or Hen and Chicken Fern.

Aster nova-belgii hybrids
MICHAELMAS DAISIES,
EASTER DAISIES

HEIGHT: 45 cm-1.2 m (18 in-4 ft)
CLIMATE: W.T., M., C.T., H.
FAMILY: Asteraceae
DESCRIPTION: They have daisy-like blooms massed along tall flower spikes and may be small or tall and white, with shades of mauve, purple and pink in late summer and early autumn. The flowers last well when cut.

Astilbe x arendsii
GOAT'S BEARD, FALSE SPIREA

HEIGHT: 60-75 vm (24-29 in
CLIMATE: W.T., M., C.T., H.
FAMILY: Saxifragaceae
DESCRIPTION: Herbaceous perennials, they tolerate sun or shade in moist soil. They die down in winter and flower in spring. The feathery flowers are carried above the shining fern-like foliage in erect panicles. Named cultivars include: 'Deutschland', white; 'Federsee', rose red; 'Mont Blanc', white; 'Rhineland', pink; and 'Rotlicht', dark red.

Begonia semperflorens
BEDDING BEGONIA

E

HEIGHT: 30 cm
CLIMATE: T.S., W.T., M., C.T.
FAMILY: Begoniaceae
DESCRIPTION: Soft fleshy perennials usually treated as annuals and grown for their green, bronze, or reddish foliage and their red, pink or white flowers. They carry male and female flowers; the females are more colourful.

Bergenia x schmidtii
MEGASEA; SAXIFRAGA;
HEARTLEAF BERGENIA

E

HEIGHT: 30 cm (12 in)
CLIMATE: W.T., M., C.T., H.
FAMILY: Saxifragaceae
DESCRIPTION: Winter-flowering with large fleshy, heart-shaped leaves and short stems of flowers in white, rose or pink, which last well as cut flowers. They suit light to filtered shade.

Blechnum gibbum
NORFOLK ISLAND WATER FERN

E ✳

HEIGHT: 1 m (3 ft)
CLIMATE: S., W.T., M.
FAMILY: Blechnaceae
DESCRIPTION: This forms a small woody trunk topped with a rosette of fresh green fronds up to 1 m (3 ft) long. Suits light to filtered shade and is fast-growing. Others are *B. minus*, the soft water fern; *B. nudum*, fishbone water fern.

Brachycome multifida
SWAN RIVER DAISY

E ✳

HEIGHT: 30 cm (12 in)
CLIMATE: T., S., W.T., M., C.T., H.
FAMILY: Asteraceae
DESCRIPTION: A tidy little plant covered throughout spring and summer with lilac-blue, daisy-like flowers about 2 cm (¾ in) wide. *B. angustifolia* is a mat-forming, suckering ground cover; *B. iberidifolia*, the Swan River Daisy, is a West Australian annual with spring flowers varying from white to blue, mauve and purple.

Campanula medium
CANTERBURY BELLS

E

HEIGHT: 1 m (3 ft)
CLIMATE: W.T., M., C.T., H.
FAMILY: Campanulaceae
DESCRIPTION: The large bell flowers hang from a tall stem. They are violet, blue or pink and last for up to 9 weeks in summer. *C. latifolia*, the Giant Bellflower, is another variety.

Cerastium tomentosum
SNOW-IN-SUMMER

E

HEIGHT: 18 cm (7 in).
CLIMATE: W.T., M., C.T., H.
FAMILY: Caryophyllaceae
DESCRIPTION: A wind-tolerant, low, spreading plant perhaps 18 cm (7 in) high and 45 cm (18 in) wide, valued for its soft, silvery-white foliage covered in fine hairs and white flowers from spring to mid-summer.

Ceropegia woodii
CHAIN OF HEARTS; ROSARY VINE.

E

HEIGHT: 1 m (3 ft) long trailers.
CLIMATE: T., S., W.T., M., C.T., H.
FAMILY: Asclepiadaceae
DESCRIPTION: Several slender, trailing 1 m (3 ft) long stems develop from a tuberous root. Round to heart-shaped leaves are greyish marked red; pinkish tubular flowers are carried in pairs. Suits light shade. *C. debilis* has small, cylindrical leaves.

Chrysanthemum
MARGUERITE DAISY

E

HEIGHT: 69-90 cm (27-35 in)
CLIMATE: T., S., W.T., M., C.T., H.
FAMILY: Compositae
DESCRIPTION: A shrubby perennial covered in spring/summer/autumn with masses of daisies, which last well indoors. There are numerous others, which include double and single daisies with yellow centres and pink, yellow or white petals.

Chrysanthemum x superbum
(syn. **Chrysanthemum maximum**)
SHASTA DAISY

HEIGHT: 30-60 cm (12-24 in)
CLIMATE: W.T., M., C.T., H.
FAMILY: Compositae
DESCRIPTION: This herbaceous perennial does not die back completely in warm climates during winter. Early-to-late-summer white daisies have a conspicuous golden centre. They last well when cut. Varieties include double and very large single Daisies.

Cineraria senecio maritima
CINERARIA

E

HEIGHT: 60-90 cm (24-35 in)
CLIMATE: T., S., W.T., M., C.T., H.
FAMILY: Compositae
DESCRIPTION: A soft-wooded perennial with felty, deeply indented, silvery foliage and heads of yellow flowers. There are many varieties available in a range of foliage shapes.

Clivea miniata
KAFIR LILY, CLIVEA

E

HEIGHT: 40 cm (16 in)
CLIMATE: T., S., W.T., M.
FAMILY: Amaryllidaceae
DESCRIPTION: Clump-forming plant with dark green, strap-shaped leaves among which are stems bearing funnel-shaped spring flowers, which last well indoors. It needs shade. *C. hybrida* has large, red flowers. *C. miniata* has salmon-orange bell flowers. White and yellow Cliveas are rarely seen.

Convolvulus mauritanicus
GROUND COVER MORNING GLORY

E

HEIGHT: 15 cm (6 in)
CLIMATE: T., S., W.T., M., C.T.
FAMILY: Convolvolaceae
DESCRIPTION: A fast-growing, wind-tolerant, prostrate plant capable of spreading 1 m (3 ft) wide. It bears 1-6 blue flowers in a cluster in spring *C. cneorum* (Silverbush) is a white flowered, silvery-foliaged, subshrub to 1 m (3 ft).

Cyclamen neapolitanum
'Album'
NEAPOLITAN CYCLAMEN

BULB: 10 cm (4 in)
CLIMATE: W.T., M., C.T., H.
FAMILY: Primulaceae
DESCRIPTION: Charming miniature cyclamen with rose-pink or white autumn flowers and prettily marked heart shaped foliage, which dies down after flowering. Bulbs are left in situ. It suits light to filtered shade. Other varieties usually available by separate colours.

137

Dahlia bedding hybrids
DAHLIA

HEIGHT: 30-70 cm (12-27 in)
CLIMATE: W.T., M., C.T.
FAMILY: Asteraceae
DESCRIPTION: Bedding Dahlias are tuberous and bloom from early summer to autumn. They have single, semi-double, and double flowers of white and shades of red, yellow and orange. Among strains available are "Hi-Dolly", "Unwin's Dwarf" and "Pom Pom Dwarf".

Dianthus deltoides
MAIDEN PINK, PINK

E

HEIGHT: 10 cm (4 in)
CLIMATE: W.T., M., C.T., H.
FAMILY: Caryophyllaceae
DESCRIPTION: This has grassy foliage forming a dense mat of grey with masses of open, 5 petalled, pink flowers, like small single carnations in mid to late summer. Numerous other Dianthus vary in flower and foliage colour.

Dampiera diversifolia
DAMPIERA

E   *

HEIGHT: 10-15 cm (4-6 in)
CLIMATE: S., W.T., M., C.T.
FAMILY: Goodeniaceae
DESCRIPTION: Almost gentian-blue flowers through spring and summer. A ground cover that roots as it spreads and becomes 1 m (3 ft) wide. There are about 60 species, most from south-west Western Australia, and nearly all with blue to purple-blue flowers.

Dendrobium kingianum
PINK ROCK ORCHID

⊛

HEIGHT: 10-20 cm (4-9 in)
CLIMATE: T., S., W.T., M., C.T.
FAMILY: Orchidaceae
DESCRIPTION: A native orchid carrying spikes of up to 10 small Lily-of-the-Valley type spring flowers in white or shades of pink. It requires light shade. There are approximately fifty species of Australian Dendrobiums in cultivation.

Dendrobium speciosum
ROCK LILY, ROCK ORCHID.

E   ⊛

HEIGHT: 45-70 cm (18-27½ in)
CLIMATE: T., S., W.T., M.
FAMILY: Orchidaceae
DESCRIPTION: Has extravagant spring display of creamy-yellow or creamy-white massed sprays of flowers. The creamy-yellow type grows happily on exposed sandstone and has flower spikes about 45 cm (18 in) long. The creamy-white form, an epiphyte from rainforests carries sprays over 70 cm (27½ in) in length. Both need light to filtered shade.

Dietes grandiflora
WILD IRIS

E

HEIGHT: 75 cm (29½ in)
CLIMATE: S., W.T., M., C.T., H.
FAMILY: Iridaceae
DESCRIPTION: The clumps of narrow, dark-green erect foliage are enlivened in summer by iris-like flowers of white with mauve and orange markings. They self-sow readily so that attractive clumps are soon built up. *D. bicolor* (Fortnight Lily) has yellow and brown flowers; *D. vegeta* is smaller than *D. grandiflora*.

Dimorphotheca hybrids
NAMAQUALAND DAISY, AFRICAN DAISY
CAPE MARIGOLD

E

HEIGHT: 15 cm (6 in)
CLIMATE: S., W.T., M., C.T., H.
FAMILY: Asteraceae
DESCRIPTION: These daisies close on cloudy days or indoors. They have spring to winter flowers in cream, yellow apricot and orange. They are drought tolerant. Others are usually sold as mixed colours in packet seeds; these will revert to perennial habit and become more or less permanent.

Doryanthes excelsa
SPEAR LILY, FLAME LILY,
GIANT LILY

E ✳

HEIGHT: 2 m (6½ ft)
CLIMATE: S., W.T., M.
FAMILY: Agavaceae
DESCRIPTION: An evergreen rosette of giant,
stiff, sword-shaped foliage above which rises a
stem 4-6 m (13-19½ ft) high with a head of red
flowers about 24 cm (9 in) across. *D. palmeri*
from Queensland reaches 3 m (10 ft).

Drosanthemum floribundum
ICE PLANT; DEW FLOWER.

E

HEIGHT: 15 cm (6 in)
CLIMATE: S., W.T., M., C.T.
FAMILY: Aizoaceae
DESCRIPTION: Glistening foliage is covered
in spring or early summer with pastel pink,
daisy-like flowers. *D. speciosum* has orange
flowers and is an annual raised from seed.
Lampranthus and Mesembryanthemums are
similar to Drosanthemums.

Echium fastuosum
ECHIUM

E

HEIGHT: 1-2 m (3-6½ ft)
CLIMATE: W.T., M., C.T., H.
FAMILY: Boraginaceae
DESCRIPTION: A furry grey, salt-tolerant
bush with spring flower spikes up to 55 cm (22
in) long of deep purple blue very like a
delphinium. It is a perennial that lives 3-5 years
and renews itself annually from seedlings. Other
species have purple, red, pink or white flowers.

Erigeron karvinskianus
(syn. Erigeron mucronatus)
VITTADENIA, SEASIDE DAISY,
FLEABANE

E

HEIGHT: 20 cm (9 in)
CLIMATE: W.T., M., C.T., H.
FAMILY: Asteraceae
DESCRIPTION: A small salt-tolerant spreading plant with dainty white daisy flowers which
become rose-pink. Main flowering time is
autumn and winter, but year round flowering
is usual in warm climates.

Euryops pectinatus
YELLOW MARGUERITE, BRIGHT EYES

E

HEIGHT: 1 m (3 ft)
CLIMATE: W.T., M., C.T., H.
FAMILY: Asteraceae
DESCRIPTION: Gay, golden-yellow spring to
autumn daisies on long, slender stems cover this
grey-foliaged, perennial shrub. It is salt and
wind tolerant.

Felicia amelloides

(syn. Agathea coelestis)
BLUE MARGUERITE,
BLUE DAISY, AGATHEA

E

HEIGHT: 45 cm (18 in)
CLIMATE: S., W.T., M., C.T., H.
FAMILY: Asteraceae
DESCRIPTION: Bright blue, yellow-centred flowers bloom almost all year round on this salt tolerant bush with its aromatic foliage and broad spreading habit up to 1.5 cm (½ in) wide. *F. bergeriana*, the blue Kingfisher Daisy is a 1.5 cm (½ in) high annual.

Freesia refracta

FREESIA

HEIGHT: 40 cm (16 in)
CLIMATE: S., W.T., M., C.T., H.
FAMILY: Iridaceae
DESCRIPTION: Strongly scented, creamy to greenish-yellow, *F. refracta*, a cormous plant, has spring flowers in one-sided spikes on thin stems and spear shaped foliage and naturalises readily. Tolerates light shade. Many strains include shades of orange, red and lilac, though not as scented as the above.

Gazania hybrids

GAZANIA

E

HEIGHT: 25 cm (10 in)
CLIMATE: S., W.T., M., C.T.
FAMILY: Compositae
DESCRIPTION: Dense, tufted, wind tolerant evergreen perennials mostly with long leaves and always with brilliant daisies in spring and early summer. Colours include pink, orange, red and yellow, including two-tone and black-centred varieties.

Geranium ibericum

IBERIAN CRANE'S BILL

E

HEIGHT: 45 cm (18 in)
CLIMATE: S., W.T., M., C.T., H.
FAMILY: Geraniaceae
DESCRIPTION: This has 2.5 cm (1 in) wide violet summer flowers in colourful open panicles and deeply lobed and toothed foliage. *G. pratense* has large blue summer flowers. There is also a white variety.

Geranium sanguineum
CRANE'S BILL

E

HEIGHT: 20 cm (8 in)
CLIMATE: S., W.T., M., C.T., H.
FAMILY: Geraniaceae
DESCRIPTION: In spring and often in summer, this evergreen, ground-covering perennial bears crimson-to-violet flowers among its deeply lobed foliage. Also see *G. ibericum.*

Gladioulus x nanus
'The Bride'
DWARF GLADIOLUS

CORM: 36 cm (14 in)
CLIMATE: W.T., M., C.T., H.
FAMILY: Iridaceae
DESCRIPTION: An easy-to-grow, small, white gladiolus with simple, funnel-form flowers in spring and narrow, sword-like foliage. Others are *G. nanus* 'Lilac', and *G. natalensis*, the Parrot Gladiolus, which is red and yellow and easy to grow. Many named dwarf gladiolus forms are available, but they are more trouble than the above.

Helianthus x multiflorus
SUNFLOWER

E

HEIGHT: 1–4 m (3–13 ft)
CLIMATE: S., W.T., M., C.T., H.
FAMILY: Asteraceae
DESCRIPTION: Sunflowers may be as much as 40 cm (16 in) across. They have flat circular flowers with a brown/black centre, a fringe of golden-yellow petals and a 6–10 week summer flowering period. The foliage is hairy. Numerous forms are available, some with double flowers and smaller height; others with bronze flowers.

Heliopsis
'Light of Loddon'
OX-EYE DAISIES

E

HEIGHT: 1–2 m (3–6½ ft)
CLIMATE: W.T., M., C.T., H.
FAMILY: Asteraceae
DESCRIPTION: Yellow, summer and autumn, daisy-like flowers cover this long flowering perennial. Flowering is prolonged if the spent flowers are removed. About 10 species and several varieties are available, varying in height, colour and flower form.

Helleborus orientalis
THE LENTEN ROSE, HELLEBORE

HEIGHT: 30 cm (12 in)
CLIMATE: W.T., M., C.T., H.
FAMILY: Ranunculaceae
DESCRIPTION: Winter and spring flowers of this herbaceous perennial are cupped at first and carried 2-6 on a stem over 30 cm (12 in) tall. They are white flushed with purple, like a single rose, though more papery. These need light to filtered shade. Others are *H. niger,* (the Christmas Rose), white flushed purple; *H. viridis,* (the Green Lenten Rose); *H. viridis* var. *purpurascens,* flowers heavily tinged purple.

Hemerocallis hybrids
DAY LILY

▢D ▢E
HEIGHT: 1-1.2 m (3-4 ft)—evergreens, 1 m (3 ft)
CLIMATE: T., S., W.T., M., C.T., H.
FAMILY: Liliaceae
DESCRIPTION: There are 2 broad types: evergreen and deciduous fibrous-rooted, herbaceous, clump-forming perennials, which flower just above the leaves. The flowers last only 1 day but are carried in groups so that one stalk may flower for a week or more. Hundreds of named varieties represent shades of blue, purple, mauve, orange, lemon, gold, red, maroon, pink, salmon and burgundy.

Heterocentron elegans
SPANISH SHAWL, TRAILING LASIANDRA

▢E
HEIGHT: 7-8 mm ($^1/_3$ in)
CLIMATE: S., W.T., M., C.T.
FAMILY: Melastomaceae
DESCRIPTION: Deep magenta, mid-summer to autumn flowers almost hide the small foliage and reddish stems of this carpeting perennial, which roots along its stems as is spreads. It is sometimes called Heeria.

Hibbertia serpyllifolia
GUINEA FLOWER

▢E ▢✱
HEIGHT: 1 m (3 ft)
CLIMATE: S., W.T., M., C.T.
FAMILY: Dilleniaceae
DESCRIPTION: Bright yellow open flowers cover this carpeting ground cover for most of the year. It suits sun and light to filtered shade. Several other Hibbertias are small yellow-flowered shrubs and one, *H. scandens,* (the Guinea Gold Flower), is a climber or vigorous ground cover.

Hippeastrum (Amaryllis) hybrids

BARBADOS LILY, GIANT ARMARYLLIS, FIRE LILY

HEIGHT: 60 cm–1 m (24 in–3 ft)
CLIMATE: T., S., W.T., M., C.T.
FAMILY: Amaryllidaceae
DESCRIPTION: The stout stems are topped with 2–5 large, funnel-shaped winter and spring blooms in white or shades of orange, red, yellow and pink. Often the wide strap-shaped leaves die down in summer.

Hosta plantaginea

PLANTAIN LILY, DAY LILY

D

HEIGHT: 30 cm (12 in)
CLIMATE: W.T., M., C.T., H.
FAMILY: Lilaceae
DESCRIPTION: Above a clump of heart-to-ovate-shaped, light green, ribbed foliage, rise short flower spikes clad with white, open, orange-scented, bell-shaped summer flowers. New spring growth rises from dense stools of thickly clustered roots. They need light to filtered shade. There are many others, for example, *H. fortunei*, which has pale lilac flowers.

Houstonia caerulea

BLUE CUSHION, BLUETS

E

HEIGHT: 6–15 cm (2–6 in)
CLIMATE: S., W.T., M., C.T., H.
FAMILY: Rubiaceae
DESCRIPTION: A dainty, spreading plant which forms a soft bright green carpet in light to filtered shade. The minute leaves are closely sprinkled in spring with tiny, salver-form, blue-to-white flowers. Others are: *H. serpyllifolia*—deep violet (or white) flowers; *H. purpurea*—purple flowers.

Impatiens hybrids

BUSY LIZZIE

E

HEIGHT: 30–150 cm (12–59 in)
CLIMATE: T., W.T., M.
FAMILY: Balsaminaceae
DESCRIPTION: These self-sow readily, popping up everywhere to cover every section of soil with colour. They can be red, pink, cerise, mauve, white in single or double flowers; some with white markings. They suit sun or shade.

Hymenocallis narcissiflora
(syn. Hymenocallis calathina)
ISMENE LILY, SPIDER LILY

BULB: 60 cm (24 in)
CLIMATE: S., W.T., M., C.T., H.
FAMILY: Amaryllidaceae
DESCRIPTION: In spring and summer green-striped white flowers, 2-5 to a stem, are held above a clump of strap foliage. *H. littoralis*, (Filmy Lily), has green-tinged, white, funnel-form flowers with long recurved segments.

Iresine herbstii
BLOODLEAF

E
HEIGHT: 75 cm (29 in)
CLIMATE: T., W.T., M.
FAMILY: Amaranthaceae
DESCRIPTION: These colourfully foliaged perennials are usually treated as annuals, particularly where frost is a problem. They have purple-red foliage with prominent veins. They suit sun or light shade. A green or green-red variety with yellow veins and several species and selections based on foliage colour and plant height are also available.

Iris
Bearded type
BEARDED IRIS

E
HEIGHT: 10 cm to 1-2 m (4 in-4 m)
CLIMATE: S., W.T., M., C.T., H.
FAMILY: Iridaceae
DESCRIPTION: Late-spring flowering, some rebloom in summer, autumn and winter, these rhizomatous perennials are classified according to flower-stem height into tall, intermediate and dwarf sections. They suit sun or light shade. The flowers have a soft, fleshy, hairy "beard" on the outer petals. Hundreds of named varieties are available in a rainbow range of colours.

Iris kaempferi
JAPANESE IRIS, WATER IRIS

D

HEIGHT: 60-90 cm to 1.2 m (24-35 in to 4 m)
CLIMATE: W.T., M., C.T., H.
FAMILY: Iridaceae
DESCRIPTION: Strong-growing, clump-forming perennial plants bearing several flower stems in late spring to early summer. Flowers fall into 2 groups: 3-petalled forms and 6-petalled forms. They suit sun or light shade. There are numerous varieties, available in white and shades of purple, violet, blue, lavender, rose and pink.

Iris unguicularis
(syn. Iris stylosa)
WINTER IRIS, ALGERIAN IRIS

E

HEIGHT: 45-60 cm (18-24 in)
CLIMATE: W.T., M., C.T., H.
FAMILY: Iridaceae
DESCRIPTION: A fragrant Iris in bloom from May to August with short-stalked flowers in white or shades of blue and violet. They suit sun or light shade. In spring and autumn, plants in bloom are available in the colours above.

Kniphofia praecox
KNIPHOFIA

E

HEIGHT: 45 cm-1 m (18 in-3 ft)
CLIMATE: T., W.T., M., C.T., H.
FAMILY: Liliaceae
DESCRIPTION: Salt-tolerant, clump-forming plants with thin, strap-shaped leaves above which rise tall inflorescenses of red and yellow in late winter. Numerous forms are available in variations on this colour theme, flowering in succession for almost year round colour.

Lampranthus aureus
(syn. Mesembryanthemum aurantiacum)
ORANGE TRAILING ICEPLANT

E

HEIGHT: 30 cm (12 in)
CLIMATE: T., S., W.T., M.
FAMILY: Aizoceae
DESCRIPTION: A fleshy leaved, ground-covering plant capable of spreading up to 1 m (3 ft) wide with brilliant orange, glistening daisy-like spring and summer flowers. Others are *L. albus*—white; *L. spectabilis*—pink; *L. citrinus*—yellow; *L. coccineus*—red; Doreanthus, Drosantheumem and Carpobrotus are closely related.

Lavatera trimestris

TREE MALLOW

HEIGHT: 60–90 cm (24–35 in)
CLIMATE: W.T., M., C.T., H.
FAMILY: Malvaceae
DESCRIPTION: Rosy, trumpet-like flowers similar to Hibiscus are carried in summer on this herbaceous, quick-growing annual with its handsome heart-shaped, serrated foliage. The variety 'Alba' is white; 'Splendens' is pink and other varieties are red-flowered.

Ligularia tussilaginea Aureo-maculata

(syn. Farfugium kaempferi)
LEOPARD PLANT

E

HEIGHT: 30–60 cm (12–24 in)
CLIMATE: W.T., M., C.T., H.
FAMILY: Asteraceae
DESCRIPTION: A cluster of slender-stemmed orbicular leaves, blotched with yellow or white topped with yellow daisy-like summer flowers. Grow in sun or light shade. *L. dentata* (syn. *L. clivorum, Fargugium kaempferi* and *Senecio kaempferi*) has dark green foliage.

Liriope muscari

LILY TURF

E

HEIGHT: 30–45 cm (12–18 in)
CLIMATE: S., W.T., M., C.T.
FAMILY: Liliaceae
DESCRIPTION: A salt and shade tolerant, grass-like plant with broad, deep green leaves forming neat clumps of mauve-lilac, summer-to-autumn flower spikes resembling those of a Grape Hyacinth. This also grows well in sun. *L. spicata* is about 36 cm (14 in) tall with finer, narrower leaves and bell-like lilac flowers from summer to autumn.

Lunaria annua
HONESTY, MONEY PLANT

E

HEIGHT: 60–75 cm (24–30 in)
CLIMATE: W.T., M., C.T., H.
FAMILY: Cruciferae
DESCRIPTION: Fragrant, purple-pink or white spring and summer flowers—for up to 10 weeks—are followed by the circular, papery seed vessels, which become silvery as the outer skin is peeled off and are much sought after for flower arrangements. The hairy, greyish leaves are heart-shaped and grow in sun or filtered shade.

Mentha requienii
CORSICAN MINT

E

HEIGHT: 2.5 cm (1 in)
CLIMATE: W.T., M., C.T.
FAMILY: Labiatae
DESCRIPTION: A peppermint-scented, minute-leaved, carpeting ground cover for light to filtered shade. It has small, mauve flower spikes, which in spring and early summer smother the foliage. There are many varieties, for example, *M. pulegium*, (Pennyroyal), and several others are used in cooking.

Moraea neopavonia
PEACOCK IRIS

E

HEIGHT: 30–60 cm (12–24 in)
CLIMATE: S., W.T., M., C.T.
FAMILY: Iridaceae
DESCRIPTION: Iris-like, clump-forming, cormous plants with narrow linear leaves and flowers of white, mauve or orange with a shining blue-black or greenish "peacock eye". It suits sun and tolerates light shade. Other varieties are 'Villosa'—bright purple flowers; 'Lutea'—yellow; *M. spathulata*—fragrant, bright yellow; *M. bicolor*—(the Butterfly Iris) —drought-resistant, sun-loving and shade tolerant with 3 petalled, creamy-centred flowers.

Narcissus species
DAFFODILS

BULBS: approx 25 cm (10 in)
CLIMATE: S., W.T., M., C.T., H.
FAMILY: Amaryllidaceae
DESCRIPTION: There are more than 8000 named cultivars of Narcissus now classified into 12 divisions. In Australia, the most popular (though not the best) Daffodil is 'King Alfred', with its large yellow trumpets. 'Fortune' has yellow petals and cup colours varying from orange to red, and flowers more consistently; 'August Pink' is a creamy white, edged with

pink; the Poet's and fragrant Pheasant's Eye types are among many worthy of investigation. Daffodils suit sun and tolerate light shade.

Narcissus bulbocodium
HOOP PETTICOAT DAFFODILS

BULB: 15 cm (6 in)
CLIMATE: S., W.T., M., C.T., H.
FAMILY: Amaryllidaceae
DESCRIPTION: A dainty, unique Narcissus with cylindrical, dark green leaves overtopping the charming upward or horizontal facing flowers. There are many garden forms and hybrids varying in shades of yellow, time of flowering, and size. They prefer sun but will tolerate light shade. *N. cantabricus* (syn. *N. bulbocodium monophyllus*) is a white-flowered species.

Narcissus x odorus
'Rugulosus'
CAMPERNELLE JONQUIL

BULB: 30 cm (12 in)
CLIMATE: S., W.T., M., C.T., H.
FAMILY: Amaryllidaceae
DESCRIPTION: A very early-flowering hybrid between a Daffodil and a Jonquil, this carries 2–3 pale yellow, fragrant, bell-cupped flowers on each stem. It suits sun and light shade. There is a rarely seen, double-flowered form.

Narcissus poeticus
'Actea'
POET'S NARCISSUS

BULB: 37–43 cm (14–17 in)
CLIMATE: S., W.T., M., C.T., H.
FAMILY: Amaryllidaceae
DESCRIPTION: A late-flowering Daffodil with uneven white petals and a flat, yellow, red-rimmed cup. The foliage is lax. It suits sun and will grow in light shade. *N. poeticus recurvens* (Old Pheasant's Eye), is late flowering, with white petals and a rich-red eye.

Narcissus tazetta
'Soleil d'Or'
JONQUIL,
BUNCH-FLOWERED NARCISSUS

BULB: 37–43 cm (14–17 in)
CLIMATE: S., W.T., M., C.T., H.
FAMILY: Amaryllidaceae
DESCRIPTION: Deep green leaves and fragrant flowers from mid-winter to early summer. This has rich yellow petals with an orange cup. Prefers sun but grows in light shade too. 'Paper White' has fragrant white blooms with grey foliage.

Nepeta x faasenii
CAT MINT

E

HEIGHT: 23-30 cm (9-12 in)
CLIMATE: S., W.T., M.
FAMILY: Labiatae
DESCRIPTION: A wind tolerant, grey-foliaged, mound forming plant up to 45 cm (18 in) wide, covered through spring and summer with pale, violet-blue flower spikes. Other varieties include 'Six Hills Giant', which has larger, brighter flowers and greyer foliage.

Nephrolepis exaltata forms
BOSTON FERN

E

HEIGHT: 3 cm-2 m (1 in-6½ ft)
CLIMATE: T., S., W.T., M., C.T., H.
FAMILY: Polypodiaceae
DESCRIPTION: Has many variations all with light to dark green pinnate foliage, much divided in some such as "Fluffy Ruffles". They need light to filtered shade. *N. cordifolia* is the very tough Sword or Fishbone Fern for shade, damp or dryish positions. It can spread too well!

Nerine bowdenii
LARGE PINK NERINE

BULB: 30 cm (12 in)
CLIMATE: S., W.T., M., C.T., H.
FAMILY: Amaryllidaceae
DESCRIPTION: Flower scapes up to 45 cm (18 in) long carry umbels of 6-12 rose-pink, lily-like flowers in late autumn on leafless plants. Their growing season is winter, their foliage dies off in spring, and the plants remain dormant in summer. They grow in sun or light shade. *N. sarniensis* (Guernsey Lily) has given rise to many handsome hybrids.

Nicotiana alata
'Grandiflora'
FLOWERING TOBACCO

E

HEIGHT: 80 cm-1 m (31 in-5 ft)
CLIMATE: T., S., W.T., M., C.T., H.
FAMILY: Solanaceae
DESCRIPTION: A perennial, which is usually grown as an annual as it is intolerant of frost. This is slender with large, soft, light green leaves and open racemes of headily scented tubular flowers from mid-summer to autumn in pure-white, mauve, purple, lime-green or crimson. It grows in sun or light shade. *N. tabacum* is the tobacco plant.

Ophipogon jaburan
WHITE MONDO GRASS

E

HEIGHT: 30 cm (12 in)
CLIMATE: T., S., W.T., M., C.T., H.
FAMILY: Liliaceae
DESCRIPTION: This forms a clump of dark green, grass-like leaves with flower scapes ending in 7.5-15 cm (3-6 in) long racemes of insignificant white summer flowers. There are forms with "blue" flowers, striped golden-yellow, white-spotted and striped white foliage. All like light to filtered shade. *O. japonicus* has violet-purple to lilac or whitish flowers. It has a variegated form.

Osteospermum ecklonis
STAR OF THE VELDT

E

HEIGHT: 45 cm (18 in)
CLIMATE: S., W.T., M., C.T., H.
FAMILY: Asteraceae
DESCRIPTION: White daisy-like spring and summer flowers are blue on the reverse of the petals and a deep electric-blue in their centres. They close up in shade and indoors. *O. barberia* 'Rosea' is pinkish-mauve with a darker reverse and royal-blue centres; *O. jucundum* is a trailing mauve-to-wine-red flowered ground cover.

Pelargonium x domesticum hybrids
REGAL PELARGONIUM,
MARTHA WASHINGTON GERANIUM

E

HEIGHT: 40 cm-1 m (16 in-3 ft)
CLIMATE: T., S., W.T., M., C.T., H.
FAMILY: Geraniaceae
DESCRIPTION: True Pelargoniums have large blooms up to 5 cm (2 in) wide, marked with veins or splashes in contrasting colours in flat heads during spring and summer. There are hundreds of varieties in white and shades of pink, mauve, purple and maroon. Grow in sun or light shade.

Pelargonium x hortorum hybrids

ZONAL GERANIUM

E

HEIGHT: 1 m (3 ft)
CLIMATE: W.T., M., C.T., H.
FAMILY: Geraniaceae
DESCRIPTION: These are grown for their foliage, variously marked in horse-shoe shaped zones of cream and yellow and deeper colours, as well as for their flowers, which may be white or shades of pink, apricot, lavender, purple, orange, red and burgundy. Others are *P. fragrans*, the nutmeg-scented Geranium, which has scented leaves; *P. tomentosum* is peppermint scented when bruised; *P. quercifolium* (Oak-leafed Geranium) has lobed, dubiously scented foliage; *P. limoneium* (Lemon Gernaium) has lemon or balm-scented, soft green or variegated foliage.

Pelargonium peltatum

IVY LEAF GERANIUM

E

HEIGHT: 2 m (6½ ft)
CLIMATE: W.T., M., C.T., H.
FAMILY: Geraniaceae
DESCRIPTION: Ivy-shaped, glossy, thick-textured, light green leaves on a plant capable of spreading 1.5 m (5 ft) wide. It remains low as a ground cover and can be allowed to climb. There are numerous singles or doubles in white, and shades of pink, mauve and "red" are available.

Penstemon hybrids

BEARD TONGUE,
BORDER PENSTEMON

HEIGHT: 60 cm (24 in)
CLIMATE: W.T., M., C.T., H.
FAMILY: Scrophulariaceae
DESCRIPTION: This herbaceous perennial has terminal spikes of tubular flowers, broad and bell-like at the opening, in shades of pink, crimson, purple, lavender and red, often with white. They appear from late spring to autumn. It suits sun or light shade.

Pentas lanceolata var. coccinea
RED STAR CLUSTER

E

HEIGHT: 60 cm-1 m (24 in-3 ft)
CLIMATE: S.,W.T., M., C.T.
FAMILY: Rubiaceae
DESCRIPTION: A compact shrub with light green foliage and rounded heads of small, red flowers from spring to autumn. Needs light to filtered shade. Varieties are available in shades of pink and pale purple.

Phlomis fruticosa
JERUSALEM SAGE

E

HEIGHT: 6o cm-1 m (24 in-3 ft)
CLIMATE: W.T., M., C.T., H.
FAMILY: Labiatae
DESCRIPTION: A dense, many-branched shrub up to 1 m (3 ft) high with wrinkled grey-green foliage, which is white and woolly on the undersides. The clear yellow flowers are carried in whorls around the stems. This is salt and drought tolerant and useful for difficult positions in sun or light shade.

Phlox paniculata
PERENNIAL PHLOX

HEIGHT: 40-60 cm (16-24 in)
CLIMATE: W.T., M., C.T., H.
FAMILY: Polemoniaceae
DESCRIPTION: This herbaceous perennial has December to April flowers which are colourful and carried in terminal panicles up to 25 cm (10 in) long, each with 50-60 salver-form flowers 4-5 cm (1½-2 in) wide. It suits sun or light shade. Named varieties in various heights and plain or "eyed" colours include blue-mauve, white with red eye, mauve, salmon-pink, crimson, white, orange, lavender and scarlet.

Phyla nodiflora
(syn. Lippia nodiflora)
LIPPIA

E

HEIGHT: 7-10 cm (3-4 in)
CLIMATE: T., S., W.T., M., C.T.
FAMILY: Verbenaceae
DESCRIPTION: A rapid ground cover, which forms a lawn-like cover. It roots at the nodes, causing its lawn-like spread. It can be mown once or twice a year to keep it 7-10 cm (3-4 in) high and will stand light traffic and a little shade, though it prefers sun. It is drought tolerant. *Lippia citriodora* is the Lemon scented Verbena (Phyla was once classified as Lippia).

Physostegia virginiana

GALLIPOLI HEATH,
FALSE DRAGONHEAD,
OBEDIENT PLANT

HEIGHT: 1 m (3 ft)
CLIMATE: W.T., M., C.T., H.
FAMILY: Labiatae
DESCRIPTION: This herbaceous perennial makes hardy dense clumps of straight stems, each ending in a spike packed with 2.5 cm (1 in) long purplish-pink flowers from mid-summer to autumn. It stands sun and filtered shade. Forms include white, deep-rose, pinks, large flowered and taller growers.

Platycodon grandiflorum

BALLOON FLOWERS,
CHINESE BELLFLOWER,
JAPANESE BELLFLOWER

HEIGHT: 60 cm (24 in)
CLIMATE: S., W.T., M., C.T., H.
FAMILY: Campanulaceae
DESCRIPTION: Blue, bell-shaped flowers pop open from balloon-like buds throughout summer on this herbaceous perennial. The plant forms an attractive clump in sun or light shade. White-flowered and variegated forms are available.

Plectranthus ecklonii

COCKSPUR FLOWER,
BLUE SPUR FLOWER

HEIGHT: 1-2 m (3-6½ ft)
CLIMATE: T., W.T., M.
FAMILY: Lamiaceae
DESCRIPTION: Purple flowers in upright racemes, sometimes 30 cm (12 in) tall provide rich autumn colours. It remains semi-evergreen in winter. Height varies according to pruning. It is drought tolerant and suits sun or light shade. *P. oertendahli*, (the Brazilian or Cockspur Coleus), is 45 cm (18 in) high, has white flowers, purple-backed leaves and a trailing habit. It is a good ground cover in shade or basket plant.

Polystichum proliferum

MOTHER SHIELD FERN,
MOTHER OF MILLIONS

E

HEIGHT: 60 cm-1 m (24 in-3 ft)
CLIMATE: W.T., M., C.T., H.
FAMILY: Polypodiaceae
DESCRIPTION: In light to filtered shade, this is a graceful, robust fern, emerald-green darkening to a deep green with arching leaf blades and buds on the pinnately divided foliage. Each bud is potentially a small plantlet and when it is in contact with the ground, it

roots and begins a new colony, but is not a nuisance. *P. reichardii* has dark green fronds; *P. setiferum* (Lacey or Soft Shield Fern) has grey-green fronds.

Primula malacoides

PRIMULA, FAIRY PRIMROSE

E

HEIGHT: 25 cm (10 in)
CLIMATE: S., W.T., M., C.T., H.
FAMILY: Primulaceae
DESCRIPTION: Low, dense rosettes of pale green foliage with 9-15 flowers on slender, 30 cm (12 in) high stems. Winter and early spring flowers are white and shades of purple, mauve, carmine or pink. It self-sows and renews itself annually in light to filtered shade.

Pteris quadriaurita

'Argyraea'
SILVER FERN,
VARIEGATED BRAKE FERN

E

HEIGHT: 30–60 cm (12-24 in)
CLIMATE: T., S., W.T.
FAMILY: Polypodiaceae
DESCRIPTION: Pale strong stalks carry feathery, much-divided green fronds with central silvery markings. Spore bearing bodies form an irregular line on the undersurface edges of foliage. Others are *P. macilenta*, with slender-stemmed light green, 1 m (3 ft) long fronds; *P. ensiformis* (Slender Brake Fern), an Australian fern with dark green fronds of finger-like segments; *P. tremula* (Tender Brake Fern), from Australia and New Zealand is found in all but T. climates. All suit light to filtered shade.

Rehmannia elata

REHMANNIA

E

HEIGHT: 30–90 cm (12-24 in)
CLIMATE: T., S., W.T., M., C.T., H.
FAMILY: Scrophulariaceae
DESCRIPTION: Terminal racemes of large bell flowers from spring to autumn are pink, purple or cream with golden throats. The softly hairy, slightly sticky, light green foliage is lobed or double-toothed. It becomes deciduous in C.T. and H. climates. It self-sows readily and suits light to filtered shade.

Rhipsalidopsis gaertneri
CHRISTMAS CACTUS, EASTER CACTUS

E

HEIGHT: 25 cm (10 in)
CLIMATE: S., W.T., M., C.T.
FAMILY: Cactaceae
DESCRIPTION: Lax, jointed, flattened stems
droop gracefully over a container to make this
a very popular basket plant in light to filtered
shade. Its scarlet-red flowers,up to 7.5 cm (3 in)
wide, are followed by red fruit. Many variations
of pink or red with white are available.

Rhodohypoxis baurii
ROSE GRASS, STAR GRASS

HEIGHT: 8-10 cm
CLIMATE: W.T., M., C.T., H.
FAMILY: Amaryllidaceae
DESCRIPTION: From a small, hard, corm-like
rootstock arise slightly hairy, grass-like leaves.
They die down for the winter. The starry, rose-
pink, 2 cm (¾ in) wide, spring and summer
flowers form a solid sheet of colour. Grows in
sun or light shade. White and a deep rose-pink
called 'Rosy Posy' are also available.

Salvia splendens
BONFIRE SALVIA, SCARLET SAGE

E

HEIGHT: 30-75 cm (12-29 in)
CLIMATE: S., W.T., M., C.T.
FAMILY: Laminaceae
DESCRIPTION: A square stemmed shrub-like
plant with terminal spike-like racemes of 20-30
scarlet summer, autumn and early-winter
flowers. Though perennial, it is usually treated
as an annual. Remove spent flowers and trim
lightly following flowering, and it will bloom
for 3 years. It self-sows readily without becoming
a nuisance. Salmon-rose, pink, dark purple,
creamy white and red with white stripes are
other forms. All prefer full sun but stand light
shade. *S. leucantha* (Mexican Bush Sage) is 60
cm-1 m (24 in-3 ft) high with grey-green mealy,
white backed foliage and velvety-purple, late-
summer and autumn flowers.

Senecio cineraria
CINERARIA

E

HEIGHT: 60–90 cm (24–35 in)
CLIMATE: T., S., W.T., M., C.T., H.
FAMILY: Compositae
DESCRIPTION: Soft-wooded shrubby perennial with felty, deeply indented, silvery foliage and heads of yellow flowers. It needs sun or light shade. Forms are available in a range of foliage shapes, but this is the most popular.

Senecio rowleyanus
STRING OF PEARLS

E

HEIGHT: 5 cm (2 in)
CLIMATE: T., S., W.T., M., C.T., H.
FAMILY: Asteraceae
DESCRIPTION: In light to filtered shade this little basket plant has small, succulent, grape-shaped leaves along weak, slender stems and tiny, white, scented, autumn flowers. Two more basket plants are *S. serpens* (syn. *Kleninia repens*)—glaucous-blue, fleshy leaves, become waxy and blue-white in full sun; *S. berreianus* (syn. *K. berriana*)—glaucous-green grape-like succulent leaves.

Silene vulgaris subsp. maritima
CATCHFLY, SEA CAMPION

E

HEIGHT: 30 cm (12 in)
CLIMATE: W.T., M., C.T.
FAMILY: Caryophyllaceae
DESCRIPTION: A small mound-like ground cover, this has oval, pale blue-grey foliage and prominent white, trumpet-shaped flowers with plump calyxes. Grows in sun or filtered shade. *S. compacta* has mauve-pink spring flowers, and is a perennial that is best treated as an annual.

Soleirolia soleirolii
(syn. Helxine soleirolii)
BABY'S TEARS, ANGEL'S TEARS

E

HEIGHT: 2.5 cm (1 in)
CLIMATE: S., W.T., M., C.T., H.
FAMILY: Urticaceae
DESCRIPTION: An emerald-green, tiny-foliaged, creeping ground cover with inconspicuous flowers, which becomes a soft carpet and moulds itself around and over rocks or baskets. It needs light to filtered shade and a moist, friable, well-drained soil.

Stachys byzantina
LAMB'S EARS, LAMB'S TONGUES

E

HEIGHT: 30-45 cm (12-18 in)
CLIMATE: W.T., M., C.T., H.
FAMILY: Labiatae
DESCRIPTION: Stachys may be 45 cm (18 in) high in cold climates and 30 cm (12 in) in warmer areas. The oblong elliptical leaves are silver and velvety to the touch. It is grown for the silver colour and spreading habit, not the purple flowers. It suits sun but will grow in light shade.

Sticherus flabellatus
UMBRELLA FERN

E

HEIGHT: 1 m (3 ft)
CLIMATE: T., S., W.T., M., C.T.
FAMILY: Gleicheniaceae
DESCRIPTION: Upright stems arising from a creeping, waterlogging tolerant rhizome, branch into two, forming an umbrella. Old fronds also produce new "umbrellas". Similar *Gleichenia microphyllus* is preferable in C.T. and H. climates. Both need light to filtered shade.

Stokesia laevis
STOKE'S ASTER

E
HEIGHT: 30-40 cm (12-16 in)
CLIMATE: W.T., M., C.T., H.
FAMILY: Compositae
DESCRIPTION: A wind tolerant, clump-forming perennial with foliage held close to the ground and flower stalks carrying blue daisies rising 30-40 cm above it from spring to autumn. Several named forms all have lavender-blue or white flowers.

Thymus vulgaris
THYME

E
HEIGHT: 30 cm (12 in)
CLIMATE: S., W.T., M., C.T., H.
FAMILY: Labiatae
DESCRIPTION: An aromatic, grey-green bushy little herb with white or pale purple flowers from spring to late summer. Prefers sun but tolerates light shade. Numerous thymes are used as ornamentals and include others with aromatic foliage, such as the lemon-scented thyme.

Tropaeoleum majus
NASTURTIUM, INDIAN CRESS

E
HEIGHT: 30 cm (12 in)
CLIMATE: T., S., W.T., M., C.T.
FAMILY:
DESCRIPTION: This has orbicular leaves, and funnel-form, 5-petalled, spurred flowers. It suits sun and tolerates light shade. Forms may be trailing, non trailing or climbing. Colours include mahogany-red, scarlet, orange, yellow, white or pink, some with brown stripes or spots.

Veronica spicata
SPEEDWELL

E
HEIGHT: 8-10 cm (3-4 in)
CLIMATE: W.T., M., C.T., H.
FAMILY: Scrophulariaceae
DESCRIPTION: Spring and early-summer flower spikes up to 15 cm (6 in) tall rise above a dense mat of dark green, narrow, toothed foliage. Grow it in sun or light shade. The flowers cut well for indoors. Several taller and lower growing species and varieties are blue or pink.

Viola hederacea
NATIVE VIOLET, AUSTRALIAN
TUFTED VIOLET

E *

HEIGHT: 10-29 cm (4-11 in)
CLIMATE: T., S., W.T., M., C.T., H.
FAMILY: Violaceae
DESCRIPTION: White, purple-centred violet
flowers appear almost year round on this mat-
forming ground cover, which covers completely
without being a nuisance. Suits sun or shade.
Pure white and blue forms are available.

Viola odorata
'Princess of Wales'
VIOLET, SWEET VIOLET

E

HEIGHT: 15 cm (6 in)
CLIMATE: W.T., M., C.T., H.
FAMILY: Violaceae
DESCRIPTION: From July to October, slender
stems carry sweetly scented, dark violet-blue
flowers. Suits sun or filtered shade. Single
flowered varieties are violet purple, rose pink
and violet blue. Parma Violets are similar
shades, double and more scented than the above.

Zantedeschia aethiopica
ARUM LILY

E

HEIGHT: 60 cm-1 m (24 in-3 ft)
CLIMATE: W.T., M., C.T., H.
FAMILY: Araceae
DESCRIPTION: This has pure white spathes
round the true flower, which is a long golden
yellow spike, and fleshy, emerald green, arrow-
shaped leaves. Suits sun or filtered shade and
spreads by tubers. Others are: 'Green Goddess,
has green and white spathes; *Z. elliottiana*
(Yellow Calla Lily) has yellow spathes, spikes
of red berries and silver-spotted foliage; *Z.
rehmannii* (Pink Calla) has multicoloured
hybrids. Both the Callas die down in winter.

Zephyranthes candida
AUTUMN CROCUS, RAIN LILY,
STORM LILY, WEST WIND FLOWER

E

HEIGHT: 30 cm (12 in)
CLIMATE: T., S., W.T., M., C.T.
FAMILY: Amaryllidaceae
DESCRIPTION: Pure white, open, rather lily-
like flowers appear with shining, thin, grassy
leaves and will last through late summer and
autumn. Grow in sun or filtered shade. Others
are *Z. citrinus* (Golden Storm Lily); *Z.
grandiflora* (Pink Storm Lily).

Swimming pool plants

For many people a native garden around the pool is the ideal. A background of dark green cypress or *Camellia sasanqua* clipped to a hedge appeals to others, but the most popular planting of all is "Tropical". The plants used are not necessarily tropical in origin but have foliage, flowers or form that suggests the tropics. Palms and tree ferns are dominant in this planting.

Those marked with an asterisk should be set 3 m (10 ft) from the pool edge to avoid the possibility of damage to the pool or its surround.

Palms look more natural in groups of 3 or more of a kind, or groups of 3 different palms—a tall, medium and short variety together as a group. For descriptions see the respective sections:

- Trees for shade and windbreaks
- Shrubs and trees for privacy
- Foundation planting around the house
- Climbers
- Colourful fill-in plants

TREES FOR POOLS

Archontophoenix cunninghamiana
✳ BANGALOW PALM

Arecastrum romanzoffianum
PLUME OR QUEEN PALM

Backhousia citriodora
✳ LEMON SCENTED BACKHOUSIA, MYRTLE

Elaeocarpus reticulatus
✳ BLUBERRY ASH

Ficus benjamina
✳ WEEPING FIG

Livistona australis
✳ CABBAGE TREE PALM

Rothmannia globosa
BELL FLOWERED OR TREE GARDENIA

Schefflera actinophylla
✳ UMBRELLA TREE

Stenocarpus sinuatus
✳ FIREWHEEL TREE, WHEEL OF FIRE, WHITE BEEFWOOD

SHRUBS FOR POOLS

Aloysia triphylla
LEMON VERBENA

Buxus microphylla var. *japonica*
JAPANESE BOX

Gordonia axillaris
GORDONIA

Hibiscus rosa-sinensis
HIBISCUS

Murraya paniculata
COSMETIC BARK TREE

Nerium oleander
OLEANDER

FOUNDATION PLANTS FOR POOL AREAS

Agave attenuata
AGAVE

✳ *Asplenium australasicum*
✳ BIRD'S NEST FERN

Aucuba japonica 'Variegata'
GOLD DUST PLANT

Bauhinia galpinii
RED BAUHINIA

Brunfelsia australis
YESTERDAY, TODAY & TOMORROW;
NIGHT & DAY FLOWER

Cyathea cooperi
✱ TREE FERN; ROUGH
BARKED TREE FERN

Cycas revoluta
SAGO PALM; JAPANESE
SAGO PALM

Dicksonia antarctica
✱ SOFT TREE FERN

Fatsia japonica
ARALIA

Fortunella japonica
MARUMI CUMQUAT, KUMQUAT

Fuchsia x hybrida
FUCHSIA

**Lepidozamia
peroffskyana**
ZAMIA; SAMIA PALM

Michelia figo
PORT WINE MAGNOLIA

Macrozamia communis
✱ BURRAWANG

Platycerium bifurcatum
✱ ELKHORN

Plumeria rubra
RED FRANGIPANI

Russelia equisetiformis
CORAL PLANT

Strelitzia reginae
BIRD OF PARADISE

**Strobilanthes
anisophyllus**
GOLDFUSSIA

Tibouchina granulosa
PURPLE SPRAY BUSH;
PRINCESSS FLOWER

**Xanthorrhoea
australis**
✱ GRASS TREE; BLACK BOYS

CLIMBERS FOR POOL AREAS

Akebia quinata
AKEBIA; FIVE-LEAVED AKEBIA

**Allamanda cathartica
'Hendersonii'**
ALLAMANDA

Antigonon leptopus
MEXICAN CREEPER; CORAL VINE;
LOVE'S CHAIN

Aristolochia elegans
DUTCHMAN'S PIPE

**Bougainvillea glabra
'Trailii'**
BOUGAINVILLEA

Campsis grandiflora
TRUMPET VINE

**Clytostoma
callistegioides**
VIOLET TRUMPET VINE

Gelsemium sempervirens
CAROLINA JASMINE, FALSE JASMINE

Hoya carnosa
WAX FLOWER

Jasminum polyanthum
PINK BUDDED JASMINE;
SWEET SCENTED JASMINE

Macfadyena unguis-cati
CAT'S CLAW CREEPER

Mandevilla laxa
CHILEAN JASMINE

Monstera deliciosa
FRUIT SALAD PLANT

Pandorea pandorana
WONGA WONGA VINE

**Phaedranthus
buccinatorius**
MEXICAN BLOOD TRUMPET

Phaseolus caracalla
SNAIL VINE

Pyrostegia ignea
FLAME VINE

Solandra maxima
CUP OF GOLD; CHALICE VINE;
HONOLULU LILY

Sollya heterophylla
BLUEBELL CREEPER

Stephanotis floribunda
CLUSTERED WAX FLOWER;
MADAGASCAR JASMINE

Stigmaphyllon ciliatum
BRAZILIAN GOLDEN VINE;
BUTTERFLY VINE

Thunbergia alata
BLACK-EYED SUSAN; ORANGE CLOCK
VINE; GOLDEN GLORY VINE

**Trachelospermum
jasminioides**
CHINESE STAR JASMINE

Plants for the footpath

This list covers a selection of trees for roadsides where space and the absence of wires allows tall, broad trees to be grown as well as smaller trees for suburban footpaths to suit smaller spaces and allow for overhead wires and underground services. Also see "Trees for shade and windbreaks" and "Shrubs and trees for privacy".

✳ indicates native plants.

Acacia floribunda
✳ WHITE SALLY, GOSSAMER WATTLE

Acer negundo
'Aureo-Variegatum'
GOLDEN BOX ELDER MAPLE

Acer palmatum
JAPANESE MAPLE

Archontophoenix cunninghamiana
✳ BANGALOW PALM

Arecastrum romanzoffianum
PLUME OR QUEEN PALM

Backhousia citriodora
✳ LEMON SCENTED MYRTLE

Bauhinia blakeana
DEEP PURPLE ORCHID TREE

Banksia serrata
✳ OLD MAN BANKSIA; SAW BANKSIA

Betula pendula
SILVER BIRCH

Brachychiton acerifolium
✳ ILLAWARRA FLAME TREE

Butia capitata
WINE PALM

Callistemon salignus
✳ WHITE OR WILLOW BOTTLEBRUSH

Callistemon citrinus
✳ LEMON SCENTED BOTTLEBRUSH

Callistemon viminalis
✳ 'Hannah Ray'
HANNAH RAY
WEEPING BOTTLEBRUSH

Camellia sasanqua
SASANQUA

Casuarina torulosa
✳ FOREST SHE-OAK

Crataegus phaenopyrum
WASHINGTON THORN

Eucalyptus haemastoma
✳ SCRIBBLY GUM; WHITE GUM;
SNAPPY GUM

Eucalyptus ficifolia
✳ RED FLOWERING GUM

Eucalyptus nicholli
✳ NARROW-LEAVED BLACK PEPPERMINT

Eucalyptus polyanthemus
✳ RED BOX

Eucalyptus sideroxylon
✳ IRONBARK; MUGGA

Fagus sylvatica
BEECH

Ficus benjamina
✳ WEEPING FIG

Fraxinus excelsior
'Aurea'
GOLDEN ASH

Fraxinus oxycarpa
'Raywoodii'
CLARET ASH

Gingko biloba
MAIDENHAIR TREE

Gleditsia triacanthos
'Sunburst'
GOLDEN HONEY LOCUST

Gordonia axillaris
GORDONIA

Grevillea banksii
✳ BANKS' GREVILLEA

Grevillea hookeriana
✳ HOOKER'S OR TOOTHBRUSH GREVILLEA

Hakea salicifolia
✳ WILLOW-LEAVED HAKEA

Hibiscus rosa-sinensis
HIBISCUS

Jacaranda mimosifolia
JACARANDA

Koelreuteria paniculata
GOLDEN RAIN TREE

Lagunaria patersonia
✳ NORFOLK ISLAND HIBISCUS

Lagerstroemia indica
'Eavesii'
CREPE MYRTLE

Leptospermum petersonii
✳ LEMON-SCENTED TEA TREE

Liquidambar styraciflua
LIQUIDAMBAR

Livistona australis
✳ CABBAGE TREE PALM

Magnolia grandiflora
WHITE OR SOUTHERN MAGNOLIA

Malus floribunda
JAPANESE CRAB APPLE

Melaleuca armillaris
✳ BRACELET HONEY MYRTLE

Melaleuca nesophila
✳ PURPLE PAPER BARK

Melaleuca quinquenervia
✳ BROAD LEAF PAPER BARK

Metrosideros excelsa
NEW ZEALAND CHRISTMAS BUSH

Nerium oleander
'Monsieur Belaguier'
OLEANDER

Nyssa sylvatica
TUPELO

Olea europaea
FRUITING OLIVE

Parrotia persica
PERSIAN WITCH HAZEL

Phoenix canariensis
CANARY ISLAND DATE PALM

Photinia glabra
'Rubens'
SMALL LEAVED PHOTINIA

Photinia x fraseri
'Robusta'
ORIENTAL RED LEAF

Photinia x fraseri
RED ROBIN

Pistacia chinensis
CHINESE PISTACHIO

Pittosporum rhombifolium
✳ ORANGE BERRIED PITTOSPORUM

Platanus orientalis
ORIENTAL PLANE TREE

Podocarpus elatus
✱ ILLAWARRA PLUM; PLUM PINE;
BROWN PINE

Prunus serrulata
'James H Veitch'
(FUGENZO), JAPANESE
FLOWERING CHERRY

Quercus palustris
PIN OAK

Rothmannia globosa
BELL FLOWERED OR
TREE GARDENIA

Sapium sebiferum
CHINESE TALLOW WOOD

Schefflera actinophylla
✱ UMBRELLA TREE

Schinus molle
PEPPERCORN TREE

Sorbus aucuparia
ROWAN TREE

Tamarix ramosissima
TAMARIX; FLOWERING CYPRESS

Trachycarpus fortunei
CHINESE WINDMILL PALM

Tristaniopsis conferta
✱ BRUSH BOX

Ulmus glabra
'Lutescens'
GOLDEN ELM

Ulmus parvifolia
CHINESE ELM

Xylosma japonicum
SHINY XYLOSMA

Planting your garden

THE SEASONS

A clement climate allows year-round planting of all container grown trees, shrubs, perennials, annuals, fruit trees, roses, in fact anything established in a container. The only provisos are the need to water until the roots establish themselves in their new position (months or weeks depending on plant and climate) and the selection of plants to suit the aspect, climate, and soil.

The year falls into two periods. In the autumn life outdoors is pleasant because flies and mosquitos are few, and the days are warm and balmy. It is a comfortable time to plant, prune and fertilise. Summer can be hot and sticky—watering, weeding, mulching and pest and disease control are the main chores.

THE BEST TIME TO PLANT

Vegetables and colourful annuals are exceptions to the above and do have planting seasons. These allow the plants to mature and make a show of colour (or produce vegetables) within their short life span (less than a year). Planting is timed to avoid frost or heat damage. See the plant lists for a table of easy-to-grow annuals.

A list is also included for the easier vegetables though in a true low-maintenance garden, vegetables would be absent as spraying for pests and diseases and fertilising are high maintenance jobs that the gardener is anxious to avoid.

Roses are sold in winter, when the widest range is available either packaged or in the bare root stage. They are dug from the field while dormant because they can stand handling at this stage without the expense of containers and the space those take up both in the growing and selling areas, not to mention the boot of your car. Potted roses have increased in popularity in recent years because many people, knowing nothing about winter planting, become interested in roses when the first spring blooms appear and want to plant immediately. The spring range of varieties is not as wide as the winter range because container grown plants occupy more space than field grown plants.

Deciduous fruits are sold in the same way and at the same time as roses. The main crop is offered in winter either as newly potted or bare-rooted plants, both dug fresh from the field. Like roses, the winter sale is due to the fact that the plants tolerate being moved in their dormant leafless stage. However, they are in greater demand in summer when the fruit shops are filled with delicious apricots, peaches, plums and nectarines, and the taste test inspires thoughts of growing your own fruit. The trees that were dug last winter are still available in summer, though now they are in containers and can be taken home, the containers removed and the trees put in, preferably without disturbing the soil. To get the best from the trees they should be pruned back to about 45 cm (18 in) of their "head" (a collection of 3 or 4 branches about 45 cm (18 in) from the ground). Ask the nursery to do this for you. You will find that in later years the tree will have a strong branch system that is able to carry the weight of fruit and not lose its branches in severe winds. The same cutting back is done with winter planted trees for the same reason.

Many field grown ornamental trees, such as ash, elms, birch, willows and flowering fruits, are available in bare root state in winter. They cost less because the cost of potting them into a container has not been incurred. But if you miss out in winter, the same range of plants, though in a diminished range of varieties and quantities will be available in containers from spring to autumn and can be planted then.

Bulbs have a definite planting season, because their life cycle is lived out in less than a year. See the plant lists for those bulbs that grow easily (in suitable climate, aspect and soil with watering).

Planting times are among hand-me-down practices from the early settlers who applied English gardening methods in Australia, but here seasons apply only to annuals, vegetables and bulbs. With care you can do pretty much as you like with everything else in the Australian garden (the Highlands and Snowy Mountains exempted), planting when you feel like it, and digging and transplanting again when the mood takes you, though preferably not on a 40°C day. Just make sure you do not disturb the roots and that you do water the plants well for several months afterwards. In Australia the importance of seasons lies in what is flowering or is at its best at that time.

In the words of the great English gardener and author Christopher Lloyd: "The best time to do anything in the garden is when you have the time."

THE PLANTING HOLE

A good start for plants is one of the surest ways to reduce maintenance.

The best planting hole is wide and shallow, rounded at the base like an orange cut in half—its depth is 10–15 cm (4–6 in) deeper than the container on the plant. If there is no container, make the hole the same depth as the previous soil level, shown by a soil mark on the stem or trunk. A 10 cm (4 in) base is sufficient depth for containers up to 200 mm (8 in) diameter, 15 cm (6 in) for larger ones.

Aerate the base of the hole by digging it over lightly with a fork or by pushing the fork down into the soil in about half a dozen places. This loosens soil and improves drainage.

On a half-and-half basis, mix the soil from the hole with organic matter, compost or well-decayed manures. Put 5–15 cm (2–6 in) of this in the base of the hole. Remove the container. Never plant a container unless it is made of cardboard or other biodegradable substance and carries a label saying it should be planted. Plastic and other rigid containers do not rot away so never buy plants in tin containers; they are a sign that the nursery is second rate. When non-biodegradable containers are left on plants, the roots cannot spread. The top growth may develop but in a strong wind the plant will be lifted out of the ground still with the soil ball around its pot-shaped tiny root system. The roots will have grown into a spiral within the container, filling it to the point where too little water has entered and the roots have strangled the plant.

Sit the plant in the hole with its soil ball intact. Fill the hole with water, let it drain away, then fill with soil to 2.5 cm (1 in) above the soil ball level. Press down *lightly* with your hands and water again. Let it drain away. Add more soil, finishing the hole with a saucer-shaped depression bounded by a small hill, which helps to keep water inside the depression.

In grass or lawn, planting holes 1 m (3 ft) wide saves trouble in the long term even when plants are only in 200 mm (8 in) wide containers. In gardens, holes should be at least two and preferably three times the width of the container. The wide hole keeps voracious grass roots away from plant roots. The fact that grass is not seen on the surface does not mean that plant roots are safe from its incursions. Grasses are greedy. The more water and fertiliser the newly planted tree or shrub has, the more encouragement grass has to grow towards it. A metre wide bed therefore protects the plant and helps it to develop more quickly. Wide beds also save plants from mower damage.

Finish the hole with a 6-10 cm (2½-4 in) deep mulch from the hill to the edge of the bed or grow annuals in this area. Their root systems will not affect those of the plant.

Before planting always water the plants in their containers. Let the water drain away and then plant. Never plant a dry soil ball even though the hole is going to be filled with water in the planting process. Not enough water will move sideways to wet the soil ball thoroughly.

Always go to the trouble of mixing the soil for the hole as described. Nursery soils are designed to drain very freely—much more so than most garden soils. Their texture is perfect for containers but quite different to that of garden soils. All too often nursery soils and garden soils will remain separate for years. An "interface" problem may occur when plants are put straight into the garden without an in-between soil such as the half-and-half mix above. The mix encourages the roots to move out from the soil ball into the intermediate "fill" soil, because that has some of the characteristics of both nursery and garden soils. From there the roots will move to the garden soil. When there is no intermediate area, the root system may develop the same spiral growth as that described for pots.

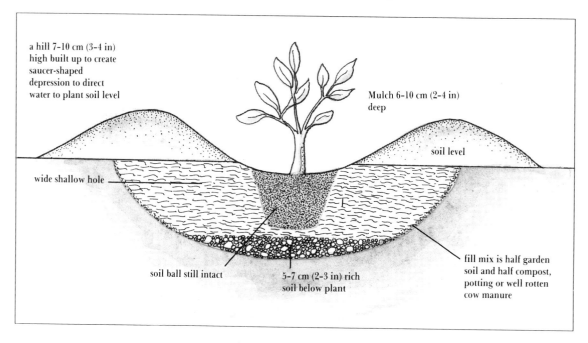

a hill 7-10 cm (3-4 in) high built up to create saucer-shaped depression to direct water to plant soil level

Mulch 6-10 cm (2-4 in) deep

soil level

wide shallow hole

soil ball still intact

5-7 cm (2-3 in) rich soil below plant

fill mix is half garden soil and half compost, potting or well rotten cow manure

PLANTING ADVANCED PLANTS   Dig a hole a metre wide or at least twice as wide as the root ball and 10-15cm (4-6 in) deeper than the pot. Dig till crumbly, add peat or sand to heavy soil. Add 10 cm (4 in) decayed old animal manure and soil to bottom of hole. Water plant and all to drain away before planting. Always remove containers.
Up-end and slide off or cut away. Keep soil intact. Never spread roots. Create a surface depression to catch water.
Keep top of root ball level with garden bed. Always keep grass 45 cm (18 in) from plant's centre.
Avoid deep planting, narrow deep holes, subsoil disturbance, heavy stamping in and fertiliser during planting.
Water frequently.

Bare root trees and roses are planted in the same way with a mound in the centre of the hole on which the base of the plant sits. Its roots are then spread down the sides of the mound.

There are many other ways to put plants in the ground. Some people, for example, like to tease the roots away from the soil ball; others like to loosen the base of the soil ball; some water only when planting is finished; and some tread the plant into place. These are variations that most plants will tolerate though the treading in is very damaging and watering after planting may not be sufficient. Plants can also not withstand deep planting.

Digging a deep hole into the subsoil, filling it with manures and organic matter and then planting, creates a sump into which irrigation, rain and drainage water will drain. Water will lie there and stagnate because it has no outlet. Conditions will be perfect for root rot diseases, which will kill the plant slowly.

Deep planting into deep holes is the biggest single cause of plant losses. Wide shallow holes help to prevent this problem. "High" planting with the soil ball above the level of the ground is as bad as deep planting because it causes drying out of the soil ball.

Fertiliser at planting time is unnecessary. The first fertiliser application can be made three months after planting or in spring or mid-summer, whichever is the earlier. Dry fertilisers, like 8-9 month Oz Gold® or Nutricote®, applied once a year are sufficient in the low-maintenance garden but are best applied *after*, not during, planting. They are easier and longer-lasting than liquid fertilisers.

Do not tread plants into the ground. It may compact the surface and make water entry difficult and it will break off delicate feeding roots. Light hand pressure and watering in are the preferable courses. Maintain regular watering for at least three months after planting and during dry periods. Indigenous tree species may tolerate "dry" planting if put in autumn.

Make sure the hill surrounding the saucer-shaped depression is built up if it has a low side, otherwise water will escape and topsoil will gradually wash away. When plants are on a gentle slope, it is worthwhile building up the low side to the same level as the high side using stone, wood or even the bases of palm fronds—anything at all that will prevent water loss and soil washaways.

On shallow soils put in plants in pots of a depth to suit the soil without digging into subsoil or leaving the soil ball above the surface of the surrounding soil. In ground that is wet or subject to periodic flooding it may be worthwhile to lay an agricultural drain pipe to take water away from the plant. This is not very difficult using fluted or slotted drain pipes or similar light, easy-to-handle drainage pipes.

The planting hole is the foundation of the plant's existence and effort spent on planting thoroughly will contribute to ease of maintenance later on. Avoid soil compaction by not digging holes in, or running vehicles over heavy, very wet soils. It is preferable to wait until the soil has drained.

Manageable garden maintenance

EQUIPMENT

Whatever you buy to help you in your garden make sure it is the best possible quality. This protects your back and saves you from nasty accidents. The handles on cheap spades break very easily. The prongs on cheap forks bend and the fork becomes useless. With both you are lucky to escape without being hurt. Check equipment for weight and "feel", because some weights suit different people. This also applies to handle lengths. It is best to buy equipment as you need it and to have a place prepared for it, so that it can be hung up at the end of the day and kept in good condition.

To clear a new garden you will need a crowbar, a pick and a mattock. Once the garden is underway, however, you will rarely need these so try and borrow them if possible. You will also need a 'D'-handled spade, which will be used for digging, cutting lawn and garden bed edges, and lifting turf. Spades may be heavy or light, small or large. Some have a turned-over edge or tread at the top of the blade as a resting place for the digger's foot, and these are very comfortable to use.

Forks are handy for lifting plants with a fibrous root mass such as perennials or weeds like paspalum. Their prong length and overall weight varies, and again it is up to the individual to choose something that suits.

Shovel This will be used to move materials around the garden, to distribute soil and mulch, manure or compost. Shovels may be round, pointed or square-mouthed. They can be light or super-lightweight as in the aluminium shovel. Narrow shovels are available for use in digging drains and post holes.

Hoe This is used with a skimming, back and forward motion as a means of chipping out surface weeds and for digging furrows and hilling up vegetable crops. There is a variety of weights, lengths and shapes available.

Rake Solid cast iron rakes are preferable to the nail type. Buy a sturdy rake because inevitably it will be used for tidying up rubbish, levelling off and fining down soil, as well as for distributing fertiliser and covering seed.

Lawn or leaf rake This can be made of bamboo or steel and is used to remove leaves and clippings from lawns. It is intended to be used with the handle fully drawn, not with a broom-like sweeping motion.

Cultivator Long handled, three or five tined cultivators are used to break up crusted soils and for weeding. Large gardens may benefit from the small mechanised cultivators or tillers that are light and easy to handle.

Edge cutter Hand operated edge cutters give lawns a professional edge. They allow the lawn to come to within centimetres of the garden edge and are much better than cord type edgers. Cord edgers are damaging and dangerous to use. They also end up separating garden from lawn by as much as 30 cm (12 in) because they require that amount of room in order to operate without damaging the garden plants. When used on lawns they damage tree trunks, creating entry points for pests and disease.

Hand trowel and hand fork These may be long or short handled but usually the short handled ones are the most practical. They are essential for planting annuals and for removing weeds.

Lawn weeder This is a two-pronged little hand fork, which allows easy removal of paspalum and summer grass.

Wheelbarrow Again, this has to be chosen to suit the person who is wheeling it. Heavy builders' barrows will be uncomfortable at the end of the day unless you are a strong person. Lighter barrows may not hold as much, but they are not as tiring.

Spray equipment This will depend on the size and extent of the garden and the degree to which you intend to carry maintenance. It is advisable to carry at least two kinds of spray equipment if weedicides are being used, one for the weedicides and the other for spraying fungicides and pesticides.

Weeding equipment This consists of a trickle bar weeding wand, or a separate sprayer for applying weedkillers. Like the weedkillers, this should be kept under clean conditions in a locked cupboard.

Watering equipment Hoses, sprinklers, a watering can and water timers are necessities. A "do-it-yourself" watering system is easy to install and there are specialist firms that will help you plan such a watering system, or will install one for you. They are not costly and save effort in the long run.

Pruning equipment This amounts to a pair of good secateurs, a pruning saw and perhaps later on a bushman's or carpenter's saw. On occasions you may need to hire a light chain saw to remove heavy limbs or stumps, but engaging a professional tree surgeon or arborist is much safer.

Pruning knife If you become very keen on the garden you may find that this will be useful, not only for pruning but for taking cuttings and grafting.

WATERING

Water is the lifeblood of the garden. When wilting is prolonged, changes within plants mean that they are unable to carry out their normal functions. When plants are stressed through too little water, growth is restricted, leaf size is reduced, older leaves are shed, root tips die and wilting occurs. Without water, plants will die.

It is imperative that gardeners avoid wasting precious water and begin to conserve it. In most cases, water wastage comes from knowing too little about the plant/water relationship and from subscribing to the popular theory that more water is better.

Water constitutes about 80 per cent of a living plant. Roots bring water into the plant. Carbon dioxide enters and oxygen leaves the plant through the open stomata. Water vapour also leaves through the open stomata. This process is called transpiration. It keeps leaves cool and helps the internal movement of nutrients from the roots to the tops. Transpiration increases in dry times, on hot, sunny days or in windy weather. Water loss is increased by the rapid movement of air across leaves.

Water that is lost through transpiration must be replaced and this can only occur when the soil is sufficiently wet. Plants must absorb water from soil. The less water soil contains, the more firmly it is held by the soil particles and the more difficult it becomes for plants to extract it. When the plant can no longer extract enough water to compensate for transpiration losses, the cells in the leaves have less water and flop or shrink to a degree. The plant "wilts" or droops and its leaves may curl inwards to protect themselves from further drying out.

Plants that wilt during the day may recover near sunset when the heat of the day is relieved and soil water flows to the roots. With prolonged dryness, wilting lasts longer and finally the plant withers and dies.

Wilting can also occur on sunny spring days in well watered soils because the ground is still cold from winter. Cold roots resist water flow and cold water is more viscous than warm water. These cold water factors result in water entry into the roots being less than the transpiration loss through the leaves.

Overwatering, however, is harmful to plants. Plants that are watered too well become "soft" in growth with shallow roots close to the surface. When they miss a watering or two during drought periods, these plants collapse quickly. Plants that have been watered deeply though infrequently do not collapse as quickly because their roots are deep in the soil and so are protected on hot days.

When infrequent deep watering is practised, drying out too quickly or too early wilting are both avoided and there is less water loss due to evaporation than is the case with over-watered plants. Excessive watering causes more plant deaths than drought. After prolonged periods of heavy rain the ground may become waterlogged. Then soil air is excluded and this creates conditions that favour the root rot diseases that kill off susceptible plants. Plants die slowly, sometimes browning off on one side and ultimately becoming brown all over. Making the soil water-receptive and retentive by adding ample organic matter saves water and promotes healthy plant growth.

Infiltration rate (the ability of soil to accept water) is variable with different soils. A dry garden loam will accept water readily, but the rate will fall off as the soil becomes wetter. Run-off will occur when more water is delivered than the soil can absorb, as can happen with heavy downpours or overwatering.

Soils vary in their capacity to absorb and retain water. In clay soils, for example, the particles may swell. This blocks the conducting pores and reduces the rate of water infiltration. Increasing the organic matter content of these soils and/or adding gypsum can make the soil more open.

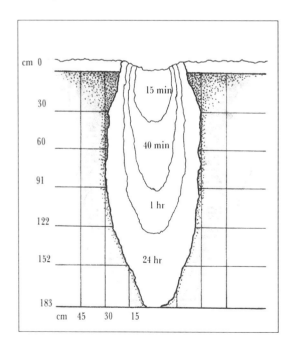

Note that water moves down in the soil. There is little lateral movement.

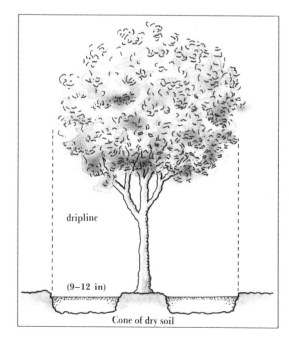

Watering basin should provide for plant's entire rooting area.

Clay subsoils may be less permeable than their overlaying topsoil. Once water reaches the subsoil level, infiltration slows up and the ground becomes boggy, yet the soil below the subsoil level will still remain dry. Applying gypsum or mechanical ripping at this level may be necessary.

A sandy layer below the topsoil may help it to drain during periods of water inundation. It may also contribute to keeping the topsoil wet as water movement into the sandy layer stops when watering or rain does.

Very sandy soils may be water repellent and can be improved by incorporating heavier soils into the sand and/or by mulching. On slopes, water is lost through run-off unless the surface is mulched, kept cultivated, or contoured to assist infiltration. Mulching reduces evaporation from the surface soil and makes plants healthier by protecting roots from heat and cold.

In many public plantings in Australia, native plants are used on the basis that if well mulched they will not require watering after the initial short establishment period of a few weeks. Usually natives belonging to the area are used, though the principle can be applied to plants that are known to adapt to the area, including exotics.

Dig a hole in the soil to find out how thorough water penetration has been and whether excess or insufficient water is responsible for plant problems. Assuming the soil has a sufficient humus content to allow water to penetrate readily and be retained, there are many ways in which home gardeners can save water without adversely affecting their gardens. Preventing run-off by altering watering applications (perhaps drip irrigation instead of sprinklers, for example) is an obvious course. Make sure soils do not repel water as may happen in some sands where there is insufficient clay and organic matter to hold water. Lawns need a high organic matter content to increase the soil's water-holding capacity. Repeated applications of lawn fertilisers to lawns on acid soils may damage structure and make the

application of gypsum necessary to soften soil and increase water penetration.

Protecting the garden from wind stress with windbreaks saves water. Watering before a forecast hot spell is more efficient than watering during it. Eliminating diseased plants and weeds also saves water as it is no longer being wasted on them.

Avoid watering with laundry effluent if it contains detergent-based washing powders, as boron problems result from some of these. Wash with either liquid detergents that do not contain boron, or "bulking agents" based on sodium in place of powders. Rinsing water and soap-based bathroom effluents can also be applied to the garden.

In severely cold areas, such as highland climates, it is wise to remove the mulch during winter to avoid increasing frost damage risk, though in all climates summer mulching makes a useful contribution to water saving. Begin your minimum watering routine on established plants at the end of the wettest part of the year. At other times, gradually increase the intervals between water applications to both lawn and garden. You will probably find that the garden's appearance remains just as attractive with less watering. Weekly watering should be sufficient on well established gardens and lawns if the soil has ample humus. About three times a week should be sufficient on new, or young gardens and lawns.

Use fertilisers sparingly on ornamentals as extra growth uses extra water, but do not allow the plants to starve. Fertilise vegetables and edible crops as these use water inefficiently when fertilised insufficiently.

Try to group plants according to their watering needs, for example, place those that require frequent watering in a different area to those that tolerate minimal watering.

Reduce lawn areas where possible as many grasses require high levels of watering. Use a mulching mower or at least return clippings to lawn as organic matter. This in turn can reduce fertiliser applications.

Put in a drip or trickle irrigation system.

These save water and because they work on low pressure, large areas can be watered in a short time with minimal waste. By wetting soil, not foliage, these watering systems help to control those foliage fungal diseases that are spread by water. Watering systems reduce evaporation loss, keep the root system at optimum water levels and are easily controlled manually or with timers and solonoid valves. They allow water with a higher saline content to be used than is possible with sprinklers, because salts in water are washed to the outside of the wetted zone.

Water stress—provided it is brief—helps a garden by preventing excessive growth and reducing disease problems common to over wet gardens. In fruit trees it encourages flower bud production, though it must not be continued once the buds appear, as then yield suffers. Mild water stress during the late ripening period improves quality by reducing fruit size and lessening the rotting of soft fruits.

HOW MUCH AND HOW OFTEN SHOULD I WATER?

These two questions cannot be answered with a set quantity because seasons, weather, plant type and age, its position in the garden, the soil, climate, even *how* you water are a few of the many factors that will vary the amount and frequency of watering. Only your aim should remain consistent—to avoid the drought or flood approaches and to water throroughly, deeply and infrequently. .

The majority of plants are deep rooted. Even lawn grass roots will run to a metre deep so obviously tall trees and shrubs will be at least as deep. Roots grow towards water, absorbing it and the nutrients plants néed. Roots function only when water and air are present in the soil.

When Should I Water?, the CSIRO's booklet published in association with Rellim Technical Publications answers the question succinctly. The amounts given are average and are only a guide. You will still have to use your judgment after taking all the relevant factors into account.

The low-maintenance gardener can make a virtue out of *NOT* watering! However, if the garden has been over watered, this decision should be put into practice slowly, gradually progressing over months towards infrequent, deep, thorough watering.

Meters that measure the availability of soil moisture are available to help you to decide when to water, but these are rarely necessary. Once you learn to watch the plants and keep an eye on weather and other factors mentioned you will soon know when to water and how much to apply.

- Digging or drilling a hole in the soil is the simplest way of quickly finding the cause of problems suspected of being due to water lack or excess.
- Plants in gardens die more often from waterlogging than from drought.
- Mulched, drought-tolerant native plants may never need to be watered after establishment.
- Generally, a well-managed lawn should need watering no more often than once a week.
- Resist a little longer the temptation to water lawns and ornamental plants. This delay will harden the plants and help them survive later difficult conditions.
- An over-watered lawn may lose 15 litres of water per square metre on a very hot, dry day; a minimally watered lawn of acceptable appearance may lose only 5 litres per square metre.
- Overwatering produces soft plants with poor ablility to cope with stress.
- Frequent light watering
  - ▶ large losses by evaporation from the soil.
  - ▶ shallow roots
- Infrequent deep watering
  - ▶ smaller losses by evaporation
  - ▶ deeper roots
  - ▶ greater drought tolerance
- To soak the top 30 cm (12 in) of a dry sand takes about 25 mm (1 in) of water.
- To soak the top 30 cm (12 in) of a dry loam takes about 40 to 50 mm (1½-2 in) of water.

- To soak the top 30 cm (12 in) of a dry clay takes about 70 mm (2¾ in) of water.
- One millimetre of rain will add 1 litre of water per square metre to a soil.
- A typical sprinkler delivering 10 litres per minute (600 litres per hour) will supply an area of 40 square metres with 600/40=15 litres per square metre per hour=15 mm per hour.
- One inch of rain is about 25 mm of rain.
- One mm of rain is about 4 points of rain.

MINIMUM AMOUNTS OF WATER (RAIN PLUS SPRINKLER) NEEDED BY LAWNS AND ORNAMENTALS TO JUST MAINTAIN THEM

(mm of water per WEEK)

PLACE	JAN	FEB	MAR	APR	MAY	JUN	JUL	AUG	SEP	OCT	NOV	DEC
Sydney	13	12	9	8	6	5	6	7	8	10	12	15
Melbourne	11	12	9	6	4	2	3	4	5	8	10	12
Adelaide	15	14	10	7	5	3	4	5	7	9	12	14
Brisbane	11	9	8	7	5	4	5	6	8	9	11	12
Perth	16	16	12	8	5	4	4	5	7	10	12	15
Hobart	9	8	6	4	2	1	1	2	4	6	7	8
Darwin	12	12	11	13	13	12	13	14	15	16	15	13
Townsville	16	13	12	12	11	10	10	12	15	18	18	17
Canberra	14	13	9	6	4	3	3	5	6	9	12	15
Alice Springs	24	21	17	13	9	7	7	10	13	18	20	22
Griffith	16	15	11	7	4	2	3	5	7	10	13	17
Tatura	13	12	9	5	3	2	2	3	5	7	10	13
Mildura	19	18	13	8	5	3	4	6	8	11	15	17
Oodnadatta	29	28	23	16	10	8	9	11	16	22	26	30
Moree	18	16	14	10	6	5	5	6	9	13	17	19
Merredin	22	20	17	4	5	4	4	5	7	11	16	20

☐ A light-coloured background indicates that in "average" years rainfall supplies enough water to maintain lawns and ornamentals.

☐ A dark-coloured background indicates that rainfall may not supply enough water, depending on the weather that year.

Rainfall since last watering should be subtracted from these figures to get the amount to be applied.

MULCHING

A mulch is a covering over the soil. Its purposes are to reduce water evaporation from the soil; to insulate roots against extremes or rapid changes in temperature; to prevent or inhibit weed growth; to stop soil from being splashed on to foliage, flowers or fruit; to make the garden look neat and to save effort on the part of the gardener.

The most effective mulches are organic because they repair and improve the soil. Organic mulches decompose into humus— the name given to the last stages of the decomposition of animal or vegetable matter. Humus is an essential part of soil. It makes soil more water-absorbent and water-retentive, and builds up the microscopic soil flora and fauna on which plant health is so dependent.

Mulching increases the earthworm population and earthworm castings are a valuable fertiliser. The earthworm eats its way through the soil, excreting perfect soil made richer and revitalised by its passage through the earthworm's intestinal tract. While you may resent earthworms in the lawn, the good they do there and in the garden is compensation enough for the appearance of the castings. As they move through the soil they aerate it, improving the drainage and texture so that water enters more easily and is retained for longer periods.

Earthworms break down and recycle mulch, creating the humus necessary to the garden. They increase and promote the availability of mineral nutrients to soil life and plants. They improve compacted soils, allow roots to penetrate more deeply into soil and stimulate aerobic soil life.

The microscopic organisms that make up aerobic soil life break down organic matter into humus, which is the key to plant growth. Without humus soils deteriorate and may become infertile. Repairing the soil by adding organic matter so that earthworms and other soil organisms can function is a responsibility common to all gardeners, including low-maintenance gardeners. Previous civilisations that have neglected the soil have left deserts behind them.

Organic mulches contribute humus to the soil, which supports aerobic soil life and earthworms, which in turn support soil and plants. Without mulching, growth suffers as soils become less fertile. Feeding with artificial fertilisers is no substitute for mulching. In unmulched soils, water absorption and retention are reduced, soil oxygen penetration is largely prevented and increased levels of carbon dioxide are retained.

Not all soil life is helpful to plants. Anaerobic soil life stabilises organic matter, rendering it unavailable to plants. This aspect of soil life prospers on poor drainage and the exclusion of oxygen from soil.

A mulch can be from 7.5 cm (3 in) to 15 cm (6 in) deep—the deeper the better, provided that it allows water through. Depth depends on the age, size and nature of the plants. Young plants require a lighter mulch. It is laid 15 cm (6 in) away from the trunks of trees and shrubs and covers the whole garden.

Aged material—that is, material that has already changed colour in its decomposing process—is preferable to new, fresh material. The latter may cause plants to turn yellow for a while as it uses the nitrogen in the soil to help in its decomposition process. If it has to be used fresh, a dressing of fertiliser before applying mulch helps.

When the mulch is being used as a weed suppressant, remove the weeds first or at least kill them with Zero® or Roundup®. If they are perennial, difficult-to-eradicate weeds such as nut or onion grasses and oxalis, apply the weedicide in spring, wait four to six weeks, reapply it and then lay a woven weed mat. Anchor it very firmly and neatly so that all light is excluded from the sides and around the plants. Cut extra pieces to overlap the planting holes, then lay enough of the organic mulch on top to hide the fabric.

The woven weed mat lasts indefinitely and

can be walked on without being damaged. It resembles shade cloth but it is more closely woven. It allows air and water through but excludes light, so that trees and shrubs survive, but weeds do not because light cannot reach their foliage.

Although it is excellent material, weed mat only works if it is put down firmly without looseness and used generously so that no clumps of weeds come up in planting holes. It should not be confused with plastic sheeting, a product that is best confined to strawberry growing. It makes a poor cover and though popular becomes a real nuisance as it deteriorates, being difficult to gather up, full of holes and tatters and a destroyer of soil. Under plastic, soil becomes hard and compacted because both air and water—two vital soil components—are excluded.

An organic mulch may be any animal or vegetable material. The following are some of the most widely used.

All Animal Manures These are smelly while fresh. Horse manure from stable-fed horses will be free of weeds. Cow manures gathered from pastures will carry the weed seeds of those pastures. These manures work best if stored until aged. Dried, processed cow manure is usually weed-free. Chicken manure is fast and hot and it is advisable to compost it before use. Sheep and goat manures are excellent. Pig manure is a cold, slow acting manure and needs composting before use. In fact most animal manures are more effective if composted with other materials, such as leaves and soil, before they are used.

Lawn Clippings Apply these thinly, a layer each week until they reach the depth required. If applied thickly while new, they become hot and slimey below, and water runs off rather than through. Thin, weekly applications build up to an effective mulch.

Mushroom Compost This is excellent on vegetable gardens. It may occasionally have a high content of salts, the residue of fertilisers used in mushroom production. Native plants are susceptible to this. Otherwise it is a first-rate, easy-to-use, readily available, cheap mulch.

Pine Needles These are good value on all acid-loving plants—azaleas, rhododendrons, camellias, daphne, strawberries and pieris.

Woodchips Suitable for most plants except vegetables, woodchips about 10 cm (4 in) deep make a good mulch—regrettably trees must die to provide it.

Sawdust Feed the soil with two cups of blood and bone to the square metre before applying sawdust to compensate for nitrogen loss. It is acidic so it will increase the acidity of soil. It is best used when at least three months old. When applied too densely, it will retard water penetration.

Seaweed A mineral and nutrient rich mulch containing a high percentage of trace elements, seaweed breaks down quickly. Collect it from the high water mark and wash before using to rid it of salt. Alternatively, purchase Seaweed Mulch.

Paper Shredded or crumpled paper makes a worthwhile, if somewhat messy mulch. Thick layers of it laid flat on the ground inhibit water penetration and they are a good, though somewhat untidy way of suppressing weeds. Layers of shredded paper in compost decompose readily and are a satisfactory way to use up newspaper.

Straw and Hay These are among the very best mulches (buy bales for convenience). Shake out each forkful to let all seeds fall on the soil, then add the straw to cover and inhibit weed growth.

Leaves Either composted or mixed with other mulch ingredients, leaves make an attractive mulch. If possible, put native plant leaves with natives and exotics with exotics, but if this is difficult, a mixed application will work.

Leaf Mould Mulch Letting leaves rot down before use—a process that can take a year or more—results in rich mulch material. Anything organic can be used—rice hulls, peanut shells, bargasse (residue of sugar cane), feathers, weeds (not perennial ones and not diseased or pest infected ones), coco bean shells, macadamia and other nut shells, spent hops, pea straw and trash—anything that grows or lives and could be spread as mulch is acceptable.

Mulch is laid on the soil surface. When fertilisers are being applied it is pulled away with a rake, the fertiliser distributed and the mulch replaced.

Apply mulch in spring or early summer to protect the roots during the heat of summer. Expect it to filter into the ground and need renewing, or at least a top-up, after 3–4 months. A top-up is a sign that your plan to repair and improve the condition of the soil is working.

When soil is correctly mulched there is no need to dig the garden. Any weeds that are blown in and grow on the mulch can be pulled out easily or treated with a weedkiller.

Mulching is the low-maintenance gardener's friend. It saves weeding, watering and digging!

FERTILISERS

Fertilising—often referred to as "feeding"— is essential to plants. It promotes growth and contributes to plant health. Because healthy plants are less susceptible to pest and disease problems, the garden looks more attractive and the gardener spends less time dealing with such problems.

ORGANIC FERTILISERS

These are manures, cotton seed meal, blood and bone or composts derived from animal or vegetable matter. These are splendid soil conditioners for all soil types; they add material that improves drainage and aeration and therefore plant health. On these accounts their value cannot be over-emphasised. Their value as fertilisers, however, is variable, altering with the age and source of the material, its storage conditions and a variety of other factors. Its actual fertiliser content cannot be quantified or repeated exactly from one application to the next as it can in the case of inorganic fertilisers. The user is therefore uncertain whether the correct fertiliser application has been made.

The best course is to follow an annual routine of adding organic matter by digging it into the soil and also applying it as a mulch, relying on inorganic fertilisers to feed the plants.

INORGANIC FERTILISERS

These contain known amounts of the primary chemicals needed by plants. They are often referred to by their N.P.K. ratios—the percentages of nitrogen, phosphorus and potassium they contain.

An analysis of the components of fertiliser is given on the container, and is often described by numbers: 10–9–8 means 10 per cent total nitrogen, 9 per cent phosphoric acid and 8 per cent water soluble potash. Each plant group needs a particular element.

Formulations that suit a wide range of plants are known as the "complete" or "all purpose" fertilisers. Others are formulated for particular plant groups, such as roses, citrus, camellias and azaleas, and indoor plants. They may be slow or fast-acting and are available in liquid, powdered or granular forms. Controlled or timed release fertilisers in a number of formulations release nutrients over a period varying from months to years. Inorganic fertilisers are a known quantity and measured amounts can be applied to suit particular plants. Unlike organic fertilisers, they do nothing at all to improve soil texture.

DRY FERTILISERS

These are preferable for all trees, shrubs, roses, fruit trees, perennials and long-lived house plants.

They are applied in spring and/or early summer. In general all fertilisers are applied when plants are in active growth. A few plants, roses included, appreciate a second summer feeding but as a general rule, one application of a dry fertiliser annually to the above plant groups though less than ideal, will keep the low-maintenance garden going.

Dry fertilisers can be sprinkled around the plant and watered in. Alternatively, a trench can be dug surrounding the plant, the fertiliser

The dripline is the outer edge of the foliage. Feeding plants are below this line.

Holes set around the dripline to receive fertiliser are best for older trees.

Surface feeding works for younger trees, though grass is a competitor and should be mowed for most efficient use of fertiliser.

placed in it and covered with soil. Large trees are fertilised by making holes at intervals following the "drip line" (perimeter of foliage) of the tree, then inserting the fertiliser and covering it with soil.

Australian native plants resent superphosphate so it is worthwhile buying formulations specifically for natives and to use these in conjunction with blood and bone.

Traditionally azaleas, camellias, rhododendrons, daphne and pieris are acid-loving plants and are fertilised with products that do not contain lime. These products are usually called "Azalea and Camellia Foods" and in well-cared-for-gardens they are applied immediately after flowering finishes and then monthly until mid-summer. In the low-maintenance garden though, one after-flowering feeding would be adequate.

There is plenty of evidence to suggest that in most soils all-purpose fertilisers can be applied to the acid-loving group without harm,

but in practice Azalea and Camellia Food is invariably recommended for these plants.

Citrus and Rose Foods are similar in formulation and can be used on crops, trees and shrubs. Ideally you should feed roses in spring, early summer and mid-summer. Feed most fruit trees about two weeks before flowering or at any time except the dormant period, and feed citrus plants in spring. Citrus plants used to be fed in autumn as well, but to help control leaf-miner, which feeds on new autumn growth, feeding at this time is no longer recommended.

The range of fertilisers available is bewildering and for convenience the low-maintenance gardener could reduce it to three: an all-purpose fertiliser for trees, shrubs, roses, citrus and long-lived house plants; Azalea and Camellia Food for that group; and finally a native plant food.

The easiest fertilisers to use are the controlled timed release coated types, for example, Chemspray's 'Native Gold' and

'Nutricote'. These are clean to handle, easy to store and do not go hard. They are purchased in a punnet, like a butter container, complete with a measuring spoon and are simply scattered on the surface of the ground and watered in.

This type of fertiliser is used by many nurseries and the small granules, mostly in a nearly transparent state are often visible on the surface of the soil when the plant is purchased. These granules break down slowly over months or even years depending on formulation. Heat and cold contribute to the break down process, on occasions causing too-sudden release. 'Native-Gold' is an exception as it is not affected by heat or cold. Like all fertilisers they should be used in accordance with the directions on the packet. The application of too much fertiliser will kill plants.

THE ELEMENTS

NITROGEN

This comes from the air, and enters the soil via rainfall or is extracted from the soil by bacteria, or from fertilisers or organic matter. It promotes vegetative growth and gives plants a rich green colour. If the label says nitrogen is present in the nitrate form, the fertiliser will be fast-acting. Ammonic or organic nitrogen is not as fast-acting but is more sustained. Of these two, ammonic nitrogen causes the faster response. This applies to all plants but is most noticeable in lawns, which are easily burnt by excess nitrogen because they are more exposed to it than deeper rooting shrubs buffered by more soil.

THE CARBON-NITROGEN RATIO

When additional organic matter high in carbon (compared to soil nitrogen) is added to soil, the organisms that digest it compete with plants for nitrogen, and yellowing of foliage and other signs of nitrogen deficiency will occur. Composted materials are therefore preferable.

Failing that straw, bark, shavings and sawdust should be mixed with a nitrogenous fertiliser to keep the carbon-nitrogen ratio in balance. Put more simply, the supplementary nitrogen helps the organic material to break down without adversely affecting growth by using too much nitrogen from the soil.

The nitrate form of nitrogen is easily lost from soil and leaches through the root area rapidly. When nitrogen is deficient, older cells turn yellow and old foliage dies and falls. Nitrogen is most active in the tender, young plant tissues of the tips of buds, opening leaves and shoots. It regulates protein production for the formation of new protoplasm in the cells.

PHOSPHORUS

Phosphorus is present in all living tissues. It is necessary for photosynthesis (the plant's food-making process) and is the means by which energy is transferred within the plant. Blood and bone, superphosphate and ammonium phosphate are sources of phosphorus.

Root tips extract phosphorus ions from soil solution, the microscopic film of water surrounding soil particles. They absorb available phosphorus, growing to new areas of soil solution and repeating the process as the phosphorus ions in an area are used up. Growth is retarded when phosphorus in the soil solution is too low or the renewal rate is too slow.

Phosphorus moves slowly in the soil as the phosphoric acid from fertiliser ionises and forms other phosphoric compounds, some of which are insoluble and unavailable to plants. "Fixation" or locking in of phosphorus is likely to occur in very acid soils rather than in alkaline or neutral soils. The problem, however, can be overcome by raising the phosphorus level of the soil to satisfy the fixing power so that other minerals do not combine with the phosphate ions.

Phosphorus is most effective when applied to the roots by "banding". This means digging a trench a few centimetres either side of and just below the level of seed rows, sprinkling fertiliser along the rows according to recommendation and covering it with soil. On trees and shrubs it can be mixed in with the soil that goes into the hole. It should not be broadcast or mixed only superficially into surface soil.

POTASSIUM

This is responsible for plant functioning, including the manufacture and movement of sugars and starch and for growth by cell division.

Muriate of potash and sulphate of potash are used to add potassium to soil. Plants need potassium and remove more of it from the soil than any other nutrients except calcium and nitrogen. Some forms of potassium are soluble in water, while others are not, but very little natural soil potassium is available to plants. By adding fertiliser that contains soluble potassium to soil, a transfer from soluble to exchangeable potassium allows this nutrient to become available to the plant.

IRON, ZINC, MANGANESE

Iron is necessary for chlorophyll formation. Manganese and zinc appear to be catalysts in the utilisation of other nutrients.

Alkaline soils in low rainfall areas can be deficient in these minor elements, a problem that is overcome by using chelated products, such as iron chelates. Chelated forms are available to plant roots and are not subject to the "fixing" that makes these unavailable in their natural state.

TRACE ELEMENTS

These are catalysts or oxidising agents that help plants in the absorption and use of major and minor elements and in the formation of various plant substances. In most soils these are present in sufficient quantity and their addition is not necessary.

Where trace element deficiency occurs, plant growth will reflect it. Such deficiencies are unusual but it is preferable to purchase fertiliser that includes trace elements.

LOW-NITROGEN OR NO-NITROGEN FERTILISERS

Some such as superphosphate and Mor-Bloom® are used on some plants to encourage flowering or fruiting without encouraging leafy growth.

SIGNS OF NUTRIENT DEFICIENCIES

Nitrogen—yellowish foliage due to lack of chlorophyll and stunted growth.

Phosphorus—bluish or purplish tinges in foliage and weak stunted growth.

Potassium—weak, undersized plants will have poor flower stems; leaf margins may be brown and shrivelled.

Calcium—foliage may be distorted with curled leaf margins or hooked leaves, brown spots or scorched areas may be present and new, young growth collapses.

Magnesium—leaves are yellowish usually between the veins—orange shades may be present and leaves fall prematurely. Dolomite, Epsom Salts (magnesium sulphate) and most composts supply magnesium.

Sulphur—yellowish leaves are smaller and sometimes rolled on the margins. The signs are similar to those of nitrogen deficiency.

Iron—usually occurs in limey or alkaline soils and shows as yellowing of the new growth. Easily corrected by applying iron chelates. Other means are adding sulphur, sulphate of aluminium, sulphate of iron or peat moss.

Manganese—buff coloured or grey marginal markings around lower leaves and dullish foliage are indicators. Corrected by acidifying soil through adding sulphur, sulphate of aluminium, sulphate of iron or peat moss.

Zinc—in citrus shows up by yellow mottling of the foliage and in apples by rosette formation of leaves. Corrected by adding zinc sulphate to the soil.

Copper—on citrus causes die-back of young shoots, "burning" of leaf margins, rosette formation of multiple buds and sometimes gum exudation. Copper sprays are the usual means of correcting this.

Boron—symptoms are hollow cores, pinkish foliage and death; hollow stem in cauliflowers, cankers in turnips; or withered sunken areas of beetroot; toughening of the skin and gumming between flesh and rind with browning in the centre of the fruit of citrus, especially in lemons. Sodium borate or borax is applied no more than once annually.

Molybdenum—this deficiency causes "whiptail" (distorted leaves) in cauliflowers and deforms new growth of forget-me-nots, pansies, and dahlias. Acid soil conditions or the use of fertilisers with high nitrogen and phosphorous content may cause this deficiency. It is corrected by spraying with sodium molybdenate (1 teaspoon per 4-5 litres (7-9 pints) of water).

Toxicity—copper, zinc, boron and manganese will create toxicity when over-used. Awareness of deficiencies and the means to correct these should not lead to an assumption that every discoloured or distorted leaf requires some action on your part. Toxicity brought about by overuse of one or more chemicals can be far more of a problem than a particular deficiency.

The low-maintenance gardener who follows a programme of annual feeding and adding organic matter will probably not have to worry too much about deficiency symptoms. As long as soil is kept in friable condition through the addition of ample organic matter and generous mulching, fertilising can be an annual event. But as fertilisers are easily leached from soil by rain or irrigation, more frequent applications give better results. Fertilisers are most effective when applied during active growth—spring or summer rather than autumn or winter—though almost any time is better than no time! They are disastrous when overused as "burning" occurs and in the worst cases plants die.

PRUNING

Low-maintenance gardeners need to know the principles of pruning, for there will always be a plant that needs shaping or a tree limb to remove. Knowing how to prune correctly will also avoid other problems.

Pruning is practised to direct growth, to improve quality and increase the yield of fruit and flowers, to strengthen the trunk and branches and to maintain plant health by pruning away weak or diseased wood. Height, width and shape are controlled by pruning. Plants that grow too high or too wide for their position, or develop an unattractive shape can be pruned to fit the space or improve their shape. Pruning can also be the means of developing particular shapes such as fruit tree cordons and ornamental espaliers to decorate walls. In fruit trees, pruning improves the quality and quantity of fruit.

For most plants the active season of growth is spring/summer. New growth arises from the terminal buds at the ends of branches and branchlets. The flow of plant energy to terminal buds is caused by the hormones and auxins within the bud. By removing or retaining terminal buds, plant growth can be directed.

When terminal buds are removed, growth energy is redirected to the buds below. Instead of the branch lengthening, with few side growths, growths develop at the buds making the branch bushier. When all-over pruning of terminal buds is practised, the plant becomes very bushy.

Tip Pruning is the pinching out of terminal buds to direct growth to the buds along the stems, stimulating production of new side branches to make plants bushier. Leaving the terminal buds on the bush promotes branch length at the expense of bushiness. This type of pruning is applied several times annually to small, quick-growing shrubs like fuchsias, salvias and many annuals, cistus, chrysanthemums—anything that is inclined to become open and straggly.

Making shrubs bushier requires removal of tip growth as above. Hard-wooded shrubs stand quite severe pruning so cutting back may mean taking a third to three-quarters off the main branches to force lower buds to develop on each branch and make the plant bushier. (On trees

Pinching out the growing points (terminal buds) keeps plants bushy.

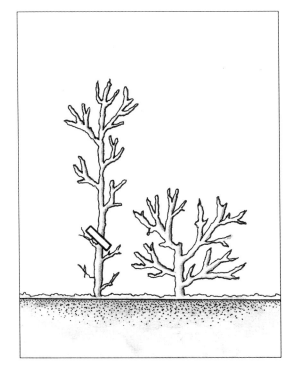

Removal of the main stem develops side growths in shrubs, but is usually not practised with trees.

this applies only to the side branches. The tip of the trunk—the "leader"—is left alone. Cutting this would interfere with tree height and shape.)

Pruning is practised only when there is a reason for it! Not everything requires pruning. Before you begin to prune, determine *why* you are pruning; this will dictate *how* you go about it. Shrubs are divided into groups determined by wood on which they bear their flowers:

SHRUBS THAT FLOWER ON NEW WOOD

These produce growth and flowers in the current season. They are quick growers and some can be spindly unless pruned. Pruning improves flower size and slightly reduces the number of flowers and controls the size of these shrubs.

The new season's growth is simply cut back to two or three buds or shoots at the base of each growth, rather like picking blooms with a long stem. This forces production of many new, flower-bearing stems. The brown, old, hard wood forming a framework at the base of

the plant is left alone except for the removal of dead or damaged branches.

Because this plant group flowers (or is at its best) usually in late spring, summer or autumn, pruning is carried out in very late winter or early spring, just before new growth occurs.

Examples

Abutilon	—Chinese Lanterns
Acacias	—Wattles
Acalypha	—(cut back by only a third of length of new growth)
Begonia	—(remove oldest shoots only at ground level)
Boronia	
Buddleia	—Butterfly Bush
Ceanothus	—Californian Lilac
Ceratostigma	—Sky Flower
Erythrina crista-galli	—Christ-thorn
Gardenia	
Grevilleas	
Hibiscus	

syriacus	—Deciduous Hibiscus
Indigofera	—Native Wisteria
Lagerstroemia	—Crepe Myrtle
Protea	
Tamarix	—Flowering Cypress

SHRUBS THAT FLOWER ON LAST YEAR'S WOOD

These plants have new growth one year and bear their flowers on that in the following year; the more new growth there is in one year the more flowers there will be in the following one.

As soon as the flowers have passed their peak, flowered stems are cut back to a shoot or new bud near their junction with the old main branches, reducing the plant to its main framework. This pruning is quite severe though its results are spectacular, long, bloom-laden growths in the next year.

Timing is quite critical. Prune as soon as most of the flowers fade. Avoid delay as the process could be complicated by new shoots.

Examples

Abutilon	—Chinese Lantern
Brunfelsia	—Yesterday, Today and Tomorrow
Calliandra	—Tassel Flower; Powder Puff Flower
Cytisus	—Broom
Deutzia	—Wedding Bush
Kerria	
japonica	—Japanese Rose
Loropetalum	—Chinese Fringe Flower
Prunus	
glandulosa	—(dwarf flowering Almond)
Prunus	
persica	—(flowering Peach)
Raphiolepis	—Indian Hawthorn
Weigela	—Diervillea

Note that though the above may be pruned in this way after flowering, not all *must* be. Brunfelsia, Loropetalum, Prunus persica and Raphiolepis are just as handsome and more natural looking when left unpruned.

REMOVAL OF THE OLD WOOD

Some shrubs need to be cleaned out in winter just before spring growth commences. Stems older than three years (hard wood) are removed at ground level, which retains only one-year-old wood and those two-year-old stems carrying side branches which will flower that year. The unflowered one-year-old stems will bloom in the coming season. Most of the two-year-old flowered stems are cut back to within a pair of leaves near the base. All flowered stems are cut back to within a pair of leaves of the base. If you find it difficult to prune so drastically, remember that new growths develop to replace those removed.

Note that the old varieties of Hydrangea are pruned in winter cutting back *all* canes but retaining old canes for a year or two more than with modern varieties.

Examples

Hydrangeas	(old varieties)
Berberis	—barberry
Cassia	
Feijoa	
sellowiana	—Fruiting Fuchsia
Forsythia	—Golden Bells
Kolkwitzia	
amabilis	—Beauty Bush
Lasiandra	
Ribes	—Flowering Currant
Rondeletia	

REJUVENATING OLD SHRUBS

Pruning rejuvenates shrub growth especially on old neglected plants. Provided they are healthy, many shrubs can be cut back really hard to within 5-10 cm (2-4 in) of ground level. First lop off a third to half of the bush with tree loppers, then with a pruning saw or bow saw, make neat, clean cuts and avoid tearing the bark. Paint all wounds with a tree dressing or wound sealant, clear grass away from the shrub, apply fertiliser and follow that with an 8-10 cm (3-4 in) mulch. The best time for this type of pruning is early spring, which allows a full growing season. Other seasons are acceptable though you may have to look at the plant in its unpruned state until growth commences in spring.

Examples

Abutilon	—Chinese Lanterns
Abelia	
Buddleia	—Butterfly Bush
Coprosma	—Looking Glass Plant
Cotoneaster	
Escallonia	
Nerium	—Oleander
Photinia	
Plumbago	—Cape Plumbago; Leadwort
Polygala	
Rondeletia	
Tibouchina	—Lasiandra

CONTROLLING CLIMBERS

Most climbers are not pruned until they become overgrown. Flowering types are then pruned immediately after flowering. Non-flowering types are pruned in late winter. They are untied from their supports, a few old stems are removed completely at ground level and then the lateral growths are removed from the other stems and the plant is retied into position. Alternatively some people take to their climbers with tree loppers, a somewhat rough but often satisfactory approach.

Examples

Akebia quinata	—Five-leaved Akebia
Bougainvillea	
Campsis grandiflora	—Chinese Trumpet Vine
Clematis	
Hardenbergia	—Sarsaparilla
Hydrangea petiolaris	—Japanese climbing Hydrangea
Jasminum grandiflorum	—Jasmine
Lonicera	—Honeysuckle
Mandevilla suaveolens	—Chilean Jasmine
Metrosideros	—(climbing form of NZ Christmas Bush)
Pandorea	—Bignonias
Passiflora	—Passionfruit varieties
Thunbergia	—Black-eyed Susan
Vitis vinifera	—Ornamental Grape
Wisteria	

REMOVAL OF DEAD WOOD AND WEAK GROWTH

Any time is suitable for the removal of dead, damaged or weak growth. It improves plant health as such wood can provide entry points for pests, especially borer, or harbour disease organisms. Any plant can be pruned in this way.

Christmas Bush benefits from routine removal of spent wood and this helps to control borer attack. Camellias, citrus trees, Euonymus, Gardenia and Nandina all need spent-wood removal at least annually.

MAINTAINING SHAPE

Many shrubs, for example Akebias, develop a better shape if lightly cut back overall in late winter or early spring after flowering has finished. This should be accompanied by selective removal at ground level of old canes and the cutting back almost to ground level of others to allow light and air to enter the bush. More severe pruning may be practised on neglected aged plants, which are rejuvenated by overall cutting back to within 30-40 cm (12-16 in) of the ground.

REMOVING SPENT FLOWERS TO MAINTAIN A SHAPELY BUSH

Immediately after flowering cut off the spent blooms of Callistemon (bottlebrush) 2-3 cm

(¾–1 in) behind the end of the brush. This will be followed very soon by soft new growth. If you wait too long, removal of spent flowers will also remove new growth. Apply this to other plants that flower at the branch ends, for example, rhododendrons.

REMOVING OLD SHOOTS TO PRODUCE MORE FLOWERS NEXT YEAR

Some plants, such as Buddleia alternifolia, flower on last year's shoots. As soon as flowering finishes these flowered stems are cut well back to encourage new shoots and therefore, more flowers to appear.

LIGHT OVERALL PRUNING OF AZALEAS

In Japan as soon as flowering finishes Azaleas are sheared all over taking off 5-10 cm (2-4 in), according to age and height. This removes straggly growth and promotes flowering on the outside of the bush, guaranteeing maximum colour. This form of pruning is applied to other plants like Coleonema and topiary subjects, buxus or conifers.

SPRING PRUNING FOR NEW WOOD AND BUSHIER SHAPE

Between September and October (the latter in frost prone areas) prune hibiscus by reducing height by one third. Hibiscus dislike the combination of cold winters and wet soil, so avoid pruning until soil begins to warm up.

Note that pruning shrubs tends to vary with age. Very young plants in their first years may be tip pruned for bushiness. As they age, one of the preceding forms of pruning will be adopted. For a good result follow pruning with fertilising, a deep mulch and a thorough watering.

Pruning cuts should always be smooth and clean, the result of cutting with sharp secateurs, loppers, or saws. Cut at a 45° angle or thereabouts, the top of the cut just above the bud, the bottom below it and the bud facing

It is preferable to thin out the crown of a tree, rather than "prune" it. A tree that is too close to a building (a) has branches removed (either all over the tree, or perhaps on one side to create a path). These branches do not grow again (b). A badly pruned tree (c) not only grows again, but is more dense and reduces the amount of light entering the building (d).

to the outside of the bush, so that growth will occur on the outside, not congest the centre.

WHAT HAPPENS IF YOU DO NOT PRUNE?

Some plants will become straggly—others will have more flowers though they will be of a smaller size and fruit may be more numerous but smaller. As long as plants are not neglected, most (with the exception of those that need tip pruning) will look attractive when unpruned. Quite often it is debatable whether pruning improves on nature anyway. To many people, Flowering Peaches and Crepe Myrtles look just as lovely unpruned. Only a few plants, for example, hydrangeas and many (though not all) roses, depend on pruning.

PRUNING ROSES

The low-maintenance gardener will be tempted by roses at some stage! Despite their high-maintenance reputation, there are many roses that give great results even when neglected (see Plant Lists). Rose pruning is uncomplicated when approached on the following step-by-step basis.

- Wear gloves. Use a small rose pruning saw and very sharp secateurs, a tree wound sealant to dress the wounds and some Dettol or other antiseptic solution to clean tools.
- Reduce bush height by cutting off 60 per cent of the top of the bush. Cut anywhere and at any angle. The objective is to clear away foliage and take a good look at the bush.
- Cut out all weak, soft or small growths and all old or dead wood.
- Assess the bush. The freshest looking limbs are this year's growth—darker limbs are last year's—old brownish limbs are three years or older. Use your saw to remove these growths—saw out at ground level. On old plants, saw old basal cuts across to remove any dead wood and expose viable growth. New shoots will spring from here.

- Go over the bush cutting back each limb to an outward facing bud to develop new shoots on the outside of the bush. Each cut shoud be at 45° to the stem, its lowest point slanting away from the bud to avoid water draining to the buds.
- Keep in mind that the object of pruning is to create an open centre in the bush to help control black spot and allow better placement of the flowers.
- There is no need to, but if you wish you can cover all large wounds (and other cuts too if you have the time) with tree wound sealant.
- Do not use blunt secateurs or saws, as jagged cuts are entry points for diseases and cause stems to brown and die back.

PRUNING CLIMBERS & WEEPERS

For the first two years of growing a climbing rose, all the long canes rising from its base should be tied to its support. The only pruning should be removal of unwanted canes, and in late autumn, the chopping off of the last 45 cm (8 in) of each cane.

This makes side growths (laterals) shoot. From these, flower stems rise. Subsequent pruning requires flower stems to be cut off 2 or 3 buds above their junction with the laterals. Picking the flowers achieves this. When a cane is worn out, cut it out at the base. A new basal cane will arise and can be trained in the same way as that already outlined for a young plant. Usually there are no blooms (or few) on climbers in their first year. Weeping roses are pruned in late summer after flowering by removing half or a third of the length of the pendulous canes. This strengthens these at the top.

TREE PRUNING

Height comes from the "leader", the tip of the trunk. If this is damaged or cut off, a side shoot will take over, but a distinct bend will remain in the trunk at the point where the damage occurred.

Trees have their own natural shapes and

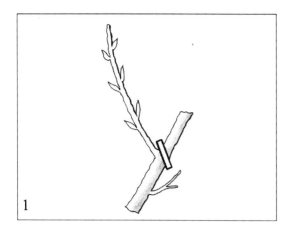

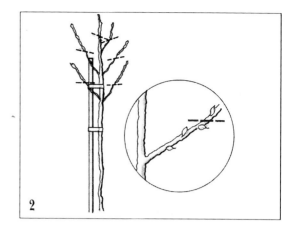

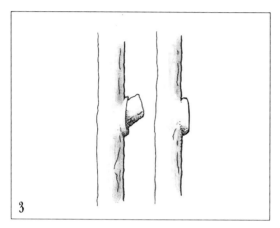

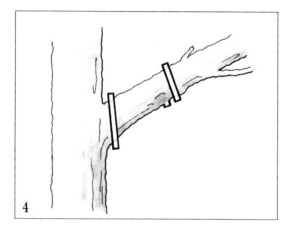

1 Cut close to a side root. 2 Shortening branches at planting times makes a better 'head' on deciduous fruit trees. 3 Remove stubs to allow bark to grow over cut of limbs from the creased area on trunk known as the healing stub. 4 Cut tree limbs as shown to avoid tearing the bark. 5 On large trees, removal of side limbs allows room to walk underneath the tree. Use the three-cut method.

most do not require pruning, though sometimes overhanging limbs must be removed or limbs that are too long cut back.

With care it is possible to remove tree limbs so that they do not regrow. This means that paths can be cut through the centre or sides of a tree to allow overhead wires to pass through, or neighbour-leaning limbs to be removed once and for all.

This takes three cuts. The first is made about 30 cm (12 in) from the junction of branch with trunk. It is only 4 or 5 cm (1½–2 in) deep and is made on the underside of the branch.

The next is made through the branch from the opposite or top side and about 6 or 10 cm (2½ or 4 in) further along the branch. When this falls, the first cut stops the bark from tearing along the stub and down the trunk.

The third cut is made through the stub just one millimetre or two beyond the crease formed by its junction with the trunk. This crease is called the "healing stub". The cut should be very clean and smooth.

It can be dressed or not with a tree wound sealant—there are arguments for and against this. The main thing is that it is clean, smooth and sloping enough not to hold water—an important point in controlling disease and pest entry.

In time bark from the "healing stub" will grow over this area completely covering the cut. If the cut is imperfect new growths may arise at this point. They can be cut off or pared off with sharp secateurs or a knife. Repeated cutting will eventually stop their growth. This form of pruning is followed to create a tall, smooth, high-branching trunk on a tree as well as for the limb removal.

Branch removal is preferable to cutting branches back to a stub as the latter practice causes a proliferation of growth and subsequent annual pruning, whereas the first method, if performed correctly, is a once-only event. To improve tree shape, branches may be shortened by cutting back to a point where a side shoot is growing in the same direction.

STAKING AND GUYING

Though plants are traditionally staked in nurseries, this is mainly done because customers expect stems to be at right angles to the ground. Plants also appear more uniform and therefore are more marketable when staked.

However, from the plant's point of view stakes are bad news, at least once plants reach 1m (3 ft) or so in height. When plants are staked, one side of the plant is shaded. If the stake is on the north side, this problem is quite serious. If you stake a plant for a year or so and then remove the stake, you will notice that the trunk now veers away from the position of the stake.

The plant in fact is anything but straight. This is because it was trying to escape the shading of one side of its trunk by the stake. If you must stake a plant therefore, do it on the south side so that the stem is not shaded.

It is far better to guy a plant, that is, to use two or three stakes placed about 15 cm

(6 in) away from the trunk. The plant is then tied to the stakes by figure-of-eight ties. This allows movement of the trunk during wind and prevents shading of the trunk, which then grows very straight. While it is often a nuisance in gardens, wind can also be beneficial. Because of wind, trunk movement at ground level occurs and plants are strengthened as a result.

The best material to use in staking or guying is anything soft. Pantihose, stockings, rubber bands or plastic are excellent. Twine and paper-coated wire will cut into stems and these are better reserved for annuals and perennials, not for long-term plants like trees and shrubs.

In large trees or shrubs, insulated wire fed through a piece of hose is effective because it prevents the wire from ever contacting the trunk.

Whatever you do when growing plants, make sure that the ties used do not cut into the plant and that stakes do not shade or rub the trunk once the plants are 1 m (3 ft) or so in height.

Some plants, however, are staked. These are the standard and weeping standard roses and

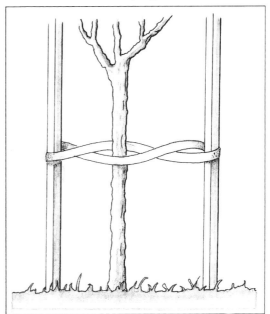

Guying is preferable to staking for plants more than 1 m (3 ft) high.
Place two stakes about 15 cm (6 in) out from the stem. Figure-of-eight ties go from one stake to the other, holding the plant in the middle.

ornamentals such as weeping cherries, apples, ash, and elms. Until their stem is very strong and capable of supporting the head, it is necessary to stake then. In their case the stake looks tidier than guying, although guying would still be preferable. These plants (roses excepted) do not have to be staked for a lifetime, only for two or three years until the stem is strong enough to stand alone. Weeping standard roses do need permanent staking to protect their "head" from wind damage and are usually supported by a rose "ring" atop a stake.

Some plants have weak stems and a floppy growth habit, for example, *Streptosolen* (Browallia). These grow from a multitude of stems and it is best to erect a small cage around them in the shape of three or four light stakes joined together by twine or light wire. The plant grows up through the middle, falls over the top layer of twine and is contained by the cage. After a while only the flowering arms of the plant are visible.

WEED CONTROL

For the low-maintenance gardener the best form of weed control is mulching. The only weeds that occur in mulch are those that are blown in or taken in with the mulch which, if it is collected from a weedy paddock, for example, will carry the weeds of that paddock. On the other hand if it is a form of processed manure, the weed seeds will have been killed and no further weeds will occur other than those blown in from neighbouring properties.

The best time to pull out weeds is after heavy rain. Pull, rather than dig, out privet, olives, ochna, pittosporum and camphor laurels left by birds. Digging would compact and harden the ground, but after heavy rain the soil around the weeds is soft and pulling out is particularly easy especially for the above.

Weed control can also be practised after moving sprinklers, when the ground is wet. Wandering Jew, for example, is easy to remove with a rake by taking away the top growth and exposing underneath, which can be treated with a weedicide.

Until a garden is established, in the first two or three years, the best form of weeding is digging with a fork. This not only removes weeds but improves the tilth of the soil making it more friable. Soils that are heavy, clayey or loamy should not be dug when wet, as they will develop hard-to-break clods.

Weeds can be crowded out by using ground covers or annuals placed so close together that light does not reach the soil and therefore weeds do not grow. However, establishing these in ground that is old, hard, shaded or in soil that has been neglected and is massed with tree and shrub roots is difficult, but not impossible. There are plants such as the annual salvia (which does best in full sun) that will cope with all of those problems and clivea, which will tolerate dry, shaded root-filled positions. The new gardener has more opportunity though to control weeds by planting not only trees and shrubs but also carefully chosen "true" ground covers and annuals, setting them out closely together in order to prevent weed growth.

Once tree and shrub roots have developed, close digging is inadvisable as it may disturb the roots or induce suckering in some species and therefore it is wise to mulch.

Chemical weed killers are a timesaver and work very well if the directions are followed carefully. It is important to read each line and to follow the instructions exactly. Using weed killers at the wrong time is not as effective as using them when the weeds are in flower or are growing very strongly as in spring and summer. Chemical weed killers are also excellent to spray around trees to stop grass growing around the trunks.

There is a plethora of weed killers available for most garden jobs from the once-a-year path weeders to selective lawn weeders. There are chemicals that sterilise the soil so that nothing occurs for months, even years, but the very best weed killers in the home garden are those that kill by contacting foliage and break down when they reach the soil. They suit planted areas. When the precautions are followed they are not harmful to animals or humans.

There are other chemicals that prevent weed

seeds from germinating, but allow plants to grow. Many of these can be used among trees and shrubs without damage. Some chemicals are specific and kill broad-leafed weeds only while others will kill all growth. Some are applied by incorporating them into the soil and others are watered or sprayed on to the foliage or dabbed on to weeds.

Satisfactory results from the use of weed killers relies on correct identification of the problem and the selection and correct application of the right chemical. Only occasionally do these work with one application. Usually, especially in the case of persistent weeds such as nut grass, oxalis and onion weed, repeated applications are necessary.

All chemicals should be used and stored with caution. Separate spray equipment and watering cans should be kept for the application of chemicals, and washed out thoroughly after use. Residual chemicals left in equipment will cause damage at a later date. A locked cupboard with the key in a safe place is the best way of storing all chemicals.

Home garden tillers—small mechanical rotary hoes—are also handy to keep down weeds in gardens and for the general preparation of garden beds and the planting of annuals, vegetables and roses. For the low-maintenance gardener with a large garden, these could be a worthwhile investment.

With the judicious use of ground covers, mulch and weed killers, hand weeding can be almost forgotten except perhaps for those weeds that the birds drop.

HERBICIDES

The best way to prevent weed build-up in gardens or lawns is to prevent weeds from flowering and seeding because that multiplies the problem.

Use selective herbicides only on the plant group they are meant to kill. For example, D.S.M.A. will kill grasses or plants with parallel leaf venation, but will not kill plants with net venation, which are nearly all broad-leafed plants. Non-selective kinds kill all plants. Herbicides should only be used for the purposes indicated on the label and should be mixed according to the instructions and only at the rate recommended.

Be particularly cautious near ornamental trees, vegetables and fruit trees and avoid spraying the root zone as many chemicals can be absorbed from the soil. Apply chemicals on warm, dry, calm days so that wind-drift will not take spray on to garden plants. Use a coarse spray nozzle as that reduces drift. Add a wetting agent only if it says to do so on the label. Rinse equipment very carefully after use. Do not use it to apply insecticides or herbicides. Rinse and then destroy empty herbicide containers to avoid their reuse. Do not burn or throw them in a garbage heap but wrap in plastic and take to recognised garbage dumps and advise them of the container's previous use. With all chemicals, avoid using old stock as shelf life is an average of two years for most products. Always read the label before use.

In the following lists the active ingredient is given. If you are unable to obtain the product by the product name, read the label and see if you can find an alternative product with the same active ingredient. Trinoc, TCA, Krenite, Hyvar and Erase are chemicals not readily available in nurseries or garden shops and may have to be ordered through agricultural suppliers.

GARDEN WEEDKILLERS					
WEED AND DESCRIPTION	WEEDKILLER	ACTIVE INGREDIENT	TYPE	CONDITIONS OF USE	COMMENTS
Paspalum	Antipas® Lawn Paspalum killer® Passtox® Swab or wipe with Zero or Roundup® (e.g., Magic Wand)	D.S.M.A. (Disodium Methyl Arsenate) Glyphosate	Selective contact killer Systemic non-selective	Is best applied to young weeds in warm weather when temperature is above 25° Swabbing with Glyphosate will kill lawn grasses if contacted	Paspalum can be dug out or cut off 2-3 cm below ground level with a sharp knife. Is applied in couch, bent and fescue lawns only, not in Queensland blue couch and buffalo
Nut grass in all lawns	Mow, dig or pull or Swab with Zero® or Roundup® (Magic Wand)	Glyphosate	Systemic non-selective	Dab only the weeds, otherwise lawn will be damaged	Regular mowing inhibits bulk growth
Parramatta grass, tufty-wire grass, rat's tail and crows foot.	Hand removal or spotting with Zero®	Glyphosate	Systemic non-selective	As above	As above
Onion grass (Romulea Rosea var. Australis), onion weed (Nothoscodeum Inodorum) and oxalis spp.	Dig or pull out, swab with Zero® or Roundup®, or as for Parramatta grass	Glyphosate	Systemic Non-selective	As for Parramatta grass	As for Parramatta grass
Sedge, Mullumbimby couch and summer grass	As paspalum	As paspalum	As above		Use only on couch, bent or fescue lawns
While root lobelia (flat, small, bronze-green foliage, white star flowers and milky sap)	Lawn Weeder and Feeder®	Urea, potassium nitrate, 2,4-D, sodium salt	Hormone (stimulates growth and alters metabolism)	Already well moistened soil	Applied liberally
Hydrocotyl (pennywort)	Lawn Weeder and Feeder® Lawn Weeder®	As above M.C.P.A. and Dicamba	As above	As above	
Summer grass or American crab grass	Hand removal or paspalum sprays or mowing	D.S.M.A.	Selective contact killer	Mowing. Winter kills it. Unchecked it smothers grass	Only germinates in warm spring temperatures (often thought to be in the grass seed but not so). Apply D.S.M.A. to bent, couch and fescue lawns only

WEED AND DESCRIPTION	WEEDKILLER	ACTIVE INGREDIENT	TYPE	CONDITIONS OF USE	COMMENTS
Bindii	Dig out or use Weedoben M® Lawn Weeder® Clover and Bindii Lawn Weeder® Bindi®	Bromoxynil Bromoxynil and M.C.P.A. M.C.P.A. and Dicamba Bromoxynil and M.C.P.A.	Bromotyril selective contact M.C.P.A. selective hormone weedkiller and Dicamba	Apply at start of active spring growth for best results	
Winter grass in bent lawns	Dig out or apply Endothal®	Endothal			Apply in late autumn or winter
Winter grass in all lawns	Dig or pull out or Swab (e.g., Magic Wand) with Roundup®	Glyphosate	Systemic non-selective weed killer	Swabbing with Glyphosate will kill lawn grasses if contacted	
Couch and kikuyu grass in all lawns	Swab (e.g., Magic Wand) with Zero® or Roundup®. Dig out pull out	Glyphosate	As above	As above	
Winter grass in couch Queensland blue couch and buffalo lawns, bent and browntop	Dig out or spray with Endothal®	Endothal			Apply in late autum winter
Creeping Oxalis and Clover	Dig out, apply lawn sand or use: Clovotox® Clovoxal® Kleen Lawn® Lawn Weeder®	Mecoprop Mecoprop Mecoprop and Dicamber M.C.P.A. and Dicamba	Selective hormone weedkiller	At active growth and when new weeds appear	Do not use on wanted plants, clover, buffalo lawns or lawns under three months
Most broad-leaved weeds in all lawns	Dig out, apply lawn and or use Lawn Weeder® Kleen Lawn® Clovotox® Clovoxal® Sulphate of Ammonia	M.C.P.A. and Dicamba Mecoprop and Cicamba Mecoprop Mecoprop	Selective hormone		
Most broad-leaved weeds in couch, bent and fescue lawns	Bindii Weedkiller® Bin-Die®	Bromoxynil and M.C.P.A. Bromoxynil and M.C.P.A.			

Pests and diseases

In a healthy garden, biological control (nature's predators and pests balancing themselves) will keep most problems at a controllable level.

When your soil is in good repair, and water and mulching are adequate, a combination of physical control (hand removal of insects, for example), biological control, and the application of environmentally preferred or low hazard chemical compounds, will probably be the best course to follow in dealing with problems.

The problems dealt with in this section could occur from time to time over a period of years. Fortunately they do not all occur together! The problems are numerous, but the controls are few and each one covers many problems. Note that garden chemicals in aerosol packs do not contain harmful propellants.

PESTS

Australia has a large range of indigenous pests plus those brought in from other countries, which is one reason why quarantine laws exist. But not every insect is a pest. Many are beneficial and should be preserved. Pests cause damage in a variety of ways according to their type. Some chew foliage or other plant tissue, others mine or burrow within the tissue, while insects such as leaf miners damage leaves and fruit fly maggots attack fruit.

Sap-sucking insects include mealy bugs, scale insects, leaf hoppers, plant bugs and aphids and many of these may carry plant virus diseases as well. Thrips and mites feed by rasping surface cells on plants and sucking up the sap. Soft scale insects, while not particularly damaging, leave a secretion on which black, sooty mould fungus grows. Mites, slugs and snails are usually included as pests. In nature, pests are kept in control by variations in weather patterns, parasitic insects and diseases. Their natural enemies are predatory insects and spiders. Insect pests may multiply into plague proportions in new environments where their natural enemies are absent, or when the natural balances are upset by clearing, by the large scale planting of single crops, bush fires or excessive spraying with insecticides that kill *everything*.

In a new garden, pests will be evident in the beginning but will become less so as their natural enemies are introduced and a balance is achieved. Birds feed on insects and are worth inviting to the garden for this reason. Butterflies are not beneficial insects as they lay eggs that become caterpillars and chew plants. However, the damage caterpillars inflict on plants is usually fairly minor and can be tolerated in view of the beauty of the butterflies. Some useful non-insect predators are spiders, gheckos, lizards and frogs.

There are many beneficial garden insects: **Ladybirds** are oval, hump-backed little beetles, often brightly coloured, which feed on aphids, scale insects and mites as larvae and adults. The common spotted ladybird is about 6 mm (¼ in) long and is yellow with 18 black spots. It feeds on aphids for several weeks. Ladybirds lay spindle-shaped eggs on leaves and along young stems.

Lacewings are yellow-green, lacy-winged insects with large eyes, which lay their eggs on long slender stalks in rows. The larvae have prominent hooked jaws and attack aphids, mites, mealy bugs, scale insects and thrips.

Praying mantis are large green insects that eat aphids while young. The adults graduate to eating larger insects such as moths, beetles, caterpillars, grasshoppers, crickets and other mantis.

Native wasps and hornets sting and carry off grubs, caterpillars, cicadas and many other insects and spiders. Small wasps lay their eggs in the bodies of caterpillars, which then become food for their hatching larvae. These move outside and pupate near the dead host, spinning tiny white or buff cocoons.

Hover flies hover over plants and flowers, their wings vibrating so quickly that they are blurred. Their eggs are laid in aphid colonies and green, or brown maggot-like larvae hatch and suck the body juices from the aphids.

Ground beetles are brown or black, long-legged beetles, which hide by day and scamper about at night to feed on grubs and caterpillars.

Assassin bugs are brown or black, narrow-bodied bugs with powerful beaks. They suck the body juices from caterpillars and large insects.

In a garden where the soil is well cared for by the regular addition of organic material, insect build-up will be reduced. Insects atttack plants in poor health, so keeping plants in good health is the first stage towards controlling insect attack.

The most serious pests in gardens are the wood borers that attack large trees. If these are left unchecked they can destroy the trees. Citrus leaf miners, fruit flies on fruit trees, mites, lace bugs, thrips and mealy bugs are among the more serious pests in gardens because they are not easy to eradicate.

Some pests can be controlled by non-chemical means. For example, aphids can be rubbed off or hosed off. Caterpillars and sawflies can be clipped off and burned, or large caterpillars and bugs can be knocked to the ground and trodden on.

"Banding" is another useful practice. This is when a double strip of hessian or other material with an open edge downwards is tied around a tree a metre or two above ground. It becomes a hiding place for insects and can be removed easily every few days. The insects can then be destroyed. This is effective for hairy caterpillars on white cedars and for many other pests.

Before attempting any control method make certain you know exactly what you are spraying for. Be sure that you are not confusing a disease with a pest problem, as the products that kill one do not kill the other. Aim to control pests to a safe limit so that there are enough pests for their predators to feed on. Eliminating both pest and predator just builds up pest problems. Spray or dust only if insect pests are present and are on the increase, otherwise excessive spraying can kill off the useful predators. Act quickly because a few days interval can allow the pests to do too much damage.

CONTROL MEASURES

These may involve the use of non-chemical insecticides or low-hazard chemical insecticides. The main difference between these is that the non-chemical insecticides are not as long lasting as the low-hazard chemical insecticides.

NON-CHEMICAL INSECTICIDES

Bacillus thuringiensis is formulated from the spores of the insect-attacking bacterium and is effective against some caterpillar pests. It is not toxic to humans. Sold as Dipel and House and Garden Bio-insecticides.

Derris dust (rotenone) is a natural compound in the roots of derris plants. This is applied as a dust or spray to kill aphids and caterpillars and other insects by coming into contact with them.

Pyrethrins are extracts from pyrethrum and chrysanthemum flowers, and are good contact sprays against caterpillars, aphids, beetles and most pests, especially flies and mosquitos indoors.

Sulphur, which is sold as wettable sulphur for spraying or dusting, has fungicidal qualities and a limited control against mites.

White and summer oils kill scale insects by blocking their air supply. They may be used alone or with a contact spray, but they should never be applied on very hot days as they will damage the foliage.

LOW-HAZARD CHEMICAL INSECTICIDES

The following are long-established chemicals with a reputation for efficiency and safety when used according to directions. Names of the active ingredient are given. Market names may be different, but the label should state the name of the active ingredient.

Bioresmethrin-bioallethrin are synthetic pyrethoides that are available as pressure pack aerosols. Useful for spraying indoor plants.

Carbaryl is effective against chewing insects and some others, but can cause an increase in mite infestation. Sold as Carbaryl dust or spray.

Dicofol is very useful against some mite pests but is not effective against insects. Sold as Kelthane.®

Dimethoate penetrates into plants and is effective against small sucking insects such as aphids on leaves, and prevents fruit fly maggot development in fruit. When injected into trees, it kills both sucking and chewing insects. Sold as Rogor®.

Endosulfan is used as a spray against a wide range of insects, such as caterpillars, aphids, thrips and bugs. Sold as Thiodan®.

Maldison has low toxicity to humans and kills many insects by contact action. Works better in conjuction with white and summer oils against scale insects and some large plant bugs. Sold as Malathion,® Maldison and Bug Aphid Spray®. It is also available as a dust.

Omethoate is a systemic insecticide available as a pressure-pack aerosol. Effective against aphids, thrips, white-flies, mealy bugs, caterpillars and mites. Sold as Folimat® .

Thrichlorfon is used against some caterpillars, especially army worm in lawns and some bugs and other pests. Sold as Dipterex®.

PESTICIDE PRECAUTIONS

Apply sprays and dust with care using them correctly and not mixing any more than is required. Most are poisons and incorrect use can be harmful to you, to useful insects in the garden, or bees, birds, fish and animals. Follow the label directions and take precautions. Above all store chemicals safely, making them inaccessible to children. Once the label becomes indecipherable, do not use; they should be used within eighteen months.

Never keep pesticides in anything other than the original labelled containers. Pesticides for the home garden are usually not highly hazardous to use when used as directed, but it is wise to follow safety procedures:

Read the label The label states what the pesticide is and what it should be used for, how to use it and any precautions needed. Use it according to the label directions.

Wear protective clothing Pesticides can be absorbed through the skin, so contact should be avoided. Wear long trousers, shirt buttoned up at throat and wrists, impervious gloves and a hat. Inexpensive disposable "suits" are available from garden shops.

Mixing up Prepare the spray according to label directions. Over-strength mixtures are unnecessary. Keep the concentrate off your skin. If accidentally splashed with concentrate, wash it off immediately.

Wash after spraying Wash face and hands and change clothes after spraying. Afterwards, wash contaminated clothing separately from other clothing.

Other precautions Never eat or smoke while spraying. Never clear blocked spray equipment by sucking or blowing with the mouth. Rinse and destroy (or dispose of) empty containers so that they cannot be used again for other purposes.

Poisoning symptoms If you use pesticides you should know the common symptoms of pesticide poisoning in case of accidents. They are nausea, headaches, giddiness, cramps, muscular trembling and sometimes blurred vision and tightness in the chest.

Residues on produce Observe the intervals between spraying and harvesting (sometimes called the "with-holding" period) that are given on container labels, then pesticide residues or harvested produce will not exceed permitted levels.

Pesticide effect on birds, fish, bees and animals Most insecticides are toxic to bees so do not use then when bees are visiting flowering plants. Cover ponds when spraying as fish are susceptible to very small amounts of some insecticides. The exception is Rogor®, which does not appear to upset fish and it can be used to get rid of aphids on waterlilies. Put pets' drinking and feeding dishes out of the way when spraying. Do not feed pesticide-treated leaves or lawn clippings to birds or stock.

Action of insecticides Insecticide sprays kill insects, usually by contact, stomach poison or systemic action. Insecticides with "contact action" are commonly used against larger sucking-type insects. They must be sprayed or dusted right onto the target pest. These do not have any persistent effectiveness. Insecticides with "stomach poison" action kill chewing insects such as caterpillars, beetles and locusts after they have fed on sprayed foliage. The effectiveness usually persists for at least several days afterwards.

Insecticides with "systemic action" are absorbed into the plant and transported through it. They are mainly effective against small sap-sucking insects such as aphids, mealy bugs and mites, and the effect usually persists for several days. They are generally not effective against chewing insects and large sucking insects.

Spray compatibility Some sprays can be applied in mixtures with others—usually as a combined attack on several pest problems. However, not all sprays will combine with others. Follow label directions.

Baits These are stomach poisons used against snails, slugs, cutworms and crickets. Most are poisonous and should be used with special care so that there is no danger to children or animals.

Deterrents Some materials deter pests or animals or both. For example, Napthalene flakes are occasionally used, though somewhat ineffectually, against a wide range of pests, especially in confined spaces like glasshouses and propagating frames. Lime stops many ground-dwelling pests. Thiram halts rabbits and hares.

Wetting agents These are additives that help sprays spread evenly over leaf surfaces. Washing-up detergent is used as a wetting agent in some instances.

Sprays and dusts Spraying with insecticides in water as the carrier is the main and usually the most effective way to control plant pests. It is essential that the spray applicator is efficient. Dusts are very convenient for short-term projects and cheap and easy to apply. They can be used with anything as simple as an old stocking.

Commercial dusts are available for a variety of purposes including derris dust (rotenone) for aphids and caterpillar control on vegetables; sulphur against mite and fungi; sulphur-carbaryl mixture, which is both fungicide and insecticide; pyrethrins for aphids and caterpillars. Apply these evenly and lightly as heavy applications do burn foliage especially in high temperatures.

WARNING It is an offence under the Pesticides Act to use a pesticide contrary to the instructions on the registered label unless a special permit has been issued under the Act to do so. However, the legally approved instructions for pesticide use may vary from time to time, so irrespective of the recommendations in this book it is essential to read and follow the registered label instructions.

SAP-SUCKING INSECTS

APHIDS

These soft-bodied sucking insects are usually found on the new growth of a variety of plants including roses, where they distort new growth and secrete honeydew. This is attractive to ants and a black sooty mould fungus grows on it. Ants protect the aphids in order to ensure a supply of honeydew. The natural enemies of aphids are ladybirds, their larvae and hover-fly

larvae. They can control aphid infestation. Aphids can be hosed off, or pulled off and squashed. For non-chemical control, spray with pyrethrum. For chemical control, spray with Dimethoate or Maldison.

SPIDER MITES

These cover a number of species and are spider-like and greenish or red, and just visible without a magnifying glass. They attack roses, beans, hydrangeas, cucumbers, strawberries and a wide range of ornamental vegetables and many broad-leafed weeds. They multiply prolifically during dry weather and feed on foliage mainly on the undersurfaces, which results in mottling. Remove broad-leafed weeds in the vicinity, and wet plant foliage. Spray with Dicofol or Dimethoate covering the undersides and surfaces of the foliage and repeat spraying seven days later.

BROAD MITES

Broad mites are colourless, and visible only under a magnifying glass. They thrive in coastal climates in warm, humid conditions and will cause damage to young shoots by distorting leaves, which gives the effect that they are suffering from weedicide application. Broad mites attack camellias, azaleas, citrus, pot plants and glass or shade-house plants. Broad-leafed weeds near the plants should be sprayed and removed. Spray both weeds and plants with Dicofol.

PLAGUE THRIPS

These can occur in very large numbers during spring and early summer when they infest roses, blossoms, gladiolus, ornamental flowers, annuals and fruit trees. These narrow-bodied tiny pests have thin, fringed wings. Control instructions as for Black thrips, with repeated applications at close intervals.

BLACK THRIPS

These are black with thin, fringed wings. They are slightly plump, elongated insects that attack fuchsias, azaleas, gladioli, glass house plants and many garden subjects. Colonies of young thrips mark foliage with unsightly silver and black blemishes. They like shady, moist conditions during summer and autumn. Control by spraying or dusting with Pyrethrins, Derris dust or Maldison and repeat the application every two or three weeks.

PSYLLIDS

There are numerous species of these attacking eucalypts and many other plants. They form a covering or lerp, which looks like a pimple on the foliage. The small insects within feed on leaves while living under the covering. They discolour the leaves and turn some sections brown. Premature leaf-fall occurs. The insects grow by shedding the skin and enlarging their covering. Spray only when the insects are present using Maldison or the tree injection method if the trees are tall.

BRONZE ORANGE BUGS

These are pests of native as well as cultivated citrus and can be found on vigorous trees with ample foliage. Remove by hand or knock into a container of water to which kerosene has been added. These pests are foul smelling. Spray with Maldison or Dimethoate plus white and summer oils.

WHITE FLIES

These tiny moth-like insects are covered with powdery wax. They congregate on the undersurfaces of leaves and suck sap, causing a yellow mottling of the upper surface. They secrete honeydew on which sooty mould will grow. When disturbed they are capable of flying but soon settle again. In the immature stage they look like scale insects. They attack a wide range of plants including glasshouse plants. Spray with Dimethoate.

SCALE INSECTS

ARMOURED SCALES

Numerous scale insects are covered with armoured scales including red and purple scales on citrus trees, circular black scale on daphne, palm scale on palms and waratah, and camellia scale on camellias. The insects are sap-sucking insects and are covered with a hard, rather flat, shell. These insects attack foliage and stems and may increase to large numbers and feed heavily, causing leaf fall and twig die-back. Control by spraying with white and summer oils alone, or combined with Maldison or Dimethoate.

WHITE WAX SCALES

The adult insects are covered quite thickly with soft white wax, which shelters red insects underneath. In early summer up to three thousand eggs hatch under each adult scale. These move onto the stems covering themselves with wax and developing into full-size scales over several months. They are best sprayed when young insects are on the leaves and before they have settled and covered themselves with peaks of wax. Usually mid-summer is the best time to spray using white and summer oils. Small numbers of the insect are easy to remove by scraping off.

BLACK SCALES

These sucking insects are the most common of several species of brown scale that occur on several garden plants. They secrete honeydew on which sooty mould develops. Two thousand eggs hatch under each adult scale during early summer. Larvae infest foliage and the stems of many trees and shrubs including citrus, passionfruit, oleander and geranium. Spraying is most effective when done before the scales reach the half-grown stage. White and summer oils are effective, or spray with Maldison or Dimethoate plus white and summer oils.

GUM TREE SCALES

These attack some eucalypts especially the Scribbly Gum (*Eucalyptus haemastoma*). As with other scales, ants are present and sugary exudations are followed by a black sooty mould on which a fungus will grow. The female scales are pink and the male scales are white. They are usually on the stem. Spray with Lebaycid or use tree injection.

MEALY BUGS

These sucking insects are covered with a soft white mealy substance, which often has white filaments. They secrete honeydew, which attracts ants and is followed by sooty mould. They are found on citrus, gardenias, ferns, orchids, house plants and garden shrubs. Outdoors they are usually destroyed by predatory insects, which can be encouraged by keeping ants under control. Possible controls indoors are touching the plants with a brush or cotton wool dipped in methylated spirits, or bringing the plant outdoors for the natural enemies to destroy the mealy bug. They can be sprayed or dusted with Maldison outdoors. These mealy bugs are also found infesting the roots and crowns of plants. They can be controlled by drenching infested plants with Maldison.

CHEWING INSECTS

VEGETABLE WEEVILS

These brown beetles shelter in the soil during the day and attack plants at night chewing leaves, stems and sometimes the roots. In their grub stage during the autumn and winter, and in the adult stage in spring, they will attack a wide range of annual flower and vegetable plants, and capeweed and many broad-leafed weeds. Control by keeping weeds suppressed and spray plants and surrounding soil with Carbaryl.

FRUIT BEETLES

These brown or black beetles damage blooms on roses and hibiscus and some flowers by entering the flowers before the petals unfold, and then feeding within. The beetles develop in fallen flowers and fallen fruit. They can be reduced by collecting this debris and destroying it. Beetles in the open flowers can be sprayed with Maldison, but control measures are not completely effective in preventing re-infestation.

FULLER'S ROSE WEEVILS

These are hard, greyish-brown weevils with faint white marks on each wing cover. They chew large pieces from leaf margins and feed on most broad-leafed cultivated plants including roses, gardenias, camellias and citrus, and on weeds. The larvae develop underground on the plant's roots and emerge as adults from the ground during summer and autumn. Soil should be sprayed with Carbaryl and repeat sprays made if more beetles emerge.

SOLDIER BEETLES

These soft-bodied beetles are black, yellow and green. They appear in large numbers and do little damage. Control measures against this insect are unnecessary when there are only a few, and impractical when there are many beetles.

HELIOTHIS CATERPILLARS

These are coloured yellow, green or red-brown, and have darker markings. They feed on many ornamentals and some vegetables. The adult is an inconspicuous moth, which lays eggs on buds or flowers. The caterpillars feed usually on or in flower buds, flowers and seed structures. Spray while the caterpillars are small with Carbaryl or Endosulfan.

TORTRIX CATERPILLARS

These green caterpillars make a shelter by curling a leaf or tying two leaves together with webbing. They wriggle when disturbed and may fall and hang suspended by a silken thread. They attack many plants and can be controlled by destroying the larvae or spraying with Carbaryl.

GREEN VEGETABLE BUGS

These green, broad bugs occur from time to time on some ornamental shrubs, vegetables and annuals. They may produce four generations between September and April. Their young stages are green, black, red and yellow. Spray with Pyrethrins, Maldison or Thiodan®, Rogor® or Lebaycid®.

SAWFLIES

Steel blue sawflies feed gregariously on eucalypts. They cluster during the day and spread out at night to feed. They are destructive in the larval stage. Remove clusters with high pruners or spray with Maldison. Usually they do not wreak enough damage to warrant spraying, and physical removal is sufficient. Other sawflies may be found on iron bark eucalypts, bottlebrush, paper barks and cypress pines. Maldison can be used on all.

LEAF MINING INSECTS

CITRUS LEAF MINERS

The adult pest is a tiny silvery white moth with yellowish markings. Eggs are deposited on leaf mid-ribs, and when the larvae hatch out, these tunnel into the leaf for five or six days causing silvery, squiggly lines.

Fully grown larvae curl a leaf into a shelter and pupate within. When unchecked, they will cause stunting of tree growth. Affected shoots should be cut off, encased in a plastic bag and disposed of in the garbage. The pest is most active in autumn. It can be sprayed with Lebaycid® or Rogor®. On mature trees the pest does not affect the yield or quality of the fruit. Fertilise in spring, not autumn, to avoid encouraging soft autumn growth, which is susceptible to the pest.

CINERARIA LEAF MINERS

These small flies insert their eggs into the undersides of leaves. The larvae then tunnel inside the leaf causing a grey or silvery wandering line on the foliage. At worst these lines will cause the plant to wilt and die when the attack is severe. Often though the plant still grows and continues to produce a good crop of flowers. Cineraria leaf miner attacks cinerarias, chrysanthemums, mist flowers and nasturtiums, lettuces and sowthistle weeds, cape weed and prickly lettuce. Spray with Rogor®.

OTHER COMMON INSECTS

CITRUS GALL WASPS

These very small black wasps lay groups of eggs in the soft young twigs, thorns, fruit stalks, or the main veins of leaves on citrus. Developing larvae cause the plant to produce extra cells, forming galls that become most noticeable in December or January, and then become larger as the wasps increase in size within. Galls should be cut off and burnt by the end of August. Galls are most noticeable on rough lemons and grapefruit, but all citrus suffer. Removal is the only control.

QUEENSLAND FRUIT FLIES

These wasp-like flies have yellow bodies and clear wings and are common on the east coast of Australia. They lay eggs in fruit a few weeks before the fruit is ripe. Maggots hatch and feed within the fruit, which then falls. Control by spraying with Rogor® (except on early peaches, apricots, Meyer lemons and Seville Oranges on which Rogor® may cause leaf drop) or Lebaycid®. Collect fallen fruit and destroy infested fruit by either burning, boiling, keeping it fully immersed in water for a few days, or by holding it in a sealed plastic bag exposed to the sun long enough to kill the maggots. Do not bury infested fruit as this increases the fruit fly population. The fruit fly infests fruit trees, ornamental fruit trees, tomatoes and capsicum. The spray used kills the tiny maggots after they hatch from the eggs laid in the fruit.

SPIDERS

Red-back spiders inhabit sheltered dry places such as meter boxes and under fences. Their presence is usually detected by strands of flimsy web.

Funnel-web spiders live below the soil surface in horizontal tunnels under large stones, bricks, timber or stumps. Their web is a finely woven, narrow tunnel. Both spiders are found in rock gardens. Permanent sites such as rockeries and the interior of meter boxes should be sprayed occasionally with a spray registered for the purpose. Defender's Spider, Cockroach and Ant Spray or Dust (active ingredient Permethrin) are registered for control of spiders.

ANTS

These insects protect sucking insects such as aphids and scale insects from their natural enemies. Ants then feed on the secretions left by these pests. Ants actually move scale insects about in order to establish colonies. To control ants spray the main nest with a pesticide registered for the purpose, for example, Defender's Spider, Cockroach and Ant Spray or Dust (active ingredient Permethrin).

BARK AND WOOD DAMAGING INSECTS

BARK BEETLES

These attack the phloem-cambium tissues just under the bark. The legless larvae are cream coloured. They mostly attack ornamental conifers, leaving small exit holes. They can be controlled by removing the limb or sometimes the whole tree. If the attack is not severe, fertilising and looking after the tree may repair the damage. Other beetles in this category are cypress bug beetles, found on *Cupressus torulosa*, and other weevils found on ornamental cypress.

JEWEL BEETLES

These come in a variety of sizes and species. They are flattened and often have bright colours and short antennae. The legless larvae are characterised by an elongated abdomen and cobra-shaped head and thorax region. The beetles eat leaves and are usually found near nectar-bearing flowers. The creamy-white larvae feed under the bark of the tree leaving tunnels packed with chewed wood. Pupation takes place in the sapwood, with the adult emerging through oval holes in the wood.

The presence of jewel beetles often shows that the tree is dead or dying, although it has not yet developed brown leaves. It is usually the result of neglect in the care of the tree. Remove affected limbs and bark areas. Apply tree surgery and improve plant health by watering and fertilising.

LONGICORN BEETLES

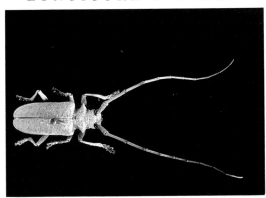

These come in a great variety of species in a range of sizes. They usually have long antennae and elongated bodies. In the larval stage they are cream coloured and legless, with robust bodies, and lack a flattened thorax region. The beetles do little damage but the larvae damage trees by boring their way into the tree leaving large oval exit holes. They usually attack trees that are under stress of some kind due to a change in circumstance, lack of water or nutrients. The best course of action is to repair the damage and fertilise the soil and promote growth in the plant.

Note: There are numerous other borers that also attack a variety of other trees in a similar fashion. Their control is as above.

WOOD MOTH

These can vary in size and most trees are susceptible to one or more wood moths. Their larvae damage sections or branch forks and stubs. The larvae have three pairs of thoracic legs and abdominal legs. As with other bark and wood damaging insects, the best course is to repair the damage to the tree, fertilise and care for the tree.

DISEASES

It is important to make a distinction between insect and disease damage. Some of the symptoms of disease damage are:

- Chlorosis or yellowing of the foliage
- Spotting of leaves, twigs, flowers and fruit
- Wilting of the aerial parts of the plant
- Rotting
- Damping off or the collapse of seedlings at ground level
- Perforations where circular patches of dead tissue drop off producing a shot-hole effect
- A water-soaked appearance
- Silvering of leaf surfaces
- Swelling of galls or other malformations
- Stunting, cankers
- Scabs
- Premature shedding of foliage, flowers or fruit
- Resin exuded by damaged tissue
- Changes in foliage colour, for example, from green to red

CAUSES OF PLANT DISEASE

As control depends on knowing the cause of the disease there is no single general control measure. There are two broad groups of diseases, those caused by non-living or environmental factors, and parasitic diseases.

Non-parasitic diseases may be caused by atmospheric influences such as excessive cold or heat, dryness or humidity and by wind, hail, lightning, the amount of light available and injurious substances. Soil influences include a deficiency or excess of water, salinity, excess of alkalinity or acidity, the presence of injurious substances such as herbicides, a deficiency or excess of nitrogen, phosphorus or potassium and a deficiency of one or more of the minor elements such as boron, calcium, copper, iron, magnesium, manganese, molybdenum and zinc.

Parasitic diseases are mainly caused by viruses, bacteria, some fungi and nematodes or eelworms. Mites and insects carry some diseases, mainly viruses, and through handling, people are responsible for the spread of others.

FUNGI

Fungi may attack any part of the plant at any stage of its growth. They are the most common disease agents. Fungi are simple plants that lack green chlorophyll, and may be saprophytic or parasitic or both. They develop a branching thread-like growth called a mycelium. Parasitic species depend on green plants for food. Fungi reproduce by spores and are diverse and variable with complicated life cycles. They are disseminated by air or water in soil and some rest in spores that may have survival periods of many years.

BACTERIA

These are single celled organisms that enter plants through natural openings, such as the breathing pores or wounds. They cause tissue death and wilting or galls. Soft rot bacteria cause decay in fresh fruit and vegetables in transit.

VIRUSES

These are reproduced only in the living cell and are transmitted from plant to plant by insects, people or pollen and (rarely) seeds. Virus symptoms are mottling, yellowing, curling, excessive branching, gall formation, rosetting, spotting of foliage or parts of the plant. Some viruses do not produce symptoms but still reduce the productivity of the plant.

NEMATODES OR EELWORMS

These are eel-shaped, unsegmented worms that are parasitic on plants or animals (including people), and form a large part of the soil fauna. Many species are parasitic on plant roots; a few feed on aerial parts of the plant. They are able to move in water.

AERIAL SYMPTOMS OF ROOT NEMATODE INFECTIONS

The symptoms are wilting and weakened yellowish growth and include root galling as with root knot nematodes and lesions for most other types. Leaf, bulb and stem nematodes cause rotting of tissue.

PLANT DISEASE CONTROL

Control measures depend on making a correct diagnosis of the disease and using a suitable control measure. The symptoms can be confusing, and accurate diagnosis may be difficult for the untrained eye.

Garden cleanliness helps restrict the spread of disease. Keeping disease-infected material removed is one step. Preventing introduction of new diseases is another. Systemic fungicides will kill internally carried fungi, or soil can be treated to destroy soil-borne pathogens. Seeds and cuttings can also be treated with various fungicides to rid them of disease causing organisms. Bulbs are heat-treated. Crop rotation or the destruciton of host plants are other control methods.

There is a large group of protectant fungicides that are suitable for a wide variety of applications. Copper compounds and sulphur are popular as are most of the modern fungicides derived from organic compounds. A few fungicides are systemic including Benomyl (Benlate®), Thiabendozole (Tecto®) and the

Oxathiin (active ingredient oxycarboxin, sold as Plantvax® systemic fungicide) compounds. Fungicides may injure man, animals or desirable plants, fish or other wildlife when they are used incorrectly. They should be applied only according to directions and leftover products and containers should be disposed of in the way outlined for Pesticides. Environmentally preferred fungicides are Kocide®, Mancozeb or Zero® aerosol fungicide.

CONTROLS FOR FOLIAGE DISEASES

FUNGUS LEAF SPOT
Leaf spotting usually follows rain and high humidity and is furthered by splashing water-carrying fungi onto foliage. Colour and size of leaf spots vary and may increase and coalesce to form large dead areas. Sometimes the centre will drop out giving a shot-hole effect. In bad cases leaves yellow and wither and die prematurely as with black spot on roses and other ornamentals. Control by spraying with copper oxychloride spray or Kocide®, which is preferred environmentally. In the case of roses, spray with Triforine®.

BACTERIAL LEAF SPOTS AND BLIGHT
These show as light or dark water-soaked spotting or streaking of foliage, stems and fruit. The spots may be grey, brown or black and the leaves may wither and die prematurely. Control using copper oxychloride fungicides or Kocide®.

BOTRYTIS BLIGHT OR GREY MOULD
This causes brown spotting or blotching of foliage, flowers, stems, fruit, tubers or roots, and is prevalent during cool, damp, cloudy periods. Furry grey mould may cover the diseased parts. Seedlings or young shoots may wilt or collapse and flowers or leaf buds may rot. Flower petals may become spotted with a ringed appearance. Older flowers rot quickly. Dead or dying plants are often affected. Control by burning infected plants and plant parts and avoid overcrowding to allow for good air circulation. Also do not over-apply fertilisers, especially nitrogenous fertilisers. Overhead watering, over-wet mulches and poor circulation or shady areas should be avoided. Remove weeds and cut off and burn affected plant parts, especially before the end of August when a new generation will develop to cause further infestation.

DOWNY MILDEW
This shows up as pale green or yellowish areas on upper leaf surfaces with mauve to light grey, downy mildewed areas corresponding on the lower surfaces. They may gradually become larger, grow yellow and turn brown, the leaves wilting and falling off prematurely. Cool, humid or wet weather favours the disease as do warm humid days and cool nights.

Control by burning infected plants and avoid overcrowding of plants, overhead watering, too much nitrogenous fertiliser and excessive humidity. Spray with copper oxychloride, covering the undersides of the leaves as well as the tops. With vegetable crops, rotate planting on a two or three year basis.

POWDERY MILDEW
Shows as a white, light grey, powdery, mealy coating developing on leaves, buds, flowers and young shoots. This causes dwarfing and curling of foliage, which may yellow and die prematurely. It is most prevalent during summer and autumn. Powdery mildew attacks a wide range of plants, but a particular species of the fungus is restricted to one host or group of related plants. Control by spraying at the first sign of the disease, covering every part of the plant. Dust with dusting sulphur or spray with wettable sulphur except on soft-foliaged plants in hot weather. Use Triforine® on roses. Other suitable fungicides are Dinocap, Powdery Mildew Killer® and Benomyl–Benlate®.

RUST
Rust shows on leaves and young stems as bright yellow, orange, red or reddish brown, brown or black or orange powdery raised pustules, usually on the lower leaf surfaces. Leaves may wither and die prematurely. The plants may be

stunted or in bad cases, wilt and die. Control by dusting with sulphur or spraying with wettable sulphur. Reduce air humidity in glasshouses and avoid watering foliage.

WHITE RUST

This fungal disease develops pale yellow areas on upper leaf surfaces with white pustules immediately below on the undersurfaces of the leaf. Gradually the yellow areas become brown and infection spreads from stem to stem and flowers, causing malformation. Gerberas and pigface (*Lampranthus*) are susceptible. Diseased plants should be removed and burnt and the balance sprayed with copper oxychloride or Kocide®.

LEAF CURL AND LEAF BLISTER

These fungal diseases cause puckered, thickened and curled foliage with a blistering effect on some leaves. It is common on peaches and is sometimes seen on Lombardy poplars. The infected shoots can be cut off and the plant sprayed with copper oxychloride plus summer and white oils in late winter as the buds begin to swell.

SOOTY MOULD

This is a black, superficial fungal coating that develops on the sugary secretion of honeydew that is left by insects such as aphids, scales, mealy bugs and leafy hoppers. It is ugly and excludes light from the green areas of the plant, so reducing its vigour and ability to make food. Keep the scale or other insects under control with appropriate sprays. The mould then dries up and disappears.

LEAF NEMATODES

Symptoms are variable, but are mostly dark brown angular discolourations bounded by the veins of the leaf. In bad cases the whole leaf may be affected. Nematodes over-winter in the soil and on infested foilage and stems and may swim up the stem in a film of water. They are spread by water from leaf to leaf and from plant to plant. Control by avoiding overcrowding of plants and spray affected chrysanthemums with Rogor®.

CONTROLS FOR VIRUS DISEASES

Virus diseases have a number of symptoms including mosaic or mottling, curling, puckering and leaf distortion. Development of light coloured veins, banding of other veins with darker green or yellow areas, yellow spotting of foliage and general yellowing is often accompanied by stem stunting and rosetting of foliage.

Virus infected plants must be removed and destroyed. A virus can be transmitted from one plant to another by aphids, thrips or other insects. Insect control is important in the control of viruses. Virus diseases can also be transmitted by plant sap on fingers or on garden implements, so make sure you wash your hands after handling plants that may be virus infected. Implements should be sterilised by heating over a flame or rinsing in trisodium phosphate. Bulbs, corms, tubers, runners, suckers and budwood from infected plants should not be used. However, seeds from virus infected plants only rarely transmit these diseases and may be used.

STEM DISEASES
DAMPING-OFF, ROOT ROT AND COLLAR ROT

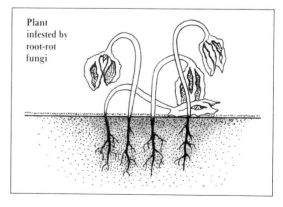

Plant infested by root-rot fungi

An example of one kind of damping-off disease.

These fungal diseases are fairly common and damping-off is the most usual, especially in seedlings that are attacked at ground level and fall over. On more mature plants, the trunk or stem is girdled at ground level and foliage colour may turn yellow. The plants begin to wilt and eventually the roots will wither and die. To control these diseases, use steam cleaned or chemically treated soil to raise seeds, or purchase vermiculite or commercial seed raising mixes, which have been so treated.

Avoid damping-off spread by drenching soil with Fongarid® or Previcur® against water moulds (Pythium and Phytophthora), and quintozene, Terraclor® against rhizoctonia. The same fungicides are also effective against collar rot but all debris from infected crops could be gathered and burned.

STEM BLIGHTS AND CANKERS
These are seen on stems, branches, twigs, trunks and are caused by both bacteria and fungi. The cankers may be swollen or sunken and can be oval or irregular, discoloured dead areas. They can crack open the bark to show the wood beneath and some will become very large and entirely girdle the stem. The parts above the diseased area will show a yellowing of leaves and will wilt or die back from the tips of the branches.

Prune off and burn all diseased parts. Scrape away bark and wound injuries and cover these with a wound dressing. Spray with copper oxychloride or Kocide®.

WILT
This is caused by lack of water, either permanently or temporarily, or diseases of the stems or roots, which stop the flow of liquids from roots and foliage.

Wilt can also be caused by viruses, bacteria and fungi. When cut the infected stems or branches will show discoloured streaks in the conducting tissue. Some plants will die as the result of the disease while others, though infected, will survive for a number of years.

FUSARIUM WILT
This is caused by a number of species and varieties of the fusarium fungus, which is a difficult-to-eradicate, soil-borne organism. Usually it is specific to a single species or to a restricted range of plants. The fungus enters the plants via the roots and grows up through the root tissue into the stem where it damages the conducting tissue. Infection is spread by wounding the root tissue through nematode attack or by other soil-dwelling animals. To control this disease collect and burn the affected plants. Always use disease-free seed in sterilised or steam-treated soil. (See "Damping-Off".)

Remove infected limbs and water plants well and keep them fertilised to promote strong growth. Rotating annual plants or vegetables or using crops that are resistant to this disease are other controls. Do not propagate from infected plants.

VERTICILLIUM WILT
This is caused by soil-borne fungus. It attacks different genera and species of plants, but has similar symptoms to fusarium wilt. Some plants may be infected with this wilt without showing obvious external symptoms. Control as for fusarium wilt.

BACTERIAL WILT
There are a variety of symptoms depending on the bacterium involved and the plants. The leaves may have water soaked areas that increase in size quite rapidly, then turn brown and become dry. The plant may be stunted. It may wilt suddenly or slowly, the wilt beginning on younger foliage, or there may be a slight yellowing of older leaves. The stems could shrivel and become dry. When cut through and squeezed, a stem shows a brownish-yellowish slime at the cut end. Wilt-producting bacteria may enter through roots or through insect, nematode or mechanical wounds. Control as for fusarium wilt.

CROWN GALL

Soil-borne bacteria cause rough-surfaced, soft, hard or spongy, swollen tumors or galls at ground level, which are often also on roots and stems. It is common to a number of plants, but particularly to members of the Rosaceae (rose family), especially peaches and roses. It is prevalent in sandy coastal soils in some areas of Sydney. Control by digging up and burning infected plants, and use No-gall® when you are planting out.

FLOWER AND FRUIT DISEASES

FLOWER BLIGHT

Flower spotting, which causes withering and rotting in fruit trees and failure to set fruit, are symptoms of flower blight and may be caused by botrytis or grey mould. This affects flowers and causes petal blight, which covers them in a furry grey coating. Powdery mildew and downy mildew fungi may also attack the flower and many viruses will cause streaking of petals.

Ovulina is a fungus that attacks azaleas and blights the petals, causing premature withering of flowers that remain on the plant, giving it an unsightly appearance. The sclerotia (the hard black resting bodies within the fungus) can be seen on the dead petals.

First use copper fungicide on the botrytis and later on Bayleton® for the petal blight. Remove infected flowers and burn.

FRUIT SPOTS

These vary with the fruit and can be small, large or scab-like, or large rotted areas. There is a variety of fungicides recommended for particular fruits and this information is available for specific fruits from the local office of the Department of Agriculture.

DISEASES OF BULBS, CORMS AND TUBERS

When these are affected the emerging shoots are weak and yellow and the roots may be discoloured and decayed. These soil-borne rots are fungal in nature and may develop on many bulbs and corms as a basal rot caused by an attack of fungi. Other fungal rots will attack the neck region. Nematodes can infest bulbs at the neck and cause rotting of the internal tissue. Most of these specialised underground organs are susceptible to bacterial soft rots. The bacteria, ever present in the soil, enter through wounds and once established can destroy a crop.

Plant only disease-free bulbs, corms and tubers and store these at the end of the season in dry, well-ventilated rooms. Protect them from superficial fungal infections by dusting or dipping with a fungicide such as Benomyl® or Thiram®. Commercial growers treat daffodil bulbs in hot water at 43°C for four hours and then dry them thoroughly before storage.

ROOT DISEASES

Most root rot diseases are caused by soil-borne fungi, which are encouraged by poor drainage. These include Phytophthora, which affects a wide range of plants from annuals to large trees. Symptoms of the diseases are:

- Foliage may lose colour gradually or quickly and the plant may develop a stunted appearance.
- Some twigs will die back or wilt.
- The plant will fail to respond to water or fertiliser and will become susceptible to drought and wind damage.
- Rot starts with the fibrous roots and progresses into the stem, causing discolouration and death of internal tissue.
- Sometimes the stem rots externally at ground level (crown rot).

This fungus is favoured by moist, poorly drained soils. Improved drainage, and soil that is high in organic matter may produce some improvement. Fongarid® may help if the disease is not too far advanced, otherwise removal and destruction of the plant is the best course.

ARMILLARIELLA

This root attacking fungus spreads through the soil by black, shoe lace-like fungal strands called rhizomorphs, which travel from one root to another. Within the roots the fungus penetrates surface tissue and causes rotting under the bark, which may extend up the trunk.

When clearing land, remove stumps of newly-felled or earlier-felled trees as these may carry armillariella. Where feasible use a pre-planting treatment of a soil fumigant, such as Methyl-bromide. This work can be carried out by pest control companies. Aerated steam at 60°C for half an hour is used commercially as a sanitary measure. In most soils clearing away the roots, aerating the soil and cultivation are probably sufficient on a home garden scale to control this disease.

Nature's law "survival of the fittest" applies in gardens as the weakest plants are infested or infected first. But pest and disease problems also have a constructive side. Their presence in most cases indicates that the plant is suffering stress from a change of circumstances (re-grading, new paths) or inferior cultural practices. Improving cultural conditions or amending any changes to suit the plant's requirements helps to reduce pest and disease problems.

Index

COMMON NAME

SCIENTIFIC NAME